Measuring for Success

What CEOs Really Think about Learning Investments

Measuring for Success

What CEOs Really Think
about Learning Investments

Jack J. Phillips
and
Patricia Pulliam Phillips

Alexandria, Virginia

ASTD Press is an internationally renowned source of insightful and practical information on workplace learning and performance topics, including training basics, evaluation and return on investment, instructional systems development, e-learning, leadership, and career development. Visit us at www.astd .org/astdpress.

Ordering information: Books published by ASTD Press can be purchased by visiting our website at store.astd.org or by calling 800.628.2783 or 703.683.8100.

Library of Congress Control Number: 2008937405

ISBN-10: 1-56286-588-9
ISBN-13: 978-1-56286-588-7

ASTD Press Editorial Staff:
Director: Dean Smith
Manager, ASTD Press: Jacqueline Edlund-Braun
Manager, Acquisitions and Author Relations: Mark Morrow
Senior Associate Editor: Tora Estep
Senior Associate Editor: Justin Brusino
Editorial Assistant: Georgina Del Priore

Copyeditor: Alfred Imhoff
Indexer: April Michelle Davis
Proofreader: Kris Patenaude
Interior Design and Production: Kathleen Schaner
Cover Design: Katherine Warminsky
Cover Illustration: Fry Design Ltd.

Printed by Versa Press Inc., East Peoria, IL, www.versapress.com

Contents

Preface

This unique book describes what senior executives of organizations need to understand about a successful learning and development function. By tapping into these executives' perspectives, the book provides rare insight into what learning and development professionals must do to provide convincing evidence of success for formal learning programs.

Among all the stakeholders in learning and development programs, the most important group is top executives—not only do they fund programs, but their commitment is necessary to sustain a viable learning process, and their support is thus essential to make programs successful. On the basis of interviews, surveys, research, and briefings with senior management teams, this book reveals what executives specifically want to see and explores their disappointment with some of the data that has been delivered to date. It also explains how learning and development leaders can meet the needs of executives and interact with them to build a world-class learning and development function that delivers results.

Why Another Book on Training Evaluation?

An obvious question is whether there is a legitimate need for another book on training evaluation. With so many books on this subject, the market is saturated. So why do we need another one? There are two main reasons.

First, though previous books have described evaluation from the perspective of learning officers, learning professionals, and evaluators, the chief executive's perspective has been limited to a few comments. This book, however, describes the perspectives of senior executives from a variety of organizations.

Second, learning and development professionals need the viewpoint from the top, because there is still confusion about which measures are most significant for those making an organization's fiduciary decisions—which matter for several important reasons:

- Top executives shape the nature, scope, and extent of learning and development in an organization. The learning and development function originates with senior executives. They provide initial funding in the early years and continue to fund the process—expecting an outcome they can understand and believe.
- Each year, top executives allocate funds to learning and development—funds that are also sought after by other groups. There is fierce competition for funds within an organization.
- Top executives' commitment is necessary to provide the appropriate resources, facilities, people, and access to make learning and development a visible and necessary part of an organization.
- Top executives model the behavior desired in all other managers. Their actions and behavior translate directly into support for learning and development. This support is sorely needed to make the function successful. Essentially, the managers in an organization will watch the senior management team for those signals, cues, and specific actions that are related to the learning and development process.
- The involvement of top executives can add to the success of learning and development programs, enabling others to clearly understand an organization's mission, vision, and value. A key aspect of this is communicating the responsibility to apply and achieve success with learning and development.

Consequently, the power and influence of this senior executive group make it an absolute must for learning and development professionals to understand and deliver the measurement and evaluation data that this group wants. But this data has not always been delivered, and other books on training evaluation have failed to properly address this issue:

- By far, the vast majority of these books provide strategies, tactics, and techniques to make evaluation work. Basically, these are the tools and processes to evaluate learning and development. These are essential references. A few books focus on the need for different levels and types of evaluation. By design, these books do not necessarily reflect the views and needs of top executives.
- Some books attempt to reflect the viewpoint of the senior executives through the chief learning officer (CLO). The traditional approach when exploring what top executives want is to ask the CLO—but this is not always the right way.
- A few books suggest that they contain the actual senior executive viewpoint—but this is difficult to obtain. When surveys are provided to senior executives in an attempt to have them detail what they desire as measures of learning success, the data can be seriously flawed. For example, many CLOs have revealed that when the chief executive receives this type of request, he or she forwards it to the CLO for response. In essence, the CLO becomes a surrogate respondent to the survey questionnaire, raising doubts about the credibility of these types of surveys and studies.

In our own work, we found tremendous disconnects between what a learning and development team thinks executives want and what executives actually want. Few researchers and authors in this field have access to top executives.

In summary, no previous book has directly addressed this issue by focusing on executives' concerns about learning and development success, and by presenting the great opportunities as well as the challenges they face. Thus, this book is needed as an additional perspective for the learning and development professional.

Why This Book Is Different

This book is different in several ways:

- ◆ The book takes the current best practices for measuring and evaluating learning and development and applies them to executives' requirements. The result is a prescription for measuring success based on the executive viewpoint.
- ◆ A large portion of the data analyzed in the book is based on a survey administered directly to CEOs—with no surrogate responses. In this survey, CEOs revealed their definition of learning and development success and offered a variety of suggestions for changes.
- ◆ Part of the input for the book was derived from interviews conducted directly with top executives. In these interviews, the executives were asked to candidly assess the current level of success with learning and development and specify what data they may need in the future.
- ◆ Part of the book's input was based on a synthesis of executive briefings conducted by the ROI Institute in the context of communicating the results of impact studies of major learning and development initiatives to senior executive audiences, including boards of directors of *Fortune* 500 companies. These briefings revealed the success measures that executives want.
- ◆ With its focus on the executive viewpoint, the book summarizes the information in a results-oriented framework for measurement and evaluation. The book also offers a scorecard that provides measures of learning and development success for all stakeholders.

The Flow of the Book

This book flows logically through 11 chapters and includes appendixes explaining the data and analysis that were used.

Chapter 1 describes in detail why the executive viewpoint matters in the learning and development process. Though most would agree that it does matter, this chapter examines the rationale for clearly understanding what executives—truly the key stakeholders in the process—want and need.

Chapter 2 sets the stage for the rest of the book by explaining the dilemma that led us to research and write this book. Essentially, this chapter shows why the book fills an important void in the literature that measures success in learning and development. It also describes our different data sources, all of which were critical for how the book was developed.

Chapter 3 summarizes the book—distilling its findings without the data that follows in the other chapters. Here, the CEO's viewpoint is thoroughly captured from all the book's sources. These sources evince not only the CEO's concerns, problems, and disappointments about the learning and development function and how it's measured and evaluated but also why CEOs are still committed to it.

Chapter 4 addresses the fundamental issue for executives' perceptions of the learning and development function: how much they are willing to invest in it. This chapter outlines five strategies pursued by executives and details the advantages and disadvantages of each. The actual executive input on this issue adds to the credibility of the presentation, and we offer descriptions for setting the investment level as well.

Essentially, chapters 5 through 9 follow a similar format in successively examining each learning and development measure. First, the chapter explains the measure's importance. Then it discusses what's wrong with the measure, the executive viewpoint on it, and how to fix it.

Chapter 5 focuses on input measures—the volumes, costs, and efficiencies in the learning and development process. These measures represent a dilemma, however; they are not the outcomes of the process, although they are often presented that way. Along with exploring this dilemma, the chapter features innovative uses of input measures.

Chapter 6 focuses on reaction, one of the most collected and reported data sets for the learning and development function. Though executives clearly judge reaction data as the least valuable, this chapter shows that there are opportunities to collect it in ways that will capture their interest.

Chapter 7 focuses on learning—the core of learning and development. Though learning is commonly seen as necessary, executives are quick to say that it's not that important to them, perceiving it as an operational measure. Also, measuring learning can be hard to manage. This chapter explores these challenges, as well as possible prescriptions for them.

Chapter 8 focuses on action, behavior, and application—all part of the on-the-job activity connected to learning and development programs, which piques some, but not all, executives' interests. This chapter considers how the very powerful data for this activity could be used creatively to strengthen learning and development.

Chapter 9 focuses on the most important data set from the viewpoint of executives: impact, results, and return-on-investment. These types of data attract executives' attention, and this chapter details all the issues related to collecting, presenting, and using them.

Chapter 10 focuses on the use of the learning scorecard and takes a fresh look at this often-neglected technique that can convey a powerful message showing the overall contribution of learning and development.

Chapter 11 considers the role of executives in learning and development. This final chapter takes a step back—examining how the relationship between learning and development can be improved and how specific actions can increase these key stakeholders' commitment, support, reinforcement, and involvement.

The appendixes supplement the book with definitions, descriptions of data collection instruments, summaries, and how the data is integrated.

Jack J. Phillips
Patti P. Phillips
2010

Acknowledgments

No book is the work of the authors alone. Because of the collaborative nature of this book, its content represents the input of many individuals and clients. We thank all the learning and development professionals we've worked with in the last two decades, as we've learned to connect learning and development to business goals. These professionals are too numerous to list here, but they are some of the best-known and most-respected individuals in the field. Many are highly esteemed chief learning officers, and we owe them a great amount of appreciation.

We also appreciate the willingness of executives to offer data on how they define measures of success in their learning and development investments. Tapping even 10 minutes of their time is a difficult feat in today's hectic and high-pressure world. But for those who were willing to respond, their recognition of this important issue is gratefully acknowledged. Unfortunately, to protect their privacy, we are unable to list their names.

Finally, we thank the top executives who, over the years, have been willing to talk and share with us, and to listen to our presentations about the connection between the important learning and development process and business outcomes. Our greatest excitement in our work is seeing executives recognize this connection. We are very grateful for the great opportunity they've given us.

With the publication of this book, our 35th with ASTD, we are honored to continue our productive relationship of almost 20 years with ASTD.

The professional publishing team at ASTD Press is a group of superb individuals, who are truly interested in making learning and development the driving force it can be within an organization. We thank Mark Morrow for bringing this book's topic to us. As manager of acquisitions and author relations, his work is outstanding, and we appreciate our great relationship with him.

Also, we appreciate the writing and editing efforts of Alison Frenzel, the best editor on our staff, past and present. We thank her for taking a significant amount of rough draft material and using her superb writing and editing skills to make it an easily understood body of work.

From Jack

My special appreciation goes to Patti for continuing the journey in our partnership to help professionals in this field. She is an outstanding teacher, researcher, writer, consultant, and business manager. But most of all, she's an outstanding partner and wonderful wife. Without her continuing support and encouragement, I don't think we could have produced 35 books with ASTD.

From Patti

As always, much love and thanks go to Jack. He invests in others more than he gets in return. What a contribution he makes! I thank him for his inspiration and the fun he brings to my life.

Jack J. Phillips
Patti P. Phillips

Why the Executive Viewpoint Matters

Regardless of what you've heard, opinions do matter. The executive viewpoint is essential, particularly with regard to learning and development. This book emphasizes that the executive point of view is the most critical perspective for today's learning and development manager—and this chapter explains why. Though past assumptions about learning and development may have been based on inaccurate, incomplete, or even false data, now it is imperative to influence executives' present and future perceptions with credible, relevant data.

This chapter provides the context needed to help learning professionals step up to the challenge of measurements that matter by providing:

- background on the changing roles, perceptions, and priorities of senior managers and other top organizational leaders
- grounding in the key factors that drive funding and resource decisions by C-level executives—that is, "chief" level, such as chief learning officer to chief executive
- cultural context to help you understand changing employee attitudes toward learning
- a reality check on the processes and politics that drive organizational funding decisions
- tips on ensuring that learning and development is valued by top decision makers.

Where It All Started: The Manager's Role

The role of the manager in the success of learning and development activities can be summarized with a brief history. In the early years of organized work, the foreman provided training to employees so they could perform their jobs. Because workers didn't read and write, on-the-job training was essential. Thus, the foreman (that is, supervisor) initiated and was responsible for job-related training. Apprenticeships became widespread in the Middle Ages as necessary knowledge and skills became more complex and specialized. Craftsmen managed the development of future experts in their trade.

Classroom training evolved during and after the Industrial Revolution and allowed many workers to be trained by a single trainer. As this type of training grew, responsibility for training success expanded beyond a specific foreman or craftsman. Rather, managers had to work together to ensure that large groups of workers received the training they needed to succeed in their various jobs.

As the growth of learning and development continued, managers throughout organizations encouraged and supported the process. At the turn of the 20th century, training became more important to organizations and the industrialization of the U.S. economy than ever before. Theoretically grounded approaches to learning evolved, and the responsibility for managing, leading, and propagating learning and development expanded even further. One of the first documented organized workshops in U.S. industry was conducted by National Cash Register in Dayton, where the chief executive summoned the sales team together near Dayton for sales training.

For centuries, supervisors, managers, and executives have seen the necessity of organized learning and development. Though today these leaders still recognize the importance of developing their people, there has been a change in perspective. For example, a respected communications company, where the learning and development team had trained 4,000 managers in leadership skills, was challenged by its CEO to show the value this significant expenditure contributed to the organization. To the disappointment of the CEO, the team had no evidence that this costly leadership development program contributed anything. The results were a tarnished image and a reallocation of departmental resources. The CEO supported the development of people, but not to the detriment of "wasted" resources. Without firm evidence of a contribution, there was little choice but to make a change.

The growth of organizations and the demand for limited resources have changed the position of learning and development from a function of absolute necessity for an organization's good to one that requires the same level of accountability as other functions. Accountability to senior executives has never been so vital.

A New Approach

Executives have changed their approach to managing organizations. This issue has been documented in thousands of books and articles. Four key issues have evolved that affect learning and development directly and, consequently, its success:

- organizational growth
- short-term results as well as long-term payoff
- competitive edge
- demonstration of value from multiple perspectives.

Most executives and industry observers suggest that growth is a must for survival. Without growth, an organization dies. With growth comes investment, including building skills to position employees to achieve goals, and learning new roles to take advantage of new opportunities. The investment is often high, leaving executives with high expectations for results.

In business, results are the most critical part of success or failure. Unfortunately, most of a business's focus is on short-term and frequent results—the "What have you done for me lately" syndrome. With this type of pressure to show immediate, routine results, an organization is forced to examine results in all areas, including learning and development. Although investment in learning and development is often positioned for a long-term payoff, some large investments in specific programs should deliver the short-term results desired by executives.

Competition, whether locally or globally, is fierce. The goal of many organizations is to defeat their competition. To achieve their mission, organizations must be efficient, competent, and effective. They have to be better than the competition; this translates to building a better team, which requires that skills and competencies be developed for success. The process for building this team armed with the appropriate knowledge, skills, and information must be timely and flawless. This translates into a strategy that includes increased investment in learning and development. Such strategic investments require accountability.

Accountability is defined by the value that investment in programs and processes brings to an organization. But the definition of "value" is changing—there is no one specific measure; instead, it now includes both quantitative and qualitative data, as well as financial and nonfinancial data. Table 1-1 highlights the new definition of value being sought for learning investments. From the executive viewpoint, value is not just defined by the financial contribution, although this is critical. Rather, value includes a clear business alignment between programs and outcomes, and the success of learning and development activities in terms of performance proficiency, teamwork, and service quality. Unfortunately, for many learning and development teams, especially within large organizations, the executive viewpoint of value is not often defined by measures of participant reaction and learning—although, from a process improvement standpoint, these measures are important.

Funding

For executives, a regular task is making decisions about major funding opportunities. Ultimately, an organization's CEO and board of directors approve its entire budget, which often includes a line item for learning and development. These funding decisions are normally made on the

Table 1-1. The "New" Definition of Value

Value must

- be balanced, with qualitative and quantitative data
- contain financial and nonfinancial perspectives
- reflect strategic and tactical issues
- represent different time frames
- satisfy all key stakeholders
- be consistent in collection and analysis
- be grounded in conservative standards
- come from credible sources
- reflect efficiency in its development
- create a call for action.

basis of the demonstrated value of either previous budget allocations or the forecasted value of a requested allocation. When these details are unavailable, decisions must still be made. Unfortunately, they are often made based on perceptions rather than data.

When budget time nears, executives examine the value and costs of the function in the context of what is planned for the future. They try to reach a conclusion as to whether or not the budget request fits their value definitions. When data is unavailable, the executives take leaps of faith that the investment level is appropriate. Fortunately, executives have done this many times and are somewhat proficient in their allocation of funds. Unfortunately, this process of resource allocation is near its end. All functions, including learning and development, must have enough data to show executives that they are delivering credible value if funds are to continue flowing in their direction.

This is particularly true in tough economic times, when the allocation of resources is even more challenging and budgets are tightening. When budgets are small and requests are modest, the pressure is released—either because executives keenly perceive the value contribution due to the organization's small size or there will be limited financial risk if the program ends up adding little value. When budgets are large, however, perceived value is often lacking and financial risk increases. Funding discussions revolve around objective data regarding results. The larger the learning and development budget, the greater the need for accountability.

Resources

Along with the need to justify funding, there is a need to justify additional resources. For the most part, funding secures the resources for the direct costs of learning and development programs. But other resources are also required to support a strong learning and development function. These other resources include facilities, internal staff, and external support.

Learning and development requires facilities. Investing in facilities is expensive, and many corporate learning campuses have been developed to house comprehensive classrooms, theaters, and offices. Today, this trend is changing. Learning and development facilities are becoming integrated into organizations' other facilities, and virtual learning is helping to eliminate the requirement for extensive brick and mortar facilities.

A second resource, which is particularly important, involves people—the learning and development team. A large team is needed to deliver a comprehensive learning and development agenda. Most benchmark studies show a ratio of 1 trainer for every 200 employees. Given this ratio, a company with 200,000 employees would usually have a learning and development team of 1,000 employees. Employees are expensive, and top executives are aware of this. Thus, when budgets are approved, staffing level is always a concern. Some companies go to extremes to avoid having to actually staff the team. This leads to the third type of resource issue: outsourcing.

Because of the high cost of maintaining employees, many organizations choose to outsource learning development, delivery, and evaluation, among other functions. This choice is often less expensive, but it still consumes precious resources and risks putting a greater disconnect between an organization's needs and programs.

Learning and development resource requirements are high. These requirements thus create pressure to show executives the value of a learning and development function—enough value to offset the costs of resources.

Changing Workplaces

Today, the attitude within the workplace has changed, because employees are not necessarily viewed as expenses but investments. Activities are not measured so much as results. This shift in the way executives view employees and practices is illustrated in table 1-2, which compares the change from an old view, which focuses on activities, expenses, and lack of contribution, to a new approach, which focuses on results, delivering value, and performance. This change in focus is causing executives to seek value in almost everything that takes place in the workplace, including investment in learning and development.

Table 1-2. The Changing Perspective of the Workplace

Old View	New View
Activity cost center	Results profit center
Expense control	Maximize value
Human resources as expenses	Human capital as investment
Rule-centered	Client-centered
We value what others value	Our value systems are unique
Tolerate overhead	Outsource or automate overhead
Add value with small pieces	Add value with integrated applications
Most of us are in a support role	All of us are in a sales role
Our measures are based on benchmarking	Our measures are based on what we need
We view value from one perspective	We view value from everyone's perspective
Just another day's work in the cubicle	We do something of value
A job	A performance
Treat old ideas as new ideas	Treat old ideas as old ideas

Changing Employee Attitudes

No change in the current workplace environment is more dramatic than the attitudes of employees regarding their work and employer. Historically, attitudes were determined with measures of job satisfaction, which recorded employees' satisfaction with their jobs, the company, immediate managers, career opportunities, compensation, and coworkers. These measures were important because job satisfaction had a positive correlation with retention and absenteeism—though not necessarily with productivity and quality.

Measures of employee attitudes now include organizational commitment and employee engagement. More than mere job satisfaction, these measures include the extent to which employees are actively involved in work processes, feel a part of the organization, or are fully engaged in decision making. Involvement and engagement have a positive correlation with both retention and productivity, measured in unit of revenue per employee.

As employee attitudes change, an important issue is evolving. Previously, employees did not necessarily seek to be involved in learning and development opportunities. The prevailing attitude was this: "If the employer thinks I need training, then they will provide it. Otherwise, I will learn on the job." Today, employees want to learn. They want to build skills. They have realized that a person's only job security in today's global economy are his or her skills and competencies. The concept of lifetime employment with a single company is gone, for the most part. Employees seek employers that provide learning opportunities, and their retention is based on the employer's continued investment in their development.

This trend has created a dilemma for executives: On one hand, they are forced to invest heavily in learning and development to keep their employees. But on the other hand, if this investment is not managed wisely to focus on job- and career-related topics that help employees succeed on the job and, consequently, help the organization succeed, the investment can be wasted. Although increased investments help with staff retention, there is a renewed emphasis on showing the value of learning and development from both the employee's and organization's perspectives.

Internal Competition for Funds

As internal budgets increase in growing companies, there is fierce competition between departments for funds. With the need for more funds, technology, and people, many parts of the organization are vying for a share of the learning and development budget, especially when there is a significant amount on the table.

In the authors' work with a large package delivery company, the top corporate learning and development officer made this comment to his senior team regarding the department's budget:

> Our direct expenditure managed by our department is over $600 million. That is a huge expenditure and would be equivalent to a medium-sized organization if we were operated independently. Today, many parts of this organization would like to have our funding diverted to their needs. The operations people would like to have it for additional trucks and airplanes. The IT Department would like to have it to invest in technology, as it is becoming an important differentiator. The sales and marketing team would like to have it to increase revenue with new marketing initiatives. With all these internal pressures to have our budget, we must show management that it's adding value. We can no longer ask them to invest on faith that things will work out.

Table 1-3 shows the functions that want a part of the learning and development budget. These functions command respect by adding and driving value. If the learning and development team doesn't enjoy the same respect, perhaps it could be in trouble at budget time.

Commitment, Support, and Involvement

Executives and managers play a critical role in the success of learning and development activities. Their commitment, support, and involvement are imperative for a sustainable learning process. But to gain their commitment, support, and involvement, the learning and development team must show executives the potential payoff for their involvement.

| | Table 1-3. Who Wants Part of the Learning and Development Budget? | |

Function	Rationale for Asking
Research and development	"R&D projects need funding. We must innovate!"
Information technology	"We must continue to automate and maintain our technology leadership."
Production	"We produce the product. We are the most critical part of the process."
Sales	"We sell the product (or service). Without us, there is no revenue."
Marketing	"We make the market and drive the brand."
Logistics	"We move people, parts, and products."
Procurement	"We ensure low cost, efficiency, and quality at the beginning point."
Quality assurance	"Quality is our most important product!"
Engineering	"Without us, nothing is built or designed!"
Finance or accounting	"We bring accountability and financial integrity to the organization."
Legal and compliance	"We defend and protect the entire system."
Human resources	"Employees are expensive. Our new performance management program needs funding."

Commitment

Executives' commitment to a particular process or function is vital to its success. Few business professionals will argue with this conclusion. Commitment is found in the allocation of resources; personal time devoted to the function; and the attitudes, behaviors, and support for the function. Without commitment, the function will not flourish as a value-added part of the organization. In the context of learning and development, value is developed because executives understand its necessity for fueling growth and enabling the organization to remain competitive. They also see the value of having skilled, competent employees. Commitment is increased when executives see routine data showing that the learning and development process is working effectively.

Support

Support for the learning and development process and programs is also very important. Failure to support these activities is a colossal problem in the industry. Support is usually described in the context of middle managers and, at times, first-level managers. Unfortunately, their failure to support these activities properly often catches the eye of not only the learning and development team but also executives. Support for these activities can be gained with a responsive team that can connect to business needs and help managers and executives drive results. Managers need data to be confident that their support is worth the investment. When positive support is achieved, it is extremely powerful, often making the difference between the success or failure of specific programs—or in some cases, even the process itself.

Involvement

Having executives involved in learning and development activities is another critical factor for success. Top executives' involvement translates into ownership and support from others. Involvement is not just teaching—although that's highly visible and important. Executives are involved when they kick off a major leadership program, write an article in support of the learning process, or coach their managers as to how they can better support learning and development activities.

To achieve this type of involvement, the value of learning and development activities must be evident. Executives must understand that these activities are relevant, necessary, and vital to their organization's success and are executed professionally and in a timely way. When this understanding is attained, the activities' image and perceived value increases. Even when other executives do not clearly understand the connection between learning and development and business results, they perceive that there is value when top executives take an active role.

The Commitment Cycle

So how does all this connect? Commitment, support, involvement, and results are revealed as forming a commitment cycle. Without results, commitment to learning and development may not exist. Without commitment, support will not be strong. Without support, involvement will not occur. Without involvement, results will be diminished. Thus, without commitment, support, and involvement, funding is at risk. This cycle may cause a downward spiral if the results are not apparent, or an upward spiral if the results are present. Obviously, the bottom line is this: Without clear results that executives appreciate and respect from the learning and development team, executives' commitment, support, and involvement vis-à-vis the learning and development process will not flourish.

Keys to Success

The key to achieving learning and development accountability is to develop measures that are important to executives because the measures reflect their perspective of value. This is not a one-shot effort but a continuous process that involves not only micro-level program evaluation but also macro-level reporting that is routinely updated.

This macro-level reporting is usually conducted via a scorecard or dashboard that can be monitored consistently. Actions are taken when the scorecard's values are unacceptable and measures need to improve. When the values are as expected or exceed expectations, the data is reviewed to determine how to sustain the momentum. This constant focus on process improvement, with a continuous stream of results, confirms to the executive that reporting value is not just for his or her sake. Instead, the learning and development team also recognizes the importance of these measures and uses them as an integral part of the learning process. This removes any perception that learning processes, including evaluation, are mere busywork activities rather than being part of ongoing business processes.

This chapter may sound like utopia to some readers—how things should be in an ideal situation. But the fact remains: Results and measures of value can be developed and communicated to senior executives to influence their perception of and decisions about learning and development.

To ensure this influence, the learning and development team must focus on six important actions:

- Spend wisely.
- Respond professionally.
- Operate proactively.
- Build productive partnerships.
- Show results.
- Take risks.

Spending Wisely

Because of the growing expenditures for learning and development, resources must be spent wisely. Efficiency is critical. There is no room for waste, which means that programs should be connected to business objectives. Steps should be taken to ensure that alignment has occurred, with unwavering focus on cost control and efficient delivery. This environment makes for a strong, productive business unit—one executives want in their organization.

Responding Professionally

Unfortunately, sometimes the learning and development team is slow to respond. Executives misunderstand why meeting an obvious need takes longer than expected. This problem is exacerbated when new products are added or there is a need for merger integration. Quick, professional responses while delivering impeccable service and building professional relationships within the organization are a must.

Operating Proactively

Today's climate requires the learning and development team not to just respond quickly but also anticipate needs. Team members must look at the organization environment and its goals for the future. Learning and development must be connected to the business in every way. This connection should consist of understanding its problems and opportunities as well as being able to examine, explore, and recommend programs that may solve problems before they are requested. Proactive involvement also ensures that the solution is properly addressed. Without this proactive approach, challenges may not be met in a timely manner, which could lead to a missed opportunity for adding value.

Building Productive Partnerships

The learning and development team must build proactive partnerships with key operating executives. Doing this is a challenge because these executives are busy and do not always prioritize partnering with learning and development staff. The challenge, then, is to work with those executives and understand their issues while delivering value that they appreciate. This effort will help make the partnership productive and earn the respect necessary for the success of the learning and development process, optimally changing this process's somewhat negative image within organizations.

Showing Results

Fundamental to influencing management's perceptions and decision making with respect to the learning and development team is that the team shows results in ways that executives appreciate and value. This endeavor is the heart of this book—presenting what is appropriate and feasible to enable the reader to focus on results important to the ultimate key stakeholders. Pursuing this results-focused approach will have tremendous influence on executives' attitudes toward and perceptions of the learning and development process.

Taking Risks

Finally, the learning and development team must take risks. Doing this may involve taking on programs when they may be unpopular, being willing to rigorously evaluate favorite programs, and overcoming the fear of negative results or a lack of success. All executives take risks, and the learning and development team should follow suit, but it can mitigate these risks by aligning potential programs with business objectives and by making immediate changes as needed. Most executives appreciate risk taking and the willingness to develop a program and evaluate it for possible value. Triumphant risk taking in the learning and development process helps demystify the field's success and, in turn, conveys the perception of a function that can provide the transparency needed to accomplish major initiatives.

Summing Up

Collectively, these six areas can ensure that executives' support of commitment, involvement, and influence is achieved. As a result, learning and development is sustained and becomes a viable important part of the organization.

◆ ◆ ◆

Final Thoughts

This chapter has explored the question of why the executive viewpoint matters and how to ensure a positive view of learning and development. The learning and development team must understand that their crucial stakeholder group is their organization's executives. And the team must deliver value as defined by these executives to secure their commitment and influence their decision-making process. This doesn't always mean financial value; it includes a variety of types of value in addition to the economic contribution. In addition, learning and development leaders must conduct their business in the same fashion as the executives driving the overall organization—by focusing on efficiencies, effective performance, partnerships, and results.

The next chapter briefly summarizes the frustrations traditionally experienced by CEOs when reviewing "successful" measurements; explains why CEOs and top learning executives often find they are not on the same page when discussing the value of learning; explains the executive survey conducted for this book and the methodologies used, briefly reviewing top-line results; and itemizes the key questions answered by this book.

 Chapter 2

The Foundation
for This Book

The goal of this book is to shed new light on what top organizational executives consider success in learning and development. The source of this new light is a set of data collected for this book that asked CEOs and other top executives what measures really mattered to them when describing the success of any learning initiative.

This chapter provides:

- a brief summary of the frustrations traditionally experienced by CEOs when reviewing "successful" measures
- a cogent explanation of why CEOs and top learning executives often find they are not on the same page when discussing the value of learning
- an explanation of the executive survey conducted for this book and the methodologies used, and a brief review of top-line results
- the key questions answered by this book.

Measuring and evaluating learning and development has earned a place among the critical issues in the learning and development and performance improvement fields. For decades, this topic has been on conference agendas and discussed at professional meetings. Journals and newsletters regularly embrace the concept and dedicate increasing print space to it.

Professional organizations have been created to exchange information on measurement and evaluation, and more than 50 books have addressed this important topic. More important, top executives have an increased appetite for evaluation data on learning and development at the level of impact and as it is related to return on investment (ROI).

Although interest in the topic has heightened and much progress has been made, it is still an issue that challenges those professionals involved in even the most sophisticated and progressive learning and development functions. The top executive group, the most important stakeholder, is the key. Though some learning and development leaders argue that developing a successful evaluation process is difficult, others are quietly and deliberately implementing effective evaluation systems and are reporting results to executives that resonate with their interpretation of success. The latter groups have gained tremendous support from the senior management teams and have made much progress.

Regardless of the position taken on the issue, the reasons for measurement and evaluation are clear. Almost all learning and development professionals share a concern that they must convincingly show the results of learning investments to senior executives. Otherwise, funds may be reduced or the function may not be able to maintain or enhance its status and influence within the organization.

The Executive's Dilemma

The dilemma surrounding the evaluation of learning is a source of frustration for many senior executives. Most executives realize that learning is a basic necessity when organizations experience significant growth or increased competition. In these cases, learning can provide employees with the basic required skills while fine-tuning those additional skills needed to meet competitive challenges. Formal learning is also important during business restructuring and periods of rapid change, when employees must learn new skills and often find themselves with heavier workloads in a dramatically downsized workforce.

Executives intuitively feel that providing learning opportunities is valuable, and they logically anticipate a payoff in important, bottom-line measures, such as productivity improvements, quality enhancements, cost reductions, time savings, and improved customer service. Yet they are also frustrated by the lack of evidence showing that learning programs really work. Though results are assumed to exist, and learning programs appear to be necessary, more rigorously calculated evidence must be reported, or executives may feel forced to reduce future funding. A comprehensive measurement and evaluation process, designed with top management in mind, represents the most promising, logical, and rational approach to accounting for the learning investment.

"You Can't Measure It"

For years, leaders in the learning and development profession have argued that one cannot measure the success of learning and development. Yet they ask executives to invest anyway. Their propensity to request funding in the faith that investment in learning is a wise decision is based on the intuition that learning adds value. Yet they don't necessarily see the direct connection between learning and development and the business. When soft-skills programs are involved, the assumption is made that the outputs either cannot be measured or cannot be credibly connected to the business.

These perceptions have caused many learning and development leaders to ignore the measurement issue altogether. This is unfortunate because the result of ignoring the issue is to leave leaders with no basis for requesting funds and executives with no basis for providing funds. As this book demonstrates, the assumptions that learning and development cannot be measured and that soft-skill outputs cannot be connected to business objectives are no longer valid. The truth is that the success of learning and development can be measured in ways that are credible, economical, and realistic within the resources boundaries of most learning and development functions.

Interaction with Top Executives

One challenge that has compounded the measurement and evaluation issues surfacing throughout the learning and development field is the lack of interaction between learning and development professionals and the senior executive team. In most organizations, this interaction is limited. Only in a few organizations does the top learning executive report to the CEO. Even in those organizations, the time the learning executive spends with the CEO is not proportional to the time the CEO spends with the others who report directly to him or her. As with all of us, senior executives have limited time; they spend time in those areas they perceive to be critical, important, and central to their organization's success.

Unfortunately, many executives do not see the learning and development function rising to this level of critical importance—and thus allocate little time to engaging in it. This problem is compounded when the learning and development executive reports through a less senior executive and only interacts with the CEO on special projects or in an occasional review of the learning and development process. Regrettably, these reviews are usually at budget time, when senior executives hope to see an immediate connection between learning outcomes and business objectives to justify increasing or sustaining budgets. It is no surprise, then, that there is confusion and misunderstanding about expectations with regard to the requirements for learning success. Our survey of CEOs, presented in appendix B and analyzed in appendix D, indicates that the head of learning and development (that is, the chief learning officer) is more than three levels below the CEO, on average.

The Disconnect

Nonexistent interaction with executives often forces the learning and development leader to guess what the top executives want in terms of measures of success. This guesswork becomes more inaccurate when filtered through multiple layers of interpretation. Asking top executives outright what specific measures they want to improve often yields ineffective or misguided dialogue. After all, top executives do not see their responsibility as defining the measures of success. Essentially, they want learning and development leaders to report improvement in measures of success that are meaningful to them in terms of business contribution.

In our work with senior executives, this disconnect has been obvious. The learning and development function does offer some measures that appear to satisfy executives, which has perpetuated a belief among learning leaders that senior executives are pleased with the results because they ask nothing more. However, in our conversations with these senior executives, the picture that has emerged is completely different. In actuality, senior executives are not necessarily pleased with the measures presented; the only reason they do not ask for more information is because they perceive that the results they seek cannot be delivered. This serious disconnect between what is being delivered and what senior executives really want was perhaps our most compelling reason for researching and writing this book.

This Issue Is Not New

Trying to understand what senior executives desire from the learning and development function is not a new issue. It has existed for many years, but has recently intensified as budgets have been trimmed or eliminated. Jack Bowsher, the former chief training officer for IBM, related his experience when he assumed the top learning and development position at IBM. As he entered into budget discussions, a senior executive explained that the previous approach of learning and development leaders was to come to the meeting with their hats in their hands asking for more money. They would say, "Invest in learning. It is needed, it is necessary, and it is a wise investment. Take it on faith that it's going to be used properly and add value."

The executive cautioned that this argument was no longer valid. Other executives approaching the same budget discussions offered concrete data in terms of their previous successes and their intended accomplishments with the future investment. Fortunately, this conversation occurs in all types of organizations. Remarkably, the discussion between Bowsher and the senior executive took place in the 1980s.

More than a decade ago, *Training* magazine published a list of the top 10 problems that keep trainers up at night. On the list were

- ◆ Getting the boss on board.
- ◆ Making training stick.
- ◆ Making training pay (prove its worth).
- ◆ Tuning in to the business.

It is telling that the top 10 problems keeping trainers up at night are still causing restless sleep for many. We and the industry need to crack this executive expectation barrier so that learning and development can focus not only on results but on the right results.

The Basic Premise of This Book

This book is not about a particular evaluation method or process. It is not a book on ROI or impact analysis. Instead, it attempts to present the types of data needed to show the value of learning and development from multiple perspectives, with its principal focus on the senior executive viewpoint. After all, these executives have more influence on the sustainability of learning and development activities than any other group.

The book is not intended to amplify the inadequacies of the learning and development process. Instead, its intent is to help learning and development teams understand what types of measures and results should be taken and reported if senior executives are to clearly understand learning and development's contribution. The book adds to the current body of knowledge in this field and seeks to substitute real data for the guesswork that has previously dominated the field.

The book seeks to unwrap the mystery of how to achieve learning and development success by reporting and analyzing actual data that we have collected (see below) and combining this data with distillations of experience and research on the field's key issues. It presents a balanced viewpoint with a focus on what executives need and want in today's economic and global climate.

Definition of Terms

As you read this book, it is important that you understand what is meant by some of the recurring terms. These terms are those that often lend themselves to confusion among learning and development professionals and leaders, as well as senior executives. These terms include familiar ones such as *return on investment* and *measurement.* Other terms such as *analytics* and *business alignment* may not be so familiar to you. The reader is encouraged to turn to appendix A for an overview of the important terms and concepts used in this book.

Sources of Data for This Book

The soundness and credibility of this book rest on its data sources, which make it unique in comparison with many others. We used eight major sources of data to develop a profile of what is needed to measure the success of learning and development in a reliable, CEO-friendly way:

- executive survey
- executive interviews
- executive briefings
- impact studies
- evaluation strategy reviews
- an analysis of learning and development successes and failures
- experience
- review of the literature.

The Executive Survey

The most interesting data set for this book are the survey responses of executives. The survey is included as appendix B, along with the letter that was sent to the first group of those surveyed, the *Fortune* 500 CEOs. We began with the complete 500 list but eliminated those organizations that were facing serious economic and organizational difficulty at the time of the study. We also selected 50 large, private-sector employers, using Hoover's Website as a guide. A small sample of small and medium-sized businesses was identified and mailed a survey, but the intent was to focus on the expectations of the CEOs of large organizations. Fifty executives of nonprofit organizations were identified from a variety of lists and mailed a survey. The response rate from these lists was very low, however, so this data was excluded from the results.

Between the *Fortune* 500 companies and the 50 large private organizations, we had a total of 451 potential respondents. Much of the data and many of the results presented in this book are based on the responses received from these executives.

Although we expected a very low response rate to the survey based on these executives' busy schedules, we were surprised to receive 96 responses, representing a 21.3 percent response rate. We attribute this level of response to a variety of factors, four of which are described in appendix D. Along with a logical appeal about the need for the data and commitment to keep results anonymous, each potential respondent was mailed a copy of our book *Show Me the Money* as a small gesture of appreciation, which was well received.

The executives were also promised a summary of the responses. There was an appeal directly and solely to the executives with a request not to pass along the survey to the chief learning officer (CLO). Though the CLO's value is appreciated, the intent of this particular book is to present the actual perceptions of the most senior executive in an organization. We also wrote a personal note on our letter if the organization had a relationship with our company, the ROI Institute.

The results of the survey provide important and insightful data from the executive perspective.

Executive Interviews
To complement the surveys, executive interviews were also conducted. The structured interview roughly emulated the survey but provided ample opportunity to probe for additional detail. Appendix C presents the interview questions.

The first group we approached for interviews were the CEOs participating in the survey. A very small group agreed; the total number of CEOs from this group was only 6. We contacted a group of about 75 CLOs to explain the research and ask if they were interested in having their CEO participate. Unfortunately, due to a lack of time and/or interest, only 5 agreed to have their CEO interviewed. We also approached clients with whom we were currently working to see if we could speak with their CEO. This generated another 8. Finally, we had 3 interviews with executives of medium-sized organizations. A total of 22 interviews were conducted from October 2008 to January 2009. These interviews allowed much insight into executive concerns, desires, and opportunities. More information about the interview process is given in appendix E.

Executive Briefings

In the last 15 years, the ROI Institute has developed a capability with individuals to conduct impact and ROI studies. Through our trademarked ROI Certification Process, almost 3,000 individuals have achieved the status of certified ROI professional. To do so, these individuals must complete an ROI study and present it to his or her organization's key stakeholders. These stakeholders often include the organization's executive team.

In some cases, an individual has asked for assistance from the ROI Institute in presenting the first study to his or her executive team. In other cases, we have coached and counseled individuals as they have prepared for their briefings. In still other cases, we have observed briefings as bystanders. Sometimes, we have received feedback on these briefings. This feedback has yielded many comments, discussions, and even debates about results and the need for results. The feedback has also provided excellent opportunities for understanding what executives want and desire from investments in learning and development. Because these programs have often involved major investments in learning and development (given that one of the criteria for selecting a program at the ROI level is that it is very expensive), they have made for very lively and interesting discussions. The observations made during the feedback have been incorporated in the book.

Impact Studies

In addition to helping others with ROI impact study briefings, the ROI Institute has conducted hundreds of studies in the last two decades and presented the results to senior executive teams. Some of these presentations have been made to CEOs and the boards of directors of *Fortune* 500 companies. These discussions have provided important insights into executive concerns and reactions to results at that level. These experiences have provided a rich source of input for this book.

Evaluation Strategy Reviews

Through its consulting network, one of the services provided by the ROI Institute is reviewing the current status of initiatives to measure the success of learning and development programs. This service often involves assessing perceptions of results and discussing what measurements are needed in the future. In some of these reviews, meetings are held separately with the members of senior executive teams to better understand their needs and desires for measures of success. These meetings have led to several important conclusions about the disconnect between what is measured by learning and development teams and what is needed by senior executives. These conclusions are presented in this book.

Analysis of Learning and Development Successes and Failures

From time to time, we have had the opportunity at the requests of major journals and other publications to analyze the success of learning and development solutions and try to understand the causes of failure and determinants of success. These reviews have led to important conclusions, which are reported in this book; some of them have also been reported in other books, journals, or magazines.

Experience

Almost two decades of working with senior executives, CLOs, and learning and development teams has given us a varied base of experience.

Each of us has served in management roles—including senior executive of one organization and head of learning and development for two major organizations. This expertise has provided us with a knowledgeable backdrop for working with senior teams to achieve the kinds of results discussed in this book.

Review of the Literature

Much has been studied and written about executives' concerns about learning and development. Although some of it is misplaced and incorrect, much literature has been published defining what does and does not work in this field. As authors, speakers, researchers, and academicians, we know the importance of copious research. For the past five years, we have studied what others have reported in this important area. These findings are included and referenced in the book.

Key Questions

When learning and development teams pursue a comprehensive process, they often have anxiety, issues, and concerns. They have important questions they want resolved. Typical questions are

- What data is desired by senior management?
- What data is not desired by senior management?
- How can I protect and enhance the learning and development budget?
- How can I enhance my influence with key executives?
- How can I make the business case for increased funds for measurement and evaluation?
- How can I move our measures up the evaluation chain?
- How can I collect data efficiently?
- What data should be collected at each level?
- How can I design a practical evaluation strategy that has credibility with senior executives?
- How can I integrate data in a management scorecard?
- How should evaluation data be used?
- How can I secure executive support for my evaluation strategy?

- How can I proceed if the evaluation reveals an unacceptable result?
- How can I use the evaluation process to implement a result-based philosophy?
- How can I make cost-effective decisions at each evaluation level?
- How can I convince executives that my program is linked to business performance measures?

Answers to and issues concerning each of these questions, as well as others, are given in detail in this book. The responses can help resolve many measurement and evaluation system challenges.

◆ ◆ ◆

Final Thoughts

After reading this chapter, you may believe that the mystery of learning and development success can be solved. And it can—but not before you know your top executives and pick up their clues along the way. In this chapter, the rationale for the book has been explored and the rich sources of data have been described to show the basis for the book. The next chapter highlights CEOs' concerns about the success of learning and development activities, opportunities CEOs see for these activities, and benefits for the learning and development leader.

Learning Investments That Matter

Executive Concerns Highlighted by the Research

If it were possible to know what your executive was thinking, then the success that he or she desires within your learning and development department could easily be achieved. But because the likelihood of your being clairvoyant is slim, the executive view remains under a veil of mystery.

This chapter highlights what the rest of this book will describe in detail: your executive's concerns and issues regarding learning and development. Thus, it focuses on three critical areas: (1) executive concerns about the success of learning and development activities, (2) the opportunities executives see for learning and development, and (3) the benefits for the learning and development executive. The presentation is based on our research, which is described and summarized in the appendixes. The comments are directly from the executives.

Executive Concerns about Learning and Development Success

Though it comes as no surprise that executives often voice concerns about learning and development, some of those expressed by the executives participating in the study are the same ones that the learning and development industry has been facing for many years. While we think we're making progress, it appears we still have work to do.

Learning and Development: A Faith-Based Initiative?

"Our budget continues to grow, and some of our projects are huge. We can no longer put this kind of money into these projects on faith that it will deliver results."

There's no doubt that executives support learning and development and see it as central and necessary for success. But as described earlier in this book, we need more data. Lack of data showing the value of the learning and development program or reflecting how it is connected with business forces the executive to take the investment on faith. Though some faith-based decisions may be permissible, when an investment is large or a project is staggering, executives need more than faith. They need data.

To a certain extent, the learning and development executive has propagated the faith-based investment. These executives often express the concerns about the measurement of success and the connection to the business. "You can't measure it," is their common reaction. Some executives, those who have asked for particular programs or supported pet projects, have reinforced this by saying, "Well, you cannot measure it, but let's do it." Now is the time to change the investment decision-making process from one based on faith alone to one based on a concrete business outcome expressed convincingly to senior executives. Without a basis for doing it, learning and development becomes a faith-based initiative, as the sidebar illustrates.

CONCEPTS IN ACTION A software supplier for the financial services industry, a *Fortune* 500 company, developed a leadership program and required all its managers to attend. The program was based on a best-selling book and was taught by the book's authors. Several hundred managers attended. Both the executives and the learning and development team assumed that results would follow, although content was not necessarily closely linked to the organization's issues, and the objectives were not focused on any specific business contribution. When making the investment decision, they concluded, "We'll implement this program on faith—faith that the managers will learn, apply, and adapt to the tremendous changes facing this organization." Unfortunately, after the program was conducted and the senior executive questioned its success, no one could see any change or value.

Increasing Costs

"The learning and development budget continues to grow, and I'm not sure exactly why. There's no other line item on our budget at that magnitude that escapes the accountability of this particular process."

Executive concern over the costs of learning and development continues to grow. As costs rise, learning and development budgets become targets for others who would like to have the money for their own projects. What was once considered a mere cost of doing business is now considered an investment, and one to be wisely allocated. Learning and development is, of course, necessary, particularly to introduce new skills and technology to employees. But without evidence of a measurable contribution to the organization, it is often viewed by executives as a frivolous expense.

In fact, as the sidebar illustrates, the hidden costs of learning and development often, if not always, outweigh the direct costs. And though it may make one feel better to only assume the direct cost, the total investment is then well understated. The learning and development executive's worst nightmare is to be audited by the internal audit office and not have a reasonable idea of the full cost of his or her programs. Audits are occurring more often, and the reports written by the internal audit team are not often very flattering. Cost is certainly an area auditors will always explore, and without full disclosure—not to mention monetary benefits to show for those costs—the report is often embarrassing.

CONCEPTS IN ACTION

Management controls of a large state agency were examined by the state auditor. A portion of the audit focused on internal learning and development costs. Costs tracked for an intervention usually focus on direct or "hard" costs and largely ignore the cost of participant time spent in the program or the cost of other stakeholders supporting the program. The costs of participant time to prepare for and attend the sessions were not tracked. For one management development program, including such costs raised the total costs dramatically. The agency stated that the total two-year costs for the specific program were about $600,000. This figure included only direct, out-of-pocket costs to the vendor and, as such, was substantially less than the cost of the time spent by the staff preparing for and attending the various meetings and sessions; accounting for preliminary work and attendance, the figure came to $1.39 million. If the statewide average of 45.5 percent for employee benefits is considered, the indirect cost of staff time to prepare for and attend meetings related to the program totaled $2 million. Finally, if the agency's direct costs of $600,000 were added to the $2 million indirect cost, the total cost becomes more than $2.6 million.

These days, the annual direct cost of organizational learning and development is estimated to be more than $100 billion in the United States. A few large organizations spend as much as $1 billion every year on corporate learning and development. Even during economic downturns, this staggering magnitude of spending on learning and development can no longer be considered a mere expense but must be seen as an investment—and many executives expect a return on this investment.

Program Failures

"Our learning and development team seems to jump on one fad after another, with almost no data showing that it's making a difference."

Almost every organization, whether for-profit or nonprofit, experiences unsuccessful programs that go astray, cost far too much, or fail to deliver on promises. Some of these disasters are legendary. Some are swept into closets and left to haunt their owners. A string of failures generates increased concerns about the value of the investment, as the sidebar suggests.

CONCEPTS IN ACTION
A firm implemented a customer service program based on requests from a midlevel operating executive. Hundreds of people attended the program. Finally, after several complaints about the program, someone

had the courage to ask about its value. When the learning and development team evaluated it at the executives' request, the findings were telling. In sum, the participants saw no need for the program, learned nothing from it, and applied nothing from it on the job—and thus it had no impact. Though the program was a miserable failure, it was a preventable disaster for the learning and development team. There had been many early flags suggesting that the program was not needed—yet it ran anyway.

Many critics of these unsuccessful programs suggest that failure could be avoided if (1) the program is conceived on the basis of a legitimate need, (2) staff do adequate planning at the outset, (3) data is collected during the program's operation to confirm that it is on track, and (4) an appropriate evaluation is conducted to detail the program's contribution. Unfortunately, these steps are sometimes unintentionally omitted, not fully understood, or purposely ignored—and hence, greater emphasis needs to be placed on accountability for these programs.

Lack of Business Alignment

"It's hard for us to see the business connection to many of these projects and programs. While a few are obvious, such as sales training, others are less obvious."

Business alignment is critical in all types of organizations. Executives require it; some even take for granted that it actually exists. The learning and development function often struggles to ensure this alignment. It typically breaks down at the beginning phase of programs, where they are not connected to a business need defined by specific measures. This is the number one reason why learning and development fails, according to our analysis of several hundred studies, which was published in *Training* magazine (Phillips and Phillips 2002). Even if the business measure(s) has been identified, quite often the solution doesn't connect or is implemented with no regard to the connection. Either way, it's disastrous.

In addition, business alignment derails during a program when all stakeholders, particularly the participants, do not see the business connection.

Impact objectives are often not developed to support the program or are not presented as key program outcomes.

Along with not identifying the business need or developing critical impact objectives, validation of alignment is often missing because the actual improvement in the business measure is not connected to the program. Essentially, the evaluation process did not attempt to isolate the effects of the program from other influences. These issues bring concerns to the executive group, requiring more analysis of major projects and programs to ensure that the alignment exists at all three program phases—as the sidebar shows.

CONCEPTS
IN ACTION

A large bank in South America was interested in improving the quality of its loan portfolio, but it had two major issues. First, the percentage of loan rejections through the underwriting process was too high. Basically, the loan officers were bringing substandard loans to the process. Second, it was taking too long to develop the loan package, causing delays and thus affecting overall volume. Through a local banking institute, the bank secured a prominent speaker, the best-known credit guru in South America, to help address the issue. A sample group of 20 of almost 1,000 loan officers was trained in a three-day pilot off-site program at an upscale hotel. This program was expensive due to consulting fees and the offsite expenses. An evaluation of the program revealed some interesting results.

The speaker did not want to capture feedback at the reaction and learning levels (for the details about the various levels, see appendix A), suggesting that his programs were always successful. "There is no need to do this," he argued. He was not interested in evaluating the program at all. However, the bank was interested, and it captured data in the follow-up, which included reaction, learning, application, and impact data.

The bank discovered at the impact level that one of the measures improved, while the other did not. The speed of processing loan packages improved when the trained group was compared with a comparison group. However, the quality of loans diminished. The actual reject rate went up, which is the opposite of what they wanted. This yielded a negative ROI, much to the surprise of the organization and the speaker. Through the analysis of the additional data, they found the content was not necessarily aligned to specific business issues faced by the bank.

Some adjustments were needed going forward, and these were made. But, without this analysis, all 1,000 people would have been trained, yielding no business connection and a negative ROI—not to mention a tremendous waste of effort.

Lack of Business Contribution

I have yet to see any business data that has been driven by our learning and development programs. I need to see something, a contribution, from a business perspective.

Another issue critical to executives is the failure of learning and development to show its business contribution. This type of data is rarely reported to the senior team in terms that are reliable and credible. Just suggesting that learning and development programs help improve productivity, profits, market share, job satisfaction, customer service, and so forth lacks credibility unless there is data that show this connection. The issue here is twofold—first, the failure to connect the major project to specific business impact measures; and second, very closely related, isolating the effects of learning and development. When a business measure changes or improves, many other factors drive it, and professionals must make an attempt to isolate the effects of learning on that measure. Without it, reporting improvement in that measure lacks credibility. Executives need evidence to respond to key questions such as "How will this help our business?" "How will this help me meet my goals?" and "How is it driving our major goals?"

CONCEPTS IN ACTION

A respected government-owned broadcasting company in Europe spent more than $5 million for a leadership program for several hundred managers. This program was implemented without any specific plan to measure the success beyond capturing traditional reaction measures in a classroom. Although the CEO requested the program, there was no attempt from the learning and development team to pin down the program's connection to job performance or business impact needs. After the training was complete, a new CEO took the helm and immediately asked the learning and development team about the program's business contribution. There was none to be found. After detailed discussions with various team members, it appeared that no apparent behavior change and certainly no business contribution could be tied to the program. This episode damaged the learning and development executive's reputation and resulted in the termination of the leadership development supplier's contract. The lesson learned here: Major projects, representing significant expenditures aimed at critical issues that attract the attention of management, should be evaluated at the impact level in an effort to show a business contribution. At a minimum, these high-cost, highly visible programs should result in change in behavior and an improvement in business impact.

Failure to "Show the Money"

"It would be helpful if the learning and development team could show us the monetary value returned from investing in our major projects. Although 'show me the money' is cliché, I think it's certainly appropriate when expenditures are significant."

Many learning and development executives are concerned that too much focus is placed on economic value of their programs. But it is the economics that allows organizations and individuals to contribute to the greater good. Monetary resources are limited, and they can and must be put to best use—not underused or overused. Executives have choices about where they invest these resources. To ensure that monetary resources are put to best use, they must be allocated to programs, processes, and projects that yield the greatest return.

For example, if a learning solution improves productivity, one might assume that it has been successful. But if the program cost more than the productivity gains are worth, has value been added to the organization? Could a less-expensive process have yielded similar or even better results, possibly reaping a more positive ROI? Questions like these are, or should be, asked on a routine basis. No longer will activity suffice as a measure of results. A new generation of decision makers is defining value in a new way.

Figure 3-1 illustrates the requirements of the new "show me" generation. "Show me" implies that executives want to see actual data (that is, numbers and measures). This accounted for the initial attempt to see value in programs and evolved into "show me the *money*," a direct call for financial results. But this alone does not provide the needed evidence to ensure that programs and projects add value. Often, a connection between learning and development programs and value is assumed, but that assumption soon must give way to showing the actual connection. Hence, "show me the *real money*" was an attempt at establishing credibility. This phase, though critical, still left stakeholders with an unanswered question: "Do the monetary benefits linked to the program outweigh the costs?" This question is the mantra for the new "show me" generation: "Show me the *real money, and make me believe it.*" But this new generation of program sponsors also recognizes that value is more than a single number—value is what makes the entire organizational system tick, and hence the need to report value based on stakeholders' various definitions.

CONCEPTS IN ACTION

A large bank in North America embarked on a leadership development program for its top 450 officers. The program was estimated to cost $100,000 per participant, resulting in a $45 million expenditure over several years. When the program was put forward to the executive board for approval, its developers suggested that the board should

Figure 3-1. The "Show Me" Evolution

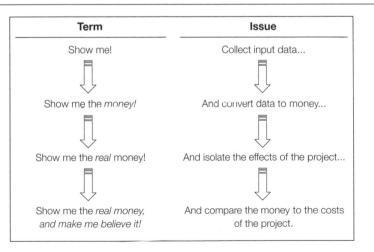

Term	Issue
Show me!	Collect input data...
Show me the *money!*	And convert data to money...
Show me the *real* money!	And isolate the effects of the project...
Show me the *real money, and make me believe it!*	And compare the money to the costs of the project.

not be concerned about its value because it would ultimately drive shareholder value. Their rationale was that the leaders were taking on particular problems of the bank that needed solving, and when these problems where solved, value would be generated. Obviously, because the board members were concerned about the cost, they suggested that the group show the ROI for the first group of 22 participants. This request from the board came as a shock to the learning and development team's members, who thought that they didn't have to "show the money." But these kinds of requests are becoming more typical, particularly when the expenditures are high, as in this program. When a program with 22 people represents expenditures of $2.2 million, it screams for an ROI evaluation. Executives can no longer allocate these types of financial resources without appropriate accountability.

Fear and Misuse of ROI

"Our group seems to be reluctant to go down the ROI path. We've asked some questions about it but have seen very little evidence. Quite frankly, I don't think they know how to do it."

Few business topics stir up emotions to the degree that ROI does. For a few misguided executives, the conclusion behind the ROI value is simple: If it is negative, they kill the program; if it is extremely positive, they do not believe it. We heard this position loud and clear in one of the interviews we conducted for this book with the CEO of a large accounting firm. The CEO said that he wants to hold his people accountable for programs in which he is investing—"If programs aren't working they need to go."

Unfortunately, this type of response from executives is what causes those concerned with the learning function to avoid the issue altogether. A familiar reaction emerges: "If my program is not delivering value, the last thing I want to do is publish a report for my principal sponsor." But if the program is not delivering value, the client/sponsor probably already knows it—or at least someone in the organization does. The best thing to do is to show the value (or lack thereof) practically, using a systematic, credible process.

With the fear of a negative ROI comes the fear of abusing both the data and the ROI concept. Will the data be used to punish people, reward individuals, or improve processes? Ideally, results should be used to improve processes. The challenge is to ensure that data is not misused or abused. The fear of ROI can be minimized when the individuals involved understand the process, how it is designed and delivered, and the value that it can bring from a positive perspective. The ROI must be reported in the context of the other measures of success so the audience understands how it evolved, and where the potential breakdowns occur. ROI has innate appeal because it blends all the major ingredients of profitability in one number; the ROI statistic by itself can be compared with opportunities elsewhere. However, for ROI to be used properly, it must be implemented to improve programs and not to evaluate performance, at least in the early years of use. Most executives support this approach.

It is important that organizations use the correct ROI formulas. The formulas used are the benefit/cost ratio (BCR) and the ROI calculation. The BCR is the program benefits divided by the costs. In formula form, the BCR is

$$BCR = \frac{\text{Program Benefits}}{\text{Program Costs}}$$

The return on investment calculation uses the net benefits divided by program costs. The net benefits are the program benefits minus the costs, then multiplied by 100 to calculate the ROI percentage. In formula form, the ROI is

$$ROI \% = \frac{\text{Net Program Benefits}}{\text{Program Costs}} \times 100$$

Deviations from, or the misuse of, this formula can create confusion, not only among users but also among finance and accounting staffs. The learning and development staff should become partners with the chief financial officer (CFO) and the financial and accounting staff as they strive to show this level of accountability. With the support, involvement, and commitment of finance and accounting leaders and staff, the learning and development team will feel more comfortable using ROI as a key measure and will be perceived as competent in its use by the larger organization.

Table 3-1 shows some misuses of financial terms in the literature. Terms such as return on intelligence (or on information), abbreviated as "ROI," do nothing but confuse the CFO, who is thinking that ROI is the actual return on investment described above. Sometimes, return on expectations (ROE), return on anticipation (ROA), or return on client expectations (ROCE) are used, confusing the CFO and others in the business community, who associate these abbreviations with, respectively, return on equity, return on assets, and return on capital employed. The use of these terms in the calculation of a payback of a program will do nothing but confuse others and perhaps cause you to lose the support of the finance and accounting staff. Other terms—such as return on people, return on resources, return on training, and return on Web—are also often used, with almost no consistent financial calculations, if any. Though these are clever abbreviations, cleverness won't get you the resources you need. The bottom line: Don't confuse the CFO. Consider this executive an ally, and use the same terminology, processes, and concepts when applying financial returns for programs.

CONCEPTS IN ACTION
Though sales training is probably one of the easiest projects to evaluate at the impact level (showing the sales increase) and even the ROI level (showing the profits from the sales compared with the cost of the program), one retail store chain instead used a measure of "ROE," which it defined as "return on expectations from clients." The members of the group felt that they could not connect the training to the sales; so instead, they developed an index based on questions that were provided to their client. These questions asked to what extent the client was satisfied with the program, using a scale of 1 to 10. The questions were averaged and presented as a percentage, with 100 percent representing a score of 10 for all questions. This ROE value was presented for one program as 85 percent ROE. Though it is good to secure client feedback, which essentially is a customer satisfaction rating, it is more helpful to see the actual value. In this example, the finance and

accounting staff was not so pleased with the result after all. ROE, in their world, is return on equity, and they objected to the use of the word "return." The lesson here is to avoid misusing accounting terms. The CFO and his or her team "own" the finance and accounting terms, and it is best to use them in the way that resonates with the owners.

Staying Relevant

"My biggest caution to the learning and development team is to make sure that they are relevant in today's world and that they are timely in what they do."

Perhaps one of the most critical issues on the executive's mind is the relevance of learning and development relevance to the organization, to future issues, to the people involved, and to the workplace environment. Ironically, program relevance can be measured usually at the reaction level by asking individuals if the program is relevant to their needs or their jobs. Executives and managers of participants may examine the content of the materials and receive feedback on a program. Through this process, they can get a perspective on a program's relevance. To most executives, staying relevant is an imperative; for an example, see the sidebar.

Table 3-1. The Misuse of Financial Terms

Term	Misuse	CFO Definition
ROI	Return of information or return of intelligence	Return on investment
ROE	Return on expectation	Return on equity
ROA	Return on anticipation	Return on assets
ROCE	Return on client expectations	Return on capital employed
ROP	Return on people	??
ROR	Return on resources	??
ROT	Return on training	??
ROW	Return on Web	??

Relevance became a critical measure when a global organization implemented a major leadership development program that cut across all its units, essentially trying to get them to operate as one unit. This program was envisioned as powerful, and it was expensive. The program was scrapped after the first group because the executives said that it was not relevant to their particular needs or the organization itself. The program was delivered completely out of the context necessary to move the organization forward. Obviously, to discontinue a major leadership program based on reaction data is extreme, but this example shows the power and importance of ensuring that the learning and development function provides relevant content on an ongoing basis.

Measures Are Not Sufficient

"I get so frustrated with the operating measures from our learning and development team. While everyone else shows how they contribute to the organization, this group shows basically how busy they are. I need to see a much better set of measures from this team."

Most executives are not satisfied with the current metrics strategy. This dissatisfaction is clear in the surveys, interviews, and observations presented in this book. Unfortunately, they don't always voice this concern to the learning and development team. These executives do raise questions and make subtle suggestions, but not usually in a forceful, demanding way until it is time to make a major organization change. Then they will require more meaningful measures. The reason that they are not so vocal is because of their concern that the learning and development team cannot measure anything beyond what they are doing now. The executives know the team is trying hard, but they wonder if it can deliver. The current measurement strategies are dominated by input measures, such as volumes, costs, and efficiencies, with some scattered reaction data. Also included in these strategies are benchmarking data, as well as some data about recognitions and awards. But this is not enough—as the example in the sidebar shows.

CONCEPTS IN ACTION A well-known telecommunications provider had one of the most recognized corporate universities and was benchmarked more than any other company. Externally, a perception existed that learning and development was connected to business impact, and that they had ample measures to show the business contribution. This perception was, unfortunately, not the case. Most of the metrics were based on input measures, with no measures showing applications or the impact of learning and development, let alone ROI. When challenged to provide measures that were more closely connected to the organization, the internal staff members resisted. After all, they had a great reputation; they were benchmarked by other companies; and they were perceived as the best corporate university in the world. However, though that was impressive to management, it was not what they needed. The executives persisted, and the learning and development team resisted, with little success. The executive responsible for planning and evaluation for this corporate university resigned and basically stated that the problem with accountability could be summed up in the phrase of an old Pogo cartoon character: "We have met the enemy, and he is us." Essentially, the organization internally did not change or want to change. Today, for all practical purposes, that corporate university is nonexistent. Obviously, all lessons are not this harsh, but this case brings out an important point: We must provide measures important to management. Sometimes, the members of the management group do not always know what specific data to include—they just know they are not happy with what is presented.

Benchmarking Limitations

"Our group provides a lot of benchmarking data, but I question the appropriateness of the data and what it really means to us in trying to understand the value of this important process."

In the past, many executives were obsessed with benchmarking. They used it to compare every type of process, function, and activity. Unfortunately, it has its limitations. First, the concept of best practices is sometimes elusive. Not all participants in a benchmarking project or report necessarily represent the best practices. In fact, some may represent just the opposite. Many benchmarking studies are developed by organizations willing to pay to participate. Also, what is needed by one organization is not always needed by another. A specific benchmarked measure or process may be limited in its actual use. Also, benchmarking data is often devoid of financial aspects—reflecting few, if any, measures of actual business contributions or ROI values. Given these weaknesses in benchmarking data, executives are asking for more specific internal measures that are more relevant to the organization. For an example of the problems that stem from relying too much on benchmarking, see the sidebar.

CONCEPTS IN ACTION	A well-known pioneering technology company in wireless communications acquired a tremendous amount of benchmarking data in learning and development. The firm's CLO presented this data every year, which included comparisons with the industry and with other organizations. Some of the important measures included the training cost per person, and the investment in learning as a percentage of payroll. Also, award recognitions received by the learning and development team were always included. Though the benchmarking data was helpful and appreciated by the management team members, they wanted to see more. They wanted to see data items that connected learning and development to the organization. Finally, the senior executives began to put pressure on the CLO to provide data and to show value. Unfortunately, that didn't occur, and this person left that post and the company.

Opportunities for Learning and Development: The Executive View

The previous section presented some of the concerns held by executives about learning and development so that improvements can be made. But executives are also optimistic. After all, they have been investing—heavily, in some cases—for years in learning and development. They must see some value and opportunity. This optimism came through in our data.

Investment Is Needed

"I think we could invest more in this area if we could only have some convincing credible arguments to provide more funding. I truly support what they're doing, and we have a great professional team. I would love to give them more, but they've got to show me something first."

Executives realize that formal learning and development is expensive, and even informal learning takes on some cost as well. Though the absolute investment value may be expensive, they realize that best practice organizations are spending about 3 percent of payroll. This may not appear to be so great for a formal learning function, particularly if the industry is growing. This cost is also relatively small considering the significant change organizations face with not only technology but also processes. And if we add mergers and acquisitions, which often require additional training and development, it seems more reasonable. So the good news is that executives recognize that learning and development does require investment, and they are often willing to provide more if they can see definite value being added.

Comprehensive Learning Is Needed for Growth

"I don't think we could have grown and expanded to our current capability had it not been for the learning and development efforts. They are on track, they respond, and they meet our requests."

Where there has been significant growth and change, executives realize the huge toll it takes on people and how these people must be prepared for their jobs. Multinational corporations also realize the huge expense of preparing people for international expatriate assignments and the costs of developing proper leaders. These corporations also know the cost of bringing in new technology, and they are willing to support and make it work.

The Learning Organization: Can It Deliver Value?

In the last two decades, organizations have experienced rapid transformation in competitive global markets and economic changes. Thus, their people must learn new ways to serve customers and use innovations and technology as they attempt to be efficient, restructure, reorganize, and execute globally. To meet this change in strategy, executives have supported the concept of a learning organization. In our interviews, 27 percent of executives identify their organizations as such. This requires organizations to use learning proactively in an integrated way and to support and enhance growth for individuals, teams, and entire organizations. A learning organization must capture, share, and use knowledge so that its members can work together to change the way it responds to challenges. Executives must therefore question old social constructs and create new ways of thinking.

With the focus on creating learning organizations—which have countless activities and processes to promote, encourage, and support continuous learning—measurement becomes important. If an organization has become a learning organization, how do we know? How are its learning activities measured? Is learning actually measured on a large scale? These issues turn attention to the measurement of learning, and as programs are initiated, learning is an essential factor.

The Corporate University: Will It Survive?

"Our corporate university seems to be functioning well. I think it could do more and play a larger role, but we have to convince our executive team that it's helping them meet some very challenging business goals."

Organizations around the globe continue to adopt the corporate university concept. Although the term *university* may conjure up a vision of a large campus with tenured faculty and a variety of academic programs, the corporate counterpart is much different. The corporate university concept is a process—not necessarily a place—where all levels of employees, and sometimes also customers and suppliers, participate in a variety of learning experiences to improve job performance and enhance business impact. In our interviews with executives, 23 percent reported they have a corporate university. The rationale for developing corporate universities varies. In some settings, the traditional training and development function has been converted to, and sometimes just labeled, a corporate university. At the extreme, some organizations have created a corporate university to meet specific challenges and address change. Although this trend began in North America, it has spread to Europe and Asia and, to a limited extent, the rest of the world.

For the corporate university concept to continue to flourish, management support is critical, including involvement in all of a university's phases and processes. Managers must willingly send employees to programs and involve them in learning activities. Senior management commitment is necessary because it usually translates into funding. Without adequate overall management support, the university concept can fail.

A comprehensive measurement and evaluation process must be in place to address accountability issues and show the contribution of the corporate university. Otherwise, the value may be questioned and the contribution will not be fully understood or appreciated. Perhaps this is the greatest challenge for corporate universities and for those organizations considering establishing them.

Executive Commitment Is Possible

"I'll be happy to get more involved in our programs and even commit additional resources in many different ways, but I need to see a little more value in what they do."

Executives suggest that greater commitment than in the past is possible. Sometimes they apologize because they haven't done as much as they could, and they realize that their influence is critical. Though time pressure keeps them from doing more, there is also pressure on the learning and development team to show more value. As was described above, the commitment often follows results, and if the results do not exist, the managers or executives do not provide commitment and personal involvement to the degree that is perhaps necessary. The danger is that they will begin to see learning and development as a necessary evil.

In one large retail store chain, learning and development essentially took on the role of providing nothing but compliance training. It became almost an extension of the Legal Department to make sure all bases were covered if problems developed. Obviously, this viewpoint vis-à-vis learning and development is disastrous and could seriously limit what it can achieve. The good news is that executives will increase their commitment, but they will probably need to see results along the way.

Management Support Is Possible

"Our learning and development team always complains about support— that they're not supported in the organization. And while I try to do my best to get the managers to support them, they have a stake in this as well. They must show these managers that they are helping them achieve their goals. When they do that, the support will come, and I will ensure that it does."

Support is usually expressed in the context of the members of the middle- and lower-level management teams. They do not always support learning and development efforts. They don't always want to send people to training. They view learning and development as more disruptive than necessary or helpful. The problem is that these executives and managers operate under tough conditions. They have goals they must meet, and their performance and sometimes their future depend on how well they can meet those goals. If the learning is perceived as disruptive in meeting their goals, it is natural for managers to resist. However, if they are convinced that the learning and development is helping them achieve their goals and is directly connected to their key performance indicators, then they will be more supportive.

Measures That Matter Are Feasible

"I'm convinced that my team is connected to the organization. They show me some data that says we're connected and that we're aligned to the business. And that's all we need."

A philosophy in the minds of many learning and development managers is that it is impossible to develop and implement meaningful business measures—at least, meaningful and credible to the executive group. Fortunately, this philosophy is not necessarily true. As will be illustrated throughout this book, it is possible to have useful measures that, when presented to managers in the right context, will be understood and supported. But first, they must be created. Managers aren't sure how to do this, but some learning and development executives are doing it, and it's paying off handsomely.

Benefits for the Learning and Development Executive

This section briefly considers a few important lessons for the learning and development team. They concern process improvement, funding and priorities, support and commitment, and image and reputation.

Process Improvement

Today's executives and administrators need information about applying knowledge, skills, and information in the workplace and their corresponding impact on key business measures. In some cases, they ask for ROI. Developing a comprehensive measurement and evaluation system is the best way to meet these requests and requirements.

Evaluation data can determine whether the upfront analysis was conducted properly, thereby aligning the program with organizational needs. Additional evaluation data can help pinpoint inadequacies in implementation systems and identify ways to improve them. Connecting learning with business objectives requires a continuous focus on critical organizational needs and results that can and should be obtained from programs.

A comprehensive evaluation system should provide information to improve the overall design of a program, including learning design, content, delivery method, duration, timing, focus, and expectations. These processes may need adjustment to improve learning, especially during new program implementation.

Learning transfer is perhaps one of the biggest challenges that the learning and development field faces. Research shows that 60 to 90 percent of the job-related skills and knowledge acquired in a program are not implemented on the job. A comprehensive evaluation system can identify specific barriers to implementing learning. Evaluation data can also highlight supportive work environments that enable learning transfer.

Funding and Priorities

Some learning and performance functions use evaluation data to support a requested budget, while others use the data to prevent the budget from being slashed or, in drastic cases, eliminated entirely. Additional evaluation data can show where programs add value and where they do not. This approach can lead to protecting successful programs as well as pursuing new ones.

Program evaluation efforts can provide rational, credible data to help support the decision to implement or discontinue a program. In reality, if the program cannot add value, it should be discontinued. One caveat: Eliminating programs should not be a principal motive or rationale for increasing evaluation efforts. Although it is a valid use of evaluation data, program elimination is often viewed negatively. The flip side of eliminating programs is expanding their presence or application. Positive results may signal the possibility that a program's success in one division or region can be replicated in another area, if a similar need exists.

A comprehensive measurement system can help determine which programs should have the highest priority. Evaluation data can show the payoff potential of important and expensive programs—the programs that support strategic objectives.

In some situations, an actual monetary value can be calculated for investing in measurement and evaluation. This is particularly true with the implementation of ROI, and many organizations have even calculated "the ROI on the ROI process." They determine the payoff from investing in a comprehensive measurement and evaluation process: the ROI methodology. This payoff is developed by detailing the specific economies, efficiencies, and direct cost savings generated by the evaluation process.

Support and Commitment

Satisfying clients is a critical objective for the learning and development function. If clients are not pleased with the data, they may decline the opportunity to use the staff in the future. If they are satisfied, they may use the program again and even recommend the program to others.

Participants' immediate managers need convincing data about the success of learning. They often do not support learning processes because they see little value in taking employees away from the job to become involved in a program with little connection to their business units. Data showing how learning can help them achieve their objectives will influence their support.

Senior executives must perceive the learning and development staff as business partners who should be invited to the table for important decisions and meetings. A comprehensive measurement and evaluation process can show the contribution of the function and help strengthen this relationship.

Image and Reputation

Collecting and using evaluation data—including application, impact, and ROI—builds respect for both learning and the learning and performance staff. Appropriate evaluation data can enhance the credibility of the learning and development and performance improvement functions when the data reveals the value added to the organization.

Middle-level managers often see learning as a necessary evil. A comprehensive evaluation process may persuade these managers to begin to see learning as a contributing process and an excellent investment. It can also help shift the perception of learning from being seen as a dispensable activity to an indispensable, value-adding process.

◆ ◆ ◆

Final Thoughts

This chapter has made the case for developing a more comprehensive, credible process to show the value of learning and development projects. Building on executive concerns about the results (or lack of results) from the learning and development team, this chapter has provided important insights for learning leaders and their teams. Executives are demanding, requiring, or suggesting more accountability, up to and including the value of learning. "Show me the money" has become a common request—and is being made now more than ever.

The chapter has also highlighted the bright spots seen by those executives who are optimistic about what can be achieved in the future with results-focused learning and development activities. A variety of forces have created this current emphasis on results. Learning and development staff members can step up to the accountability challenge, create a process that can make a difference, develop data that is credible for a variety of important stakeholders, and pursue a process that will improve programs in the future. The rest of this book seeks to delineate these efforts. The next chapter explores the first challenge: establishing the investment level.

Investing in Learning and Development

The Survey Reveals Strategies That Resonate in the C Suite

Ultimately, top executives set the investment level for learning and development. Though some rely only on benchmarking, others adopt more well-defined strategies. The executive view of the investment strategies captured in our survey can be found in appendix D. Table 4-1 shows the results from our survey for the question on approaches to investing in learning and development. Of those CEOs responding to the survey, 96 provided a response. As expected, the use of benchmarking was the dominant rationale for determining the investment level, with 39 percent of respondents selecting this option. Surprisingly, 20 percent invest only the minimum, what is absolutely necessary for job-skill training. Equally surprising was that 18 percent base their investment on the value received. Overall, the results provide a valuable and rare insight into CEOs' perception of the investment strategy issue.

With the results of the survey in mind, this chapter describes the five strategies for determining the investment level in learning and development that are most often used by the organizations researched for this book:

1. Avoid the investment altogether.
2. Invest in only what is absolutely necessary.
3. Use benchmarking to guide the appropriate investment.

4. Spend as much on learning and development as requested.
5. Invest when there is value returned.

Although an investment level may be set initially, using one or more of these five strategies or some other process, addressing the process of determining how much to spend in learning and development is an issue that should be reviewed periodically.

Avoid the Investment

Some executives prefer to take a passive role when investing in employees, attempting to minimize the investment altogether. Though appearing somewhat dysfunctional, this approach has proven effective for certain organizations, depending on the strategic focus and current status—although only 4 percent of our survey respondents indicated that this is their preferred investment strategy.

Table 4-1. CEO Input: CEO Rationale for Investing in Learning and Development (*N* = 96 large public and private firms)

Which of the following best describes your approach to investing in learning and development? Check the one best answer:

Action	Percent Answering Positively
We try to avoid the investment if possible, hiring employees on a contract basis, hiring fully competent people who do not need training, and using temps when necessary.	4
We invest only the minimum—what is absolutely necessary for job-skill training.	20
We invest at levels consistent with our benchmarking studies, using measures such as amount of learning and development as percent of payroll.	39
We invest heavily in learning and development, essentially meeting all needs that are identified in the organization.	10
We invest when we can see some type of benefit for investing, essentially investing when we see a payoff.	18
Don't know / Did not respond.	9

This strategy is implemented using one or more of three approaches. The first approach is to employ competent employees who need minimal exposure to developmental opportunities. This approach avoids much of the learning and development investment required by progressive organizations. The second approach is to use contract and temporary employees rather than permanent staff. This arrangement allows the organization to increase or decrease staffing as needed, thus reducing the expense connected to employee acquisition, training, development, and termination. The third approach is to use outsourcing to get the job done, often at lower cost. Taken to the extreme, an organization can outsource most functions that would be performed by its regular full-time employees.

Several factors motivate executives to pursue one or more of these approaches:

- *The cost of developing employees.* Some executives cannot—or will not—build the infrastructure to support formal learning and development.
- *The need to bring stability to the organization, particularly as expansion and decline occur in cyclical or seasonal industries.* Avoiding investment by hiring employees with the requisite skills and knowledge enables leaders to balance employment levels, address particular needs, and, at the same time, control costs.
- *Expertise may be unavailable in the organization.* It may not be practical to develop the experience needed, so executives will take advantage of external expertise.
- *Some executives pursue this strategy for survival.* They cannot afford to invest in developing their people, at least not to the extent needed to build a successful team.

Recruiting Competent Employees

In the early years, Microsoft took the approach of hiring highly competent employees who needed little or no training. Consequently, it placed little emphasis on formal learning and development. Later, it discarded this approach. Now it invests heavily in formal learning and development.

Most executives realize that the acquisition and maintenance of employees is expensive. Because of the magnitude of these costs, executives want to avoid them. Recruiting trained employees avoids the cost of socialization, initial training, development, and on-the-job training—although the salary and benefits may be higher than that of less-skilled employees. Ultimately, however, this approach may be more costly than training current employees, because new employees will need to be hired as new skills are needed.

Employing Temporary and Contract Workers

Because of the high cost of attracting and retaining employees, particularly in cyclical industries, some firms employ contract workers. This practice is based on the belief that the nature of the employment cycle can create unnecessary expenses when acquiring and removing employees. Table 4-2 shows the cost categories related to turnover. In recent years, the costs of departing employees have become significant as employers have spent large amounts on severance packages and services to enable employees to find other jobs. Coupled with the high cost of attracting and developing employees, some organizations conclude that a highly capable contract employee is the best option.

Many executives manage business fluctuations by reducing the number of employees, often through a "last-in/first-out" process, which is frequently used by unionized organizations. This leaves the most senior and highest paid, but not necessarily the most productive, employees on the payroll. The use of temporary and contract workers allows the organization to maintain positive employee morale by reducing perceived pay and job risk.

Outsourcing

Recognizing the high cost of maintaining employees, particularly on a long-term basis, some organizations have resorted to outsourcing to keep their employee head count to a minimum. For other companies, this is a strategy that enables them to remain highly flexible, adaptive organizations. This approach essentially creates a smaller number of core employees and a comprehensive network of subcontractors providing services

Table 4-2. Turnover Cost Categories

Orientation/Training Costs	Departure/Exit Costs
Preemployment training	Exit interview costs
Development	Administration time
Delivery	Management time
Materials	Benefits termination/continuation
Facilities	Pay continuation/severance
Travel (if applicable)	Unemployment tax
Overhead (administration)	Legal expenses (if applicable)
Orientation program	Outplacement (if applicable)
Development	
Delivery	**Replacement Costs**
Materials	Recruitment/advertising
Facilities	Recruitment expenses
Travel (if applicable)	Recruitment fees
Overhead (administration)	Sign-up bonuses
Initial training	Selection interviews
Development	Testing/preemployment examinations
Delivery	Travel expenses
Materials	Moving expenses
Facilities	Administrative time (not covered above)
Time off the job	Management time (not covered above)
Travel (If applicable)	
Overhead (administration)	**Consequences of Turnover**
Formal on-the-job training	Work disruption
Development	Lost productivity (or replacement costs)
Job aids	Quality problems
Delivery	Customer dissatisfaction
Management time	Management time
Overhead (administration)	Loss of expertise/knowledge

that regular employees provide in other firms or that regular employees previously performed. Outsourcing usually costs less and can bring in much-needed expertise and specialization. The external providers of outsourcing are usually responsible for most employee learning and development, avoiding the investment from the organization.

Invest in Only What Is Necessary

Although the strategy of avoiding investing altogether in learning and development is workable for some organizations, an alternative strategy for others is to invest in only what is necessary to get the job done. Twenty percent of our survey respondents have adopted this strategy. A few organizations adopt this strategy by choice; others do it out of economic necessity. Either way, this is a viable investment strategy for some organizations.

Basic Approach

This strategy involves investing the minimum in learning and development, providing training only at the job-skills level, with almost no development and preparation for future jobs. Executives adopting this philosophy operate in a culture that is sometimes reflective of the industry and the competitive forces within the industry. These organizations experience high turnover and usually adjust processes and systems to take into account the constant churning of employees.

This strategy should not be confused with efficient resource allocation. Obviously, efficiency is gained by keeping costs to a minimum. The strategy presented here is a deliberate effort to allocate only the minimum investment in the development of people. This strategy is about facing the inevitable in some situations, or making a deliberate attempt to invest as little as possible in employees.

Forces Driving the Strategy

The primary forces driving this strategy can be put into three words: cost, cost, and cost! Some organizations work in such a low-cost, low-margin environment that a minimal investment appears to be their only option. Low-margin businesses, such as Wal-Mart, operate on volume to make significant profits. Competition forces this issue in many cases, and it is inherent in some industries such as retail stores or restaurants.

In some cases, the minimum investment strategy is adopted out of the need to survive—the organization must invest as little as possible to make it, particularly in the short term. These organizations are often managed by executives who see little value in their employees and view them only as a necessary cost to deliver the service. They consider employees to be dispensable, easily recruited, and quickly discharged if they are not performing appropriately.

The Cost of Turnover

Organizations investing only the minimum amount in learning often do not understand the true cost of turnover. They see the direct cost of recruiting, selection, and initial training, but they do not take the time to understand turnover's other effects. The total of both the direct and indirect costs of turnover must be taken into consideration. This total cost is rarely calculated in organizations investing minimally in their human capital. Thus, the cost of turnover is often underestimated. More important, estimations of the total cost are not communicated throughout the organization, leaving the management team unaware of the potential costs.

As mentioned above, table 4-2 is a complete list of turnover cost components. This table contains a list of cost items that can be derived directly from cost statements as well as others that have to be estimated. Essentially, the costs on the left side of the table can easily be derived, whereas those on the right side typically have to be estimated. When considered in total, excessive turnover is expensive and disruptive. When the total cost of turnover is developed and expressed as a proportion of annual pay for the particular job group, the cost can range from 30 percent of pay for a fast food worker to 400 percent of pay for a computer software designer.

Advantages and Disadvantages

There are many advantages to this strategy of investing in only what is necessary. The first and most obvious is low direct costs. Executives taking this approach strive to be the low-cost provider of goods or services. In doing so, they must invest at minimum levels. Another advantage is that this strategy requires simplistic jobs, tasks, and processes. These job elements make recruiting, training, and compensation relatively easy. Finally, this may be the best strategy for survival, particularly on a short-term basis. Given the nature of their business, some organizations must operate with a minimum commitment to employees.

Despite these advantages, investing the minimum in learning and development can result in negative consequences for organizations. First, a minimum investment strategy must be considered only in the context of simple, lower-level jobs. Automation is desired if the jobs can be eliminated. If not, they must be broken down into simple steps.

Second, organizations using this strategy must be able to cope with a high turnover rate. With little investment, employees will tend to move on to another organization offering just a slight increase in pay. Executives must ensure that hiring costs are minimal and initial training costs are low. For example, McDonald's keeps its jobs simple and its training efficient, resulting in low costs. With these costs at a minimum, its executives expect high turnover and are willing to live with and adjust for it.

Third, this approach can have a long-term negative impact as the turnover costs cause the organization's efficiency and quality of service to deteriorate. This is not a major issue in a fast food chain where jobs can be broken down into small parts and administered efficiently. However, for a manufacturing organization or a large customer call center, it may be difficult to deal with the high turnover inherent with this strategy on a long-term basis. Learning and development executives in these companies are typically trying to increase investments in their function. This is a difficult road to travel; however, with the right internal champions, changes can be made. Using benchmarks, demonstrating value-added contributions, and aligning with business goals will help make the case for increasing investment in learning and development.

Use Benchmarking to Guide the Appropriate Investment

Most executives prefer to invest in learning and development at the same level as other peer organizations. This approach to determining appropriate investment levels was selected most often by survey respondents, with 39 percent choosing it. This approach involves collecting data from a variety of comparable organizations, often ones perceived as implementing best practices, to determine the extent to which those organizations invest in learning. The benchmarking data is used to drive improvement or changes, if necessary, to achieve the benchmark level. In essence, this strategy aligns the organization with a level of investment that the benchmarked organizations achieve.

Forces Driving the Strategy

There has been phenomenal growth in benchmarking in the last two decades. Practically every function in an organization has been involved in some type of benchmarking to evaluate activities, practices, structure, and results. Because of its popularity and effectiveness, many learning and development leaders use benchmarking to show the value of, and investment level for, learning and development. In many cases, the benchmarking process develops standards of excellence from "best practice" organizations. The cost of connecting to existing benchmarking projects is often low, especially when considering the available data.

However, when a customized benchmarking project is needed, the costs are high. Organizations such as ASTD have a benchmarking forum that uses a standardized tool for evaluating learning and development practices and compares them by industry, company size, and geographic location. Other helpful benchmarks come from articles in *Training*, *Chief Learning Officer*, and *T+D* magazines. These sources provide excellent opportunities to understand and validate investments in learning.

An important force driving this invest-with-the-rest strategy is that it is safe. Benchmarking has been accepted as a standard management tool, often required and suggested by top executives. It is a low-risk strategy. The decisions made as a result of benchmarking, if proven to be ineffective, can easily be blamed on faulty sources or processes, not the individuals who initiated or secured the data.

Benchmarking can be used in conjunction with other strategies. With its low-cost approach, it can provide another view of the learning and development function and the required investment.

Benchmark Measures

Investment benchmarks are captured in a variety of benchmarking studies focused on a few measures. For example, it may be helpful to understand how much is invested annually or quarterly for a particular employee category or group. According to ASTD's *2008 State of the Industry Report* (Paradise 2008), $1,103 was invested each year per employee; and the best practice was $1,609 per year. The 2008 *Training* magazine benchmarking places the value at $1,075.

Another measure is the investment in learning and development as a percentage of the total employee payroll. The numbers typically range from 1.5 to 3.5 percent. The best practice is on the high side. A similar measure is the total investment in learning and development as a percentage of revenue. This is particularly helpful in the knowledge industry, where the individual employee is generating revenue in many cases—in large consulting firms, for example. This shows how much is being invested in the learning and development of those individuals who are actually driving the revenue. A measure used less often—but one that may be helpful in some situations—is to consider learning and development as a percentage of operating costs. This measure recognizes that most learning and development programs support the operational issues in an organization and compares these program costs with other operational expenditures.

The total investment in learning and development can be divided into different job groups, categorized by department, division, region, or unit. Still other ways to analyze the investment are by functional categories, such as analysis and assessment, design and development, implementation and delivery, coordination and management, and measurement and evaluation. The investment number must represent a meaningful value for the organization, particularly when it comes from organizations representing a best practice.

Concerns

Several issues that often inhibit the benchmarking process should be addressed. Benchmarking involves two challenges. The first one is to understand the current sources for benchmarking studies. Respected organizations are needed as sources for benchmarking studies because having credible data is important. It is even more difficult to benchmark at the international level. A replication process is necessary for benchmarking in each country.

The second challenge is the character and accessibility of the benchmark data. The measures must be meaningful, respected, and comparable. Some benchmark reports contain data that is not easily replicated or obtained. Data must come from organizations recorded as best practice examples and those that compare with other organizations. Not all benchmarking sources represent best practices. Often, they reflect an organization's willingness to pay the price to participate. Organizations use "competitive intelligence" to drive business decisions based on comparative and competitive data. It is important for each learning and development executive to determine the right measures for his or her own organization and management. Once shared, the measure should be used routinely to make comparisons. Measures should be replicable and easily obtained.

Creating a Custom Benchmarking Project

The concerns about benchmarking may leave executives with little choice but to develop a customized benchmarking project. Although this can seem unnecessary and expensive, it may be the only way to match the organization's interests and needs with those organizations pursuing the comparison. Incidentally, if more organizations developed their own benchmarking studies, there would be more available data from the various partners. Figure 4-1 shows a seven-phase benchmarking process that can be used to develop the custom-designed benchmarking project. Other sources provide more detail on the phases of benchmarking (Phillips 2005).

Advantages and Disadvantages

Benchmarking satisfies a variety of needs and is used in several important applications. It is helpful in strategic planning for the learning and development function and in the decision-making process when determining the desired investment level. Information and measures derived from the benchmarking process can enable executives to meet strategic objectives.

Figure 4-1. Phases of the Benchmarking Process

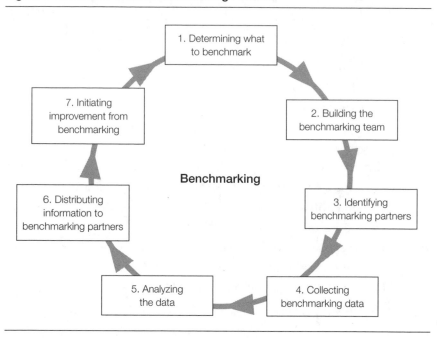

Benchmarking is also useful in identifying trends and critical issues for learning and development management. Measures from benchmarking can become the standard of excellence for an activity, function, system, practice, program, or specific initiative. It has become an important measurement tool for senior executives.

The benchmarking process is not without its share of problems, consequences, and issues. Benchmarking must be viewed as a learning process, not necessarily as a process to replicate what others have accomplished. Each organization is different; what is needed in one organization may not be the same as in another. Also, developing a custom-designed benchmarking project is time consuming. It requires discipline to keep the project on schedule, within budget, and on track to drive continuous process improvement. Determining the best practices is an elusive goal; benchmarking can create the illusion that average data, taken from a group willing to participate in a study, represents best practices. The sources and reliability of national and international data are a difficult issue that often limits benchmarking as a global tool. Finally, benchmarking is not a quick fix; it is a long-term improvement process, and one that needs to be continually replicated to be valuable and taken seriously.

Spend Money on Everything

Although some organizations invest at the same level as other organizations, many operate under the premise that more is better. They overinvest in learning and development. Of those responding to our survey, only 10 percent selected overinvestment as a strategy. The results of such an approach can be both disappointing and disastrous. A few executives do this intentionally; most do it unknowingly. Either way, this strategy deserves serious attention, because the investment in learning is beyond what is needed to meet the organization's goals and mission. Executives using this strategy approve almost every learning program they see and teach every new idea that comes over the horizon.

Rationale for the Strategy

Some advocates suggest that overinvesting in employees is not an important issue—after all, they think, the more you invest, the more successful your organization can become. However, others will argue that overinvesting occurs regularly and is unnecessarily burdening organizations with excessive operating costs. Overinvesting puts pressure on others to follow suit, thus creating an artificial new benchmark. This is often not a deliberate strategy. Executives are unaware that the increase in spending is not adding value.

Signs of Overinvesting

Many signs indicate that companies are overinvesting in learning and development. For example, consider the comments of the CEO of Sears, Roebuck, and Company when announcing disappointing financial performance. In an interview with a major publication, the CEO indicated that the company's poor performance was due, in part, to the excessive amount of training. Employees enjoy training, they want to take any course that is offered, and store managers support the training.

The result: There is not enough staff to serve the customers, causing customer dissatisfaction and ultimately loss in revenue.

Some companies make a deliberate attempt to invest a certain number of hours or days in training. Consider, for example, Saturn Corporation, once the shining star at General Motors. Saturn had a commitment that each employee in the plant would spend more than 100 hours each year in training. Manager bonuses were attached to this goal and trimmed significantly if targets were not met. As expected, employees attended all types of training. Some employees complained that they were attending unnecessary training programs—often unrelated to their work—simply to meet their training hourly goals. What had once been designed to show a commitment to learning and development turned into an expensive practice and, in some cases, a major turnoff in the eyes of employees.

Forces Driving This Strategy

Several forces cause excessive spending. Some are realistic challenges; others are mythical. Either way, they cause firms to routinely overinvest. During the 1990s, retention became the main battle cry of organization leaders. The labor market was tight, skilled employees were scarce, and executives would do almost anything to keep employees or attract new ones. This often led to investing excessively in learning and development, well beyond what would be necessary or acceptable in many situations. The conventional wisdom was that offering all types of learning opportunities helps keep turnover low and is necessary for business survival. However, many organizations—and even whole industries—were able to maintain low turnover without having to resort to this strategy.

Some executives spend excessively to remain competitive in the market. They must attract and maintain highly capable employees and are willing to invest in them. They sometimes offer all types of programs, which can cost the company too much. They want certain capabilities and are willing to invest to keep the talent. The talent becomes an important part of the competitive strategy.

Some executives have an appetite for new fads. They have never met one they did not like, so they adopt new fads at every turn, adding additional costs. The landscape is littered with programs stemming from such books as *Open-Book Management, The Seven Habits of Highly Effective People, The Carrot Principle, Who Moved My Cheese?, Fish,* and dozens of leadership solutions. Once a fad is in place, it is hard to remove, adds layers of programs, and goes beyond what is necessary or economically viable.

Spending too much on learning can occur because executives are unwilling or learning leaders are unable to conduct the proper initial analysis to see if learning is needed. A proper analysis will indicate if learning and development is the right solution to a particular problem or concern. Without this analysis, programs are conducted when they are not needed, wasting money.

Some executives spend an excessive amount on learning because they can afford to do so. Their organizations are profitable, enjoying high profit margins and ample growth, and they want to share the wealth with employees. During the 1990s, many high-technology companies made tremendous amounts of money. Some spent excessively on learning and development because they felt they could afford it. But when the economy turned, these companies could not sustain some of these expenditures.

Concerns

Obviously, spending excessively is not a recommended strategy. Many of the problems depicted in this section are the by-products of this strategy, not only for an organization but also for an industry. The most significant disadvantage of overinvestment is less-than-optimal financial performance. By definition, this strategy entails investing more than necessary to meet the objectives of the organization. Though some increases in investment yield additional financial results, there is evidence of a point of diminishing returns, where the added benefits peak and then drop as investments continue. This relationship between performance and investment in people is depicted in figure 4-2. Excessive investing can eventually cause the organization's performance to deteriorate, particularly in industries where the human capital expense is an extraordinarily high percentage of the total operating cost.

Figure 4-2. The Relationship between Investing and Learning and Development

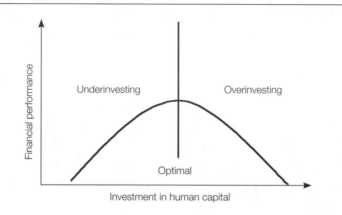

Invest When There Is Value Returned

Some executives prefer to invest in learning and development when there is evidence that the investment is providing measurable benefits. This was made evident by the fact that 18 percent of survey respondents indicated that this is their approach to learning investment. They often compare the monetary benefits of learning programs with the costs of learning. This strategy is becoming more popular following the increased interest in accountability, particularly with the use of ROI as a business-evaluation tool. With this strategy, all learning programs are evaluated with a few key programs evaluated at the ROI level. The ROI in these programs is calculated the same way as the ROI for investments in buildings or equipment.

The Strategy

This strategy focuses on implementing a comprehensive measurement and evaluation process for expenditures in an organization. This involves the possibility of capturing the types of data in the learning value chain, as shown in figure A-1 in appendix A.

Using this philosophy, only a small number of programs are taken to the level of ROI impact analysis, whereas every program is evaluated with data on reaction and satisfaction. Also, when business impact and ROI are developed for a program, one or more techniques need to be used to isolate the program's impact on the business data.

The Veterans Health Administration, part of the U.S. Department of Veterans Affairs (VA), is the largest health care organization in the world. The VA takes a very comprehensive approach to evaluating learning initiatives. Data is collected for each program implemented by the learning and development function. All programs are evaluated for employee reaction; 50 percent of them are evaluated for learning; 30 percent of them are evaluated for application (behavioral change); 10 percent of them are measured for their impact on business measures; and 5 percent of them are evaluated at the ROI level, where the actual monetary value is compared with the program costs. Table 4-3 shows the breakdown in terms of percentages of programs developed at each level.

Forces Driving Change

Although the trend toward additional accountability has been increasing over the last decade, there are several reasons why this strategy is critical at this time. In the last few years, demonstrating the value of learning and development to the organization has been at the forefront of the executive agenda. With this mandate, learning and development team members have had to develop the skill to communicate with other managers the contribution to the financial bottom line in the language of business. In a world where financial results are measured, a failure to measure learning

Table 4-3. Evaluation Targets for the Veterans Health Administration, U.S. Department of Veterans Affairs

Level of Evaluation	Percentage of Programs Evaluated at This Level
1 Reaction	100
2 Learning	50
3 Application	30
4 Business results	10
5 ROI	5

success dooms this function to second-class status, oversight, neglect, and potential failure. It has become apparent that the CLO needs to be able to evaluate, in financial terms, the costs and benefits of different strategies and individual practices.

The increasing cost of learning is another driving force. As has been discussed throughout this book, investment in learning is quite large and growing. As learning budgets continue to increase—often outpacing those of other parts of the organization—the costs they represent alone are requiring some executives to question their value. Consequently, these executives are often requesting or suggesting that the impact of learning be determined or forecasted. In some cases, the ROI is required at budget review time. A production manager, for example, proposes investing in new technology and incorporates into his proposal the projected increases in productivity and resultant decreases in unit production cost. With this in mind, learning and development professionals must compete for scarce organizational resources using the same language as their colleagues and must present credible information on the relative costs and benefits of their proposed programs.

This situation is not new. Several years ago, a special research report from *CFO* magazine, in collaboration with Mercer Human Resource Consulting, provided input on ROI from the perspective of the CFO:

> There is an argument to be made for trying to calculate the ROI. Taken as a whole, … human capital is an unavoidable cost of business. When considered as a collection of smaller investments, though, there are clearly choices to be made. Which training programs are worth investing in? If managers can gain some sense of the return on these different options, then they can ensure that money is being put to the best use. This may not mean putting a dollar value on the different choices, but perhaps understanding their effect on key non-financial indicators, such as customer or employee retention. (Durfree 2003, 24)

More learning leaders are managing the learning and development function as a business. These executives have operational experience and, in some cases, financial experience. They recognize that learning should add value to the organization and, consequently, these executives are implementing a variety of measurement tools, even in the hard-to-measure areas.

These measurement tools have gradually become more quantitative and less qualitative. ROI is now being applied in learning just as it is in technology, quality control, and product development. (For example, on managing talent retention and ROI, see Phillips and Edwards 2009.) A decade ago, it was almost unheard of to use ROI in this area. Now, business-minded executives are attempting to show value in ways that top executives want to see. Top executives who are asking about the value of the investment, including ROI, are viewing learning and development differently than they have in previous years and are no longer willing to accept the programs, projects, and initiatives on faith. This is not to suggest that they do not have a commitment to learning, but now they see that measurement is possible—ROI is feasible—and they want to see more value.

The ROI Methodology

To develop a credible approach for calculating the ROI in learning and development, several components must be developed and integrated, as depicted in figure 4-3. This strategy comprises five important elements:

1. An evaluation framework is needed to define the various levels of evaluation and types of data, as well as how data is captured. (These are defined in figure A-1.)
2. A process model must be created to provide a step-by-step procedure for developing the ROI calculation. Part of this process is the isolation of the effects of a program from other factors to show its monetary payoff.
3. A set of operating standards with a conservative philosophy is required. These "guiding principles" keep the process on track to ensure successful replication. The operating standards also build credibility with key stakeholders in the organization.
4. Resources should be devoted to implementation to ensure that the ROI methodology becomes operational and routine in the

Figure 4-3. The Key Elements of the ROI Process

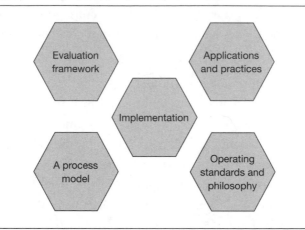

organization. Implementation addresses issues such as responsibilities, policies, procedures, guidelines, goals, and internal skill building.

5. Successful applications are critical to show how ROI works with different types of programs and projects.

Together, these elements are necessary to develop a comprehensive evaluation system that contains a balanced set of measures, has credibility with the various stakeholders involved, and can be easily replicated. Because of the importance of, and interest in, this ROI strategy, references focus directly on the ROI methodology.

Advantages and Disadvantages

The ROI methodology has several important advantages. With it, both the learning and development staff and the client will ascertain a program's specific contribution in a language the client understands. Measuring the ROI is one of the most convincing ways to earn the respect and support of the senior management team—not only for a particular program but for the learning and development function as well. The client, who requests and authorizes a learning program or project, will have a complete set of data to show the overall success of the process.

Because a variety of feedback data is collected during the program's implementation phase, the comprehensive analysis provides data to drive changes in processes and make adjustments during implementation. Throughout the cycle of program design, development, and implementation, the entire team of stakeholders focuses on results. If a program is not effective, and the results are not materializing, the ROI methodology will prompt modifications. On rare occasions, the program may need to be halted if it is not adding the appropriate value.

This methodology is not suitable for every organization and certainly not for every program. It has some very important barriers to success. The ROI methodology adds additional costs and time to the learning budget, but not a significant amount—probably no more than 3 to 5 percent of the total direct learning and development budget. The additional investment in ROI should be offset by the results achieved from implementation.

However, this barrier often stops many ROI implementations early in the process. Many staff members may not have the basic skills necessary to apply the ROI methodology within their scope of responsibilities. The typical learning program does not focus on results but on qualitative feedback data. It is necessary to shift learning and development policy and practice from an activity-based approach to a results-based approach. Some staff members do not pursue ROI because they perceive the methodology as an individual performance evaluation process rather than as a process improvement tool.

◆ ◆ ◆

Final Thoughts

This chapter has explored five different strategies used to set the investment level in learning and development. Though some strategies appear to be dysfunctional, there are often logical reasons for using any one of them. Avoiding much of the investment is a strategy to avoid investing altogether. For some, this fits the overall mission of the organization and may be an appropriate method to achieve a corporate strategy. Investing the minimum may be a requirement for survival for many organizations, although it often leads to serious turnover issues. Using benchmarking is the most popular approach, although the data may not truly represent best practice organizations. Spending excessive amounts can be harmful to both the organization and the profession. Fortunately, only a few executives take this approach. Finally, investing when there's value added by learning and development is an emerging strategy to assure the organization of the return on its investment.

Input Measurements

Time, Effort, Cost—
Low Importance to Executives

Measuring volume, costs, and efficiencies is the first step in capturing data about learning and development programs. For some organizations, these input measures are the principal type of data collected for the learning process. Executives quickly observe that this data represents activity, and they are concerned that the learning and development team is confusing activity with results. Knowing the activity involved in the learning process is important because it represents the investment commitment. But knowing the outcomes of that investment is more important. Regardless, the input leads to outcomes. This chapter highlights some of the more common input measures and provides the executive view on their importance.

The Executive Viewpoint

What do executives say about data on volume, costs, and efficiencies? It is the largest data set but considered the least valuable—for many reasons. Table 5-1 shows the response from the CEOs of large public and private companies, which verifies that input and efficiencies are the most reported data set; 94 percent of the respondents indicated that inputs are reported, and 78 percent indicated that measures of efficiencies are reported. According to 86 percent of the respondents, inputs should be reported; 82 percent indicated that efficiency measures should be reported. Though both inputs and efficiencies are reported and should be, they also both rank low on the importance scale. Using a scale of 1 to 8, with 8 as least important, the respondents indicated that inputs ranks 6 out of 8, with an average of 6.73; measures of efficiency were ranked 7 out of 8, with an average of 6.92. As described in the next chapter, only measures of reaction ranked lower.

Activity Is Not Results

"We have lots of data and our team is representing stats that all look like process or perhaps activities. We'd like to see more focus on results."

The learning and development staff must be reminded that input data does not represent results. It only shows what goes into the learning process and in no way reflects any of the outcomes described in the subsequent levels. However, this data is necessary and should be reported.

Table 5-1. CEOs' Views of Inputs and Efficiencies (*N* = 96 large public and private companies)

Below is a list of measures. For each measure, an example is provided to help you understand the type of data captured with the measure. Please check if you are measuring this now (check all that apply). Next, indicate if the measure should be included in the future (check all that apply). Finally, rank the importance of the measure to you, with "1" as the most important and "2" as the second most important and so on, with "8" as the least important.

Measure	We currently measure this (percent)	We should measure this in the future (percent)	My ranking of the importance of this measure	
			Average	Rank
Inputs: "Last year, 78,000 employees received formal learning."	94	86	6.73	6
Efficiency: "Formal learning costs $2.15 per hour of learning consumed."	78	82	6.92	7

Input Data Reported to Executives Should Be Minimized

"What I need is just a few data sets that show me that this is making a difference. Yes, I can spend a little more time reviewing data if it gets my attention. Unfortunately, what I see doesn't get me excited."

Executives care little about input data. In a broad sense, though they are curious about measures of volume and efficiencies, they want to see data on application, impact, and maybe ROI. Consequently, the learning and development team should pick the few input data sets that resonate with executives, or it should emphasize some of the areas under consideration or that need attention. Above all, in reporting, the space and time used to present this type of data should be minimized.

Inputs and Efficiencies Must Represent Operational Concerns

"I'm impressed that the scheduling is getting done here. There's a tremendous amount of volume taking place in our corporate university. I just wish I knew a little more how it links to the business."

The stakeholders who most value input data are the learning and development team members charged with managing the learning process. For them, these data items represent costs, inputs, efficiencies, and other key business aspects that must be known to organize and streamline this process—and maximize its effectiveness and efficiency.

Why We Need Input Data

Although, as the executive perspective reported above shows, there is some debate over the importance of input data, few would say that it is not needed. Inputs and indicators are an important first step in showing insight, commitment, and support for the learning and development function.

The set of measures included in this category represents the beginning of the learning process. It shows what is put into the process in terms of energy, effort, cost, and time. In the early days of formal learning and development, only this category of data was presented to show the basis for learning investment. Unfortunately, it is still the dominant type of data used by some, although this situation is changing. As expected, executives view this as one of the least important data categories.

Reflects Commitment

For some organizations, the amount of input reflects their commitment to and support for learning and development. This is particularly helpful for industries and organizations where the commitment is quite weak. Often, the executives in these organizations boast about the strength of their commitment to learning, indicating such statistics as the total number of people trained, the number of hours, the cost as a percentage of employee compensation, and other impressive measures showing the amount of resources allocated to the effort. A few organizations prefer not to measure the consequences of learning but instead simply invest heavily, hoping that the money will be spent wisely and used appropriately to deliver the desired results.

Facilitates Benchmarking

This level of data represents the most common benchmarking data—it's easy to count. In most organizations, input measures are part of the budgeting and cost control processes and, therefore, are necessary data items. Consequently, input measures dominate benchmarking, as illustrated in annual industry reports for magazines such as *T+D*, *Training*, and *Chief Learning Officer*.

Explains Coverage

An important consideration for organizations is to make sure that appropriate individuals receive the learning and development assistance that they need, and that learning programs contain relevant content. From the participant's perspective, the goal is to have content that is "just in time," "just for me," and "just enough." By tracking inputs and indicators, managers can show where these efforts are being applied and used by job function, by area, by topic, and in a variety of other areas. This helps management to understand what is being achieved and to identify gaps or necessary adjustments.

Highlights Efficiencies

An important consideration is how the investment in learning and development is being used and managed. A variety of types of data can be captured to indicate the extent to which an organization's processes are being streamlined, its deadlines and cycle times are being met, and it is operating on a lean basis—with a constant focus on improving its overall efficiencies and effectiveness. The learning and development function must do its part to show that it is being properly managed. Also, many of the data items measuring efficiencies focus on the length of time taken to accomplish certain tasks. This responsiveness to clients is often an important measure of customer service.

Provides Cost Data

Every organization should know how much money is being spent on learning and development. Although comparisons are difficult to make because of differing ways of doing cost calculations, many organizations calculate this expenditure and make comparisons. Some executives require learning and development costs be reported as a percentage of payroll and set targets for increased investment.

Measures Defined

As we dive into this issue, it's helpful to define the measures in this category. These are actually input measures (sometimes called indicators) that focus on the principal categories of volumes, costs, and efficiencies of the learning design, development, and delivery processes. The number of specific data categories can be significant, representing the largest data set collected and reported in most learning and development functions. These include tracking the following:

- volume
- hours
- coverage by talent

- topics and programs
- delivery
- costs
- efficiencies
- outsourcing.

Tracking Volume

The obvious place to start with input is by tracking the people involved. Several measures may be important to show the impact of learning and development activities throughout the organization. The first measure, total number trained, is the actual number of participants in a formal, organized, learning or development activity. This can also be expressed as a percentage of total employees. Ideally, all employees, or at least the vast majority, would be involved in some type of learning activity. The sheer number of people can also be divided into different categories. For example, it is interesting to report the demographics of program participants in terms of age, gender, and race.

Tracking Hours

Although tracking participants is important, tracking the time they spend participating in formal programs is more revealing in terms of investment. This is one of the most common sets of measures for benchmarking. Some learning and development executives track the total participation hours to create an impressive figure indicating the amount of time that participants are spending in programs. A more appropriate measure is the hours per person, targeting a particular amount of activity for certain jobs. Still others track the number of hours involved by various demographic categories. A few organizations make a commitment for an average number of hours per person. Though this is an admirable goal, it may create more activity than improvement.

Tracking Coverage by Talent

Perhaps the most important way to track people and hours is to track the coverage by jobs, job groups, and/or even functional areas. With the current focus on talent management, some organizations track the critical talent coverage. This involves tracking the numbers and hours of individuals who serve in critical talent categories. This varies among organizations. For some, such as pharmaceuticals, the research and development staff makes up one of the critical talent categories. For others, such as Amazon.com, the critical talent may be in the IT Department. For still others, it may be in the frontline sales team, such as the couriers for FedEx. In any case, showing an organization's amount of formal learning and development activity for this critical group indicates its commitment and coverage.

Another way to illustrate the coverage is by a particular function. This involves coverage by people and hours according to the different functions of the organization, from research and development to sales, marketing, and customer support. This helps to show which part of the organization is receiving most of the learning and development investment, particularly if gaps need to be addressed. Another way to express coverage is by specific job level, such as first-level managers, middle-level managers, and top executives.

Tracking Topics and Programs

Sometimes, it can be helpful to show how the content of learning and development activity is divided into different categories. Typical categories include sales, customer service, IT, leadership, empowerment, technical, and administrative. Tracking the percentage of the budget dedicated to each topic can be insightful—for example, the percentage of the budget devoted to leadership.

Tracking Delivery

The use of technology to deliver learning is one of the most interesting phenomena worth paying attention to. Although significant progress is being made in transforming content delivery from using traditional, instructor-led processes to more technology-based methods, progress has been slower than forecast by most experts. For an organization attempting to make dramatic shifts in how it delivers learning, this becomes an important area to monitor.

Tracking Costs

The cost of providing learning and development is increasing—creating more pressure to determine exactly how and why money is being spent. The total direct cost of learning and development is usually reported as a percentage of the payroll. This makes sense because organizations use learning to develop their employees, whose salaries are represented in the total payroll number. However, this can also be misleading—sometimes organizations with low salaries will show a higher expenditure as a percentage of the payroll because of the payroll's low cost. Only direct costs are reported in both *Training* magazine and the ASTD *State of the Industry Report*. If all costs must be included, this presents significant challenges for the learning and development function. The difficulty is that some of these costs—if not most—are incurred by other functions, yet they represent the total learning and development investment.

Tracking Efficiencies

Efficiency, an important issue for the learning and development function—particularly in larger organizations—can be measured in different ways and from different viewpoints. One primary efficiency measure is the use of the learning and development staff, such as the number of employees per staff member or the learning hours provided per staff member. Another measure is the average cost for each hour of learning consumed. Other measures focus on the average time needed to accomplish certain tasks, such as conducting a needs assessment, designing an hour of classroom content, and designing an hour of e-learning content.

Tracking Outsourcing

More organizations are outsourcing part of—and sometimes almost all—the learning and development function. For an organization moving in this direction, it is helpful to track the extent of outsourcing. The most common area is outsourcing delivery, showing the percentage of programs delivered by external services compared with internal ones. Another measure is the percentage of training programs developed by external contractors compared with internal staff.

What's Wrong with These Measures?

At this point, it is helpful to review what's wrong with these measures. The following comments come from executives, professionals, learning executives, researchers, and consultants who have a variety of perspectives on these issues:

- too much data
- too much emphasis
- activity = results?
- automation is insufficient.

Too Much Data

Obviously, the number of possible input measures produces too much data in proportion to other data categories. Measures can be sliced in a variety of ways, and some learning and development functions do this to the point where it becomes mind-boggling. Though it is good to know what's going on with inputs and processes, too much information is confusing and counterproductive. With so many data items, it is difficult to focus on the really important information.

Too Much Emphasis

Along with the fact that there simply is too much input data, a great deal of emphasis is placed on input measures. They always make up the first set of data reported, and unfortunately it is often the principal set. This must change. Because they are under pressure to justify their existence, members of learning and development teams would be well advised to answer this important question: "What percent measures represent input and what percent represent outcomes?" Some learning staff members suggest that probably 80 percent or more of the measures represent input. This high percentage is unacceptable to many executives. Although input measures are easy to track and monitor, they receive entirely too much emphasis.

Activity = Results?

Input measures reflect activity—busy people are involved, classrooms are full, e-learning enrollments are up, registrations are maxed out, and new programs are being developed. Unfortunately, however, there is a perception—particularly by those involved—that this busyness equals results. If all this activity is taking place, it must be generating something good. After all, these programs are all designed and implemented with good intentions. But mere activity-based programming is unacceptable these days. Results are the focus, and this means that outcome measures are relevant to all stakeholders.

Automation Is Insufficient

Because of the sheer volume of input data, it must be automated as it is captured, integrated, and reported. Fortunately, many learning management systems provide mechanisms for capturing most of the data sets described in this chapter. Because these data sets represent the greatest amount of data but the least value to executives, they must be captured in the most efficient way; thus, automation is critical. However, sometimes this automation is disjointed, requiring too much time from learning and development team members.

Innovative Uses of Input Measures

Although CEOs and learning executives are concerned with reporting excessive amounts of input data, this data is still very important. To meet this challenge, savvy learning and development team members can pursue innovative uses of input measures that will set them apart from others and perhaps capture the attention of the management team:

- Link to strategy or operational problems.
- Consider tracking by requests.
- Consider disclosing all costs.
- Report costs by functional group.
- Track for the scorecard.

Link to Strategy or Operational Problems

Learning and development coverage can be focused on specific strategic objectives. Often, the learning and development function is aligned with particular strategic objectives. When this is the case, certain programs are designed to support them. The total hours and people involved can be specific to a particular objective, showing current alignment with an important strategy, and this can be revealing to executives. Likewise, when a strategic objective has little or no coverage, it can spur immediate action to devote resources to it.

It may also be helpful to show how coverage focuses on particular operational problems, specifying people and hours. For example, one organization was experiencing serious problems with customer service, and thus several learning and development programs were aimed at improving this service, reporting the number of people trained and hours involved. Senior executives were pleased because they saw appropriate coverage in this critical area.

Consider Tracking by Requests

An often-overlooked issue is the percentage of programs requested and the reasons for these requests. Unfortunately, some learning and development programs are implemented for the wrong reasons—or at least questionable ones. Coding each program based on where and how it originated can provide insightful information about why a specific learning and development program was implemented. Table 5-2 shows the tracking of reasons for learning and development programs at one large financial services firm. What is revealing in this example is that over 50 percent of the programs are being implemented for questionable reasons—that is, reasons 4, 5, 6, 8, and 11 in the table. By tracking this information over time, the learning and development team and executives can see how requests are being filled and how the need for programs is evolving.

Consider Disclosing All Costs

Today, there is increased pressure to report fully loaded training costs. This requires a cost profile that goes beyond the direct costs and includes other costs, such as the time that participants are involved in programs. For years, managers have realized that many indirect costs of learning and development are accumulated. Now they want these costs included. Table 5-3 is a complete list of cost categories representing the fully loaded costs of learning and development.

Table 5-2. Sources of Learning and Development Requests	

Source	Percent Requests
1. An analysis was conducted to determine need.	12
2. A regulation requires it.	8
3. It appears to be a serious problem.	5
4. Management requests it.	23
5. Other organizations in industry have implemented it.	11
6. The topic is a trend.	13
7. It supports new policies and practices.	6
8. The learning and development team thought it was needed.	2
9. It supports new equipment, procedures, or technology.	10
10. It supports other processes such as Six Sigma, transformation, continuous process improvement, etc.	6
11. A best-selling book has been written about it.	4

Communicating the costs of learning and development without presenting the benefits is dangerous. Costs are presented to management in all types of ingenious ways, such as the cost of the program, cost per employee, and cost per development hour. When most executives review learning and development costs, the logical question is: "What benefits were received from the program?" This is a typical management reaction, particularly when costs are perceived to be high. Because of this, some organizations have developed a policy of not communicating learning and development cost data for a specific program unless the program's benefits can be captured and presented if needed. Even if such benefits data is subjective and intangible, it is included with the cost data. At the very least, an explanation should be available of how the benefits can be developed (that is, the method).

Report Costs by Functional Group

Another important way to think about learning costs is in following how the program unfolds. Figure 5-1 shows the typical learning and

Table 5-3. Categories for Fully Loaded Costs of Learning and Development

Cost Item	Prorated	Expensed
Needs assessment and analysis	✔	
Design and development	✔	
Acquisition	✔	
Delivery/implementation		✔
Salaries/benefits – facilitators		✔
Salaries/benefits—coordination		✔
Program materials and fees		✔
Travel/lodging/meals		✔
Facilities		✔
Participants' salaries/benefits		✔
Contact time, travel time, preparation time		✔
Evaluation		✔
Overhead	✔	

development cycle, beginning with the initial analysis and assessment and progressing to the evaluation and reporting of the results. These steps represent the typical flow of work during a program's cycle. As a performance problem is addressed, a solution is developed or acquired and implemented within the organization. Implementation is often grouped with delivery. The entire process is reported to the client or sponsor, and evaluation is undertaken to show the program's success. Costs are also incurred for supporting the process—administrative support and overhead costs. To fully understand costs, the program should be analyzed in these different categories.

This grouping of costs reveals two critical issues in this field: (1) the lack of investment in needs assessment, and (2) the lack of investment in evaluation. By reporting these costs, it is easy to see how little is spent on these two important components of the learning process. Often, the challenge is to allocate more funding in these two categories, even if it is at the expense of a program's design, development, and delivery. Additional investment in analysis generates huge returns, ensuring that the program is appropriately aligned with the business, is the proper solution, and is

Figure 5-1. The Typical Learning and Development Cycle

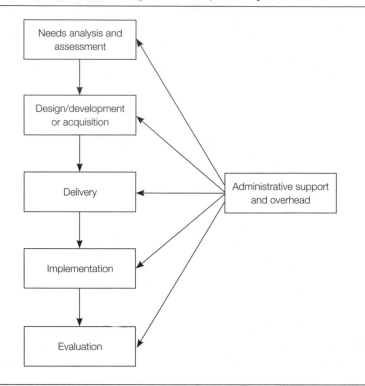

delivered just in time to the intended audience. Likewise, investing more in evaluation can make programs more efficient and effective.

Track for the Scorecard

The data collected for each program is at the micro level. In essence, data can be collected for each program for the types of measures included in this book. With this approach, each program is then measured at the micro level, keeping in mind that not all programs will be evaluated to the higher levels. Another issue is to show the combined contribution of all programs. For learning and development teams within very large organizations, there may be 500 to 1,000 or even more programs. Executives and managers need scorecard information that shows the total contribution across all programs. The approach is to select appropriate sets of micro-level data and include them in an overall scorecard, representing

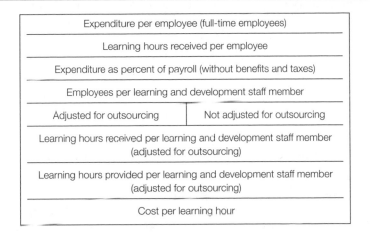

Table 5-4. Essential Level 0 Input Measures for Macro-Level Scorecard

Expenditure per employee (full-time employees)	
Learning hours received per employee	
Expenditure as percent of payroll (without benefits and taxes)	
Employees per learning and development staff member	
Adjusted for outsourcing	Not adjusted for outsourcing
Learning hours received per learning and development staff member (adjusted for outsourcing)	
Learning hours provided per learning and development staff member (adjusted for outsourcing)	
Cost per learning hour	

a macro-level viewpoint. Only a few data sets at each level would be captured to include in the macro-level scorecard.

Table 5-4 shows micro-level data suggested for Level 0, inputs, in the large macro-level scorecard. (For the details on Level 0 through Level 5, see appendix A.) For the most part, this data mirrors what is recommended by ASTD and represents essential inputs. Although many other measures could be presented, as explained in this chapter, these are some of the critical measures. Of course, the decisions as to which measures to include in the scorecard are based on the management team's priorities and the need to emphasize particular parts of the process.

Chapter 10, "The Learning Scorecard," will show how this overall macro-level scorecard concept works. However, each of the next four chapters will have a recommendation that will then be included in the overall scorecard.

◆ ◆ ◆

Final Thoughts

This chapter is the first of several chapters describing the different levels of data. At Level 0, volume and costs describe what goes into the learning process. Abundant amounts of information are available to be captured, analyzed, and reported to various stakeholders. These include data items about people, the number of hours, coverage of jobs and functions, tracking programs, topics, and issues.

In addition, it is important to track volumes, costs, and efficiencies for a variety of uses and applications. These types of data help the members of the learning and development team manage their resources carefully, consistently, and efficiently. They also allow for comparisons among different elements and cost categories. In many situations, costs will be fully loaded to include both direct and indirect aspects. However, from a practical standpoint, including certain cost items may be optional, given the organization's guidelines and philosophy.

Not all is rosy for input data. If there's too much emphasis on it, executives lose interest—but, unfortunately, it dominates learning and development reporting. Efforts must be made to streamline the types of input data gathered, report on them more selectively, use them in more innovative ways, and not put so much emphasis on them. The next chapter focuses on the first outcome level: reaction.

Reaction Measurements

Executives Are Only Slightly Interested

Regardless of your approach to gathering feedback from participants in a program, you want data that is helpful to its success. Collecting reaction data at the end of the program's operational phase is the first step toward reporting results. However, it is also the first step at which the chain of impact can be broken if participants see little or no value in the program. Unfortunately, though participant feedback can be a powerful type of data, this group of measures is often overused, misused, and misunderstood. Executives rate this level of data as least valuable. Yet reaction data is more likely to be reported to executives than any other type. This chapter explores ways to use this information for maximum value.

The Executive Viewpoint

Our research shows that executives place very little value on reaction data. They do recognize that it is important, and it probably helps the learning and development team, but it is not so useful to them when making decisions about learning and development. Here are a few details.

Not Much Value

> *"The reaction data means very little to our senior team. Yes, it's important for people to be satisfied with experiences, but it's more important to see what they do with what they are experiencing."*

Of all the data sets, though reaction to programs is reported frequently, it has the least value among top executives. In our CEO survey, reaction was ranked last (8 out of 8). In terms of use, 53 percent of CEOs said that reaction data was reported to them; yet only 22 percent stated that it should be reported. See appendix D for more details.

Unfortunately, the overall satisfaction measure has little value. Many executives wonder what it means when the overall satisfaction is low, or when it is high. When comparing this rating with other measures, such as the relevance of content, there is often a negative relationship, which reinforces the limited value of this particular measure.

Necessary for Someone

> *"Reaction data is helpful. At least, it will tell us something about the learning process."*

In spite of the points noted above, many executives do recognize the value of reaction data and thus believe that someone must pay attention to it. They understand that this data represents a process or an operational issue that makes it necessary to monitor learning and development from this perspective. And the learning and development team needs this type of data to improve processes.

Some Measures Are OK

> *"I'm quite pleased with reaction data, particularly when individuals tell us that learning has value to them. I look at this like customer satisfaction. We know good things will happen if we keep that number up."*

A few learning and development teams have abandoned the idea of reporting overall data on satisfaction and only report a few measures, such as relevance, importance, and the perceived value of learning and development programs. These measures are content related and begin to have more utility for an executive trying to understand the value of investing in learning and development.

It's All We Have

"I'm concerned with the importance we place on this type of data. Even our own learning and development team says that because people are satisfied doesn't mean that they are using anything from the programs. Thus, it appears to be almost irrelevant."

Regrettably, a few top executives have replied that this type of data, when combined with the Level 0 (inputs), is all the data that is available. (For the details on Level 0 through Level 5, see appendix A.) With some concern, they underscore that reaction data is better than having no outcome data. This dilemma highlights a major problem in this field—a lack of opportunity or desire to move beyond what is comfortable. Input data represents the cost of learning and development. Costs can be cut. Reaction data is easy to collect and summarize, but it is limited in how it portrays the value of learning and development. When this type of data is the only one used, it dominates the story of program success, making it easy for senior executives to reallocate resources to other departments and processes.

Why Reaction Is Important

It is difficult to imagine conducting a learning program without collecting feedback from participants. Their feedback is critical for understanding their perceptions of the program. Because of its importance, this level of evaluation is usually recommended for every program.

Customer Satisfaction

With the constant focus on customer service, measuring customer satisfaction with each program is important. Participants are important customers. The reaction from participants is perhaps the most important type of customer satisfaction data, because it is the participant who has to learn new skills, tasks, and behaviors if the program is to be successful. This feedback is critical to making adjustments and changes in the program as it is implemented.

Feedback Is Necessary for Adjustments

Sometimes, a new program ends up being the wrong solution for the specified problem. Immediate feedback provides an early warning sign that there is a disconnect between the program and the problem. Ultimately, this information helps to avoid misunderstandings, miscommunications, and, more important, misappropriations of resources.

The concept of continuous process improvement suggests that a program is adjusted and refined throughout its duration. Obtaining feedback, making changes, and reporting changes to the groups who have provided the information—the survey-feedback-action loop—is critical for any program.

Comparing Data with Other Programs

Some organizations collect data on reactions and planned actions using standard questions. The data is then compared with data from other programs so that norms and standards can be developed. This approach is particularly helpful in the early stages of a new program. Overall satisfaction data is collected and compared. Some firms even base part of the learning team's success on the level of client satisfaction, making reaction data important to the success of every program.

Measures Defined

Measures of reaction are vast due to the number of elements involved in a typical program. Feedback is needed for almost every major step of program development and delivery to ensure that outcomes are successful.

Table 6-1 shows the typical major areas of feedback data for most programs. The table shows the key success factors in a program, beginning with the objectives and moving through a variety of related issues.

Table 6-1. Typical Major Areas of Feedback Data for Programs

Category of Data	Reason for Collecting	Data Components
Participant demographics	Audience served versus needs assessment Trends in attendance Future planning Diversity	Job/role Department/division Education Experience Length of service Reason for participation
Logistics and service	Facility adjustments Customer satisfaction Critical to solution effectiveness	Location Room/comfort Communication Access to food and refreshments
Readiness	Right participant Right timing Ready to learn	Appropriate experience Prerequisites Motivation to learn Opportunity to use the program Timing of program
Objectives	Proper objectives Progress	Clarity of objectives Appropriateness of objectives Success with objectives
Learning materials	Adjustments Design Stimulate interest	Usefulness of materials Appearance of materials Amount of new information
Facilitator	Performance data Complaints Contractors New facilitator New material	Facilitator experience Knowledge and expertise Communication success Responsiveness to participants Involvement of participants Pacing of program
Media/delivery	New media Comparison of types of media Effectiveness of media	Delivery Media effectiveness Timeliness Applicability to content

(continued on next page)

Table 6-1. Typical Major Areas of Feedback Data for Programs (continued)

Category of Data	Reason for Collecting	Data Components

Value of content	Alignment with business
	Future planning
	Adjustments
	Design
		Alignment with business need
		Why learning solution was
		  selected
		Relevance of content to job
		Importance of content to job
		  success
		Input into business strategies
		Customer satisfaction

Practice and laboratories	Effectiveness Transferability to job	Applicability to content Similarity to job
Value of program	Marketing Pricing Commitment Support	Good investment in me Good investment of my time Fair price for program Overall satisfaction
Planned use	Follow-up Adjust Transfer learning Support	Planned actions Intent to use Recommend to others Barriers to implementation Enablers of implementation Willingness to provide data
Future needs	Planning	Additional needs Other programs
Marketing and registration	Source of enrollment Decision-making process Pricing Ease of registration	Source of enrollment Decision-making process Pricing Registration process
Open comments	Opportunity to identify unknown issues	Other comments

Source: Adapted in part from Barksdale and Lund (2001). Used with permission.

An important consideration in capturing reactions is to obtain data about the content of the program. Too often, feedback data reflects aesthetic issues but may not capture the substance of the program at hand. In this regard, here are five important content areas:

1. *Amount of new information.* In too many situations, programs simply rehash old material. Sorting out what is considered new information and what is old information can be helpful.

2. *Program relevance.* Participants want to learn skills and knowledge relevant to their work. Consequently, exploring the relevance of the material to their current work or future responsibilities is helpful. These types of data focus on a critical issue, helping ensure that the skills and knowledge will be used on the job. If they are relevant, more than likely, they will be used.

3. *Program importance.* Participants need to see that the content is important to their job success. This answers their question "What's in it for me?" Results with this measure also are indicative of the extent to which participants will use the content when they return to work.

4. *Intention to use the material.* Asking participants about their intentions to use the material can be helpful. The extent of planned use can be captured, along with the expected frequency of use and the anticipated level of effectiveness when using the skills and knowledge. Their intention to use the material usually correlates to actual use and is important for enhancing the transfer of learning to the job.

5. *Planned improvements.* Sometimes, gathering specific, detailed information about how participants will use what they learn on the job is helpful. A supplementary form can ask them to identify their intended actions and the consequences of those actions. These supplementary questions are not appropriate for every program, but they are often helpful when participants are in professional, supervisory, managerial, or technical positions. The responses provide an opportunity to show the anticipated value of the program.

What's Wrong with Reaction Data?

Reaction data, though important, is subject to much use and misuse. This data is usually collected for every program, but it has only a limited value from the executive's point of view. Reaction data is often the focus of jokes and unflattering comments. In this regard, here are a few issues related to reaction data:

- There's an image problem.
- This data is not taken seriously.

- ◆ There's too much data.
- ◆ There's too much time.
- ◆ There may be a deceptive feedback cycle.

Image Problem

Surveys used to collect reaction data suffer from an image problem. Often referred to as "happy sheets," "smiley feedback," or "happiness rating," the feedback from these tools is perceived to be a measure of participants' happiness. Though happiness can be a rating, it has very little use as a measure by itself. Unfortunately, happiness doesn't equate to learning. Content-related measures are essential.

Not Taken Seriously

Most stakeholders do not take reaction data seriously. Participants rarely provide quality feedback and often take little or no time to respond to a reaction questionnaire. Evaluators rarely use the data in a systematic way to make adjustments. The facilitators take the data and use it to feed their ego if comments are positive and discount it if comments are negative, filing it away with little regard. Program designers often don't have a chance to see the data and consequently fail to miss the opportunity. Even if they do see the data, they are often too busy to do anything other than put out the next fire. Participants' managers rarely see the data—unless, of course, it is positive. As was described above, the executives don't take it seriously either, often preferring not to have this type of data.

Although there are many ways to use reaction data, in practice, it is used very little. The data is generated but not often used to make adjustments to programs. Reports are generated and sent to various stakeholders, but unless there is something exceptional, the data in them is often not used at all.

Too Much Data

Approximately 80 to 90 percent of programs in an organization are evaluated using reaction data. This is entirely too much data collection when compared with the value of the data. The process consumes resources, leaving many organizations without the resources to collect and analyze data higher on the value chain.

Too Much Time

Because so much reaction data is collected, the process consumes time for the staff to design the feedback questionnaires, administer the questionnaires, process the data, and report it to a variety of stakeholders. Also, the participants take time from the program's agenda to provide the data. It's questionable whether the quality of data is worth the time it takes to develop the data.

The Deceptive Feedback Cycle

There is a danger of placing too much reliance on reaction, particularly to use it for facilitator evaluation. If the objective is for the participants to enjoy the program, the facilitator is the centerpiece of that enjoyment. As shown in figure 6-1, when the participants enjoy the program, the facilitator ratings are often high. Consequently, in many organizations, facilitators are rewarded on those ratings. When this occurs, facilitators naturally focus their behavior on the enjoyment factor (Dixon 1990). Of course, nothing is wrong with enjoying a program. A certain level of enjoyment and satisfaction is an absolute must. But if the focus is entirely on enjoyment and even entertainment, we run the risk of losing sight of the content and learning. As some of our professional colleagues say, "We quickly migrate to the business of entertaining instead of the business of learning."

How to Improve These Measures

To improve reaction measures requires actions to address what is wrong with the measures. Several tactics can be undertaken to create a renewed appreciation for reaction measures:

- ♦ Manage the measures.
- ♦ Minimize the deceptive feedback cycle.
- ♦ Delay the evaluation.
- ♦ Improve the response rates.

Figure 6-1. The Deceptive Feedback Cycle

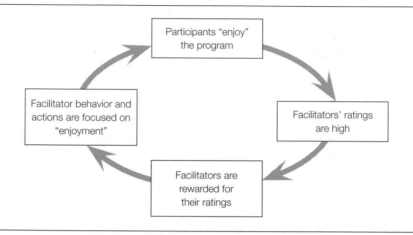

- ◆ Ask for honest feedback.
- ◆ Use the data.
- ◆ Collect information related to improvement.

Manage the Measures

An easy action is to report only a few measures that reflect the contribution of the program rather than the process improvement data. Content-related measures have more meaning to executives and other key stakeholders. This may mean leaving out some measures of overall satisfaction, facilitator ratings, and the quality of the experience, which have very little meaning from a value perspective.

It may be helpful to trim the total number of measures collected— perhaps reducing the amount of noncontent measures, and even considering evaluating only a sample of programs that run routinely with the same facilitators and participants. For large organizations, reaction data should be automated to the fullest extent; otherwise, data collection becomes too expensive.

Minimize the Deceptive Feedback Cycle

To avoid the potential problem of the deceptive feedback cycle, several actions can be taken. Facilitators' performance should be based on overall effectiveness and not so much on facilitator ratings. Perhaps facilitators should be evaluated on learning, application, and occasionally impact measures. This approach keeps a balanced perspective and prevents an overreliance on reaction data. Most of the evaluations should focus on content-related issues, as described in this chapter. Consider using these ratings to evaluate the facilitators. This approach moves away from relying too much on feedback focused on the facilitator's skill and entertainment.

The value of reaction data must be routinely put into perspective. From the point of view of the client and sponsor, it is not valuable. As noted above, many CEOs consider it essentially worthless. For other stakeholders—the designer, developer, facilitator, and participants, for example—reaction data is important. But for funding decisions, reaction data contributes little.

Delay the Evaluation

An increasingly common approach is to delay the reaction evaluation until a few days after the program has ended. This approach avoids the pressure to provide positive feedback to an anxiously waiting facilitator and reduces the influence of the excitement that participants feel at the end of a program. After participants have returned to work, the evaluations may be more objective.

Technology can help with email or Web-based surveys. A downside to this approach may be a low response rate. To overcome this, some of the techniques described next can help create the desire to provide information. Realistically, a 100 percent response rate is not necessary. A 50 percent response rate on a postprogram reaction may be acceptable, particularly if the quality of data increases. But don't delay collecting participant reaction too long after the program. If too much time passes, the data may not be as useful in making immediate change to the program content, design, or facilitation.

Improve the Response Rates

Several actions can be taken to ensure an impressive and appropriate response rate for reaction surveys and questionnaires:

- ◆ Early in the process, let participants know that they will need to complete a questionnaire.

- Indicate how the data will be used and perhaps how it has been used in the past.
- Design the instrument for a quick response, usually not to exceed 10 to 20 minutes.
- Make responding to the questionnaire easy, using forced-choice questions.
- Make it look professional.
- Communicate the estimated amount of time required to complete the questionnaire.
- Tell participants they will receive the summary of the results within an allotted time period.
- Routinely report to participants how the data is used to improve the learning and development process.
- Collect the data anonymously.

For more actions, see other references, such as Phillips and Stawarski (2008).

Ask for Honest Feedback

Too often, facilitators do not explain the value of participant feedback. Facilitators must stress the need for honest feedback and that this feedback is being used to improve processes. Participants should know that the information they provide is used to rectify problems and make adjustments. When asked to be open, honest, and candid with their feedback, participants may increase the quality and quantity of their responses.

Use the Data

Unfortunately, reaction data is often collected and immediately disregarded. Too often, facilitators use the information to feed their egos and then let it quietly disappear into their files, forgetting the original purpose behind its collection. Successful evaluation requires action with the data. The information collected must be used to make adjustments or validate early program success; otherwise, the exercise is a waste of time. A few of the common uses for collecting reaction and satisfaction data are

- Monitor customer satisfaction and make adjustments.
- Identify programs' strengths and weaknesses.

- Evaluate facilitators.
- Determine participants' needs.
- Evaluate planned improvements.
- Develop norms and standards.
- Link with follow-up data.
- Market future programs.

The point is to use the reaction data, routinely and consistently.

Collect Information Related to Improvement

Consider collecting data about results, including expected impact and monetary contribution. Although obtaining realistic input on a feedback form related to profits, cost reductions, or savings is difficult, it is worth the effort. The results may be surprising. Just a simple question may spur participants to concentrate on the monetary values of improvements resulting from their actions. A possible series of questions might be

1. Please estimate the monetary values that will be realized (increased productivity, improved methods, reduced costs, and so on) as a result of this program over a period of one year.
2. Please explain the basis of your estimate.
3. Express as a percent the confidence you place on your estimate (0 = no confidence, 100 = certainty): _____ .

This series of questions is sometimes used to forecast the economic contribution of a program, as described in the next section.

Innovative Approaches with Reaction Measures

Although the use of reaction data provides an initial view of a program's success, some organizations are attempting to provide more meaning for these measures, with approaches that include

- using different intensities
- building reaction measures into macro-level scorecards
- developing predictive capability
- forecasting impact and ROI.

Using Different Intensities

Because different programs need different types of questions and questionnaires, it can be helpful to think of three types of reaction feedback instruments. The first type is a survey instrument with low intensity and usually represents five to eight questions that are simply worded with value-based feedback. These are for programs that are short in duration, ranging from 30 minutes to four hours, where quick feedback is needed. These surveys use a scale that is suitable for automated analysis and avoid written comments.

The second type is a questionnaire of moderate intensity and would cover most of the necessary Level 1 feedback. This involves 10 to 20 questions and covers many of the issues described in table 6-1. The questions are designed for easy tabulation—using the 5-point Likert Scale, true/false questions, or multiple-choice questions. Few open-ended questions are included.

The third type of questionnaire is a high-intensity one used to gather detailed feedback. This is designed for pilot programs, where high-quality, in-depth feedback is needed. Sometimes, a detailed questionnaire of up to 40 or 50 questions may be necessary. In-depth interviews or focus groups could also be used. The purpose is to secure high-quality, high-content feedback, taking one hour or less. Because of the time and expense, this type of questionnaire is reserved for situations where feedback is critical to the program's future. Key introductions or the initial offerings to the first group of a pilot program would be a typical application of this type of data collection (Barksdale and Lund 2001).

Building the Macro-Level Scorecard

As described in chapter 5, a macro-level scorecard, showing the combined contribution of all learning and development programs, is recommended. This involves collecting data at each level to be included in the overall scorecard. Because up to 30 or 40 items can be selected, the challenge is to select only those measures that have value to the senior management team. These reaction questions represent measures that provide insight into the value of programs and are ideal for macro-level scorecards:

- ♦ How relevant is this to my job at the present time?
- ♦ How important is this to my job success?
- ♦ How much of the information is new information?
- ♦ I intend to use the materials from this program.
- ♦ This is a good investment in me.

Developing Predictive Capability

A recent application of reaction data is using it to predict the future success of programs. This involves asking the participants in a program to rate several key measures and then compare the results with their success with application at a later time. Figure 6-2 shows the relationship between data points, where reactive feedback correlates with application data.

The reaction measures are taken as the program is conducted, and the success of the implementation is later judged using the same scales (for example, a rating of 1 to 5). When positive, significant correlations are developed, reaction measures can predict the future use of the knowledge, skills, and information acquired during a program. Countless studies have been conducted to validate this correlation with certain reaction

Figure 6-2. Correlations between Reaction Data and Application Data: Seeking a Connection

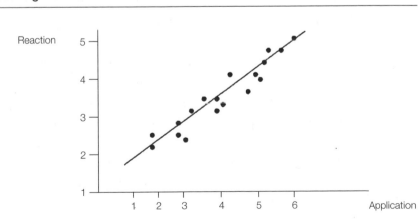

measures. Some of the measures that have been shown to have predictive capabilities are:

1. The program is relevant to my job.
2. This program is necessary for my job.
3. The program is important to my success.
4. The program contains new information.
5. I intend to use the skills and knowledge in this program.
6. I would recommend this program to others in similar jobs.

Although other measures have predictive capabilities, these consistently develop strong, positive correlations and consequently become more powerful feedback than typical measures of overall satisfaction.

Forecasting Impact and ROI

One of the most important executive-friendly approaches to using reaction data is to try forecasting impact and ROI. Here, the program participants indicate the extent to which they will use what they learned and the success that it will achieve. When this success is captured in one or two measures, then this can be forecasted into impact and actual ROI.

This process can best be described with a case. Global Engineering and Construction Company designs and builds large commercial projects, such as plants, paper mills, and municipal water systems. Safety is always a critical matter at the company and usually commands much management attention. To improve safety performance, a safety improvement program was initiated for project engineers and construction superintendents. The program focused on safety leadership, safety planning, safety inspections, safety meetings, accident investigation, safety policies and procedures, safety standards, and workers' compensation. Safety engineers and superintendents (participants) were expected to improve the safety performance of their individual construction projects. A dozen safety performance measures used in the company were discussed and analyzed at the beginning of the program. At that time, participants completed a feedback questionnaire that probed specific action items planned as a result of the safety program and provided estimated monetary values of the planned actions. In addition, participants explained the basis for estimates and placed a confidence level on their estimates. Table 6-2 presents the data provided by the participants. Only 19 of the 25 participants supplied data. (Experience has shown that approximately 50 to 90 percent of participants will provide usable data on this series of questions.) The estimated cost of the program, including participants' salaries for the time devoted to the program, was $358,900.

The monetary values of the planned improvements were extremely high, reflecting the participants' optimism and enthusiasm at the end of an impressive program, from which specific actions were planned. As a first step in the analysis, extreme data items were omitted (one of the guiding principles of the ROI methodology). Data such as "millions," "unlimited," and "$4 million" were discarded, and each remaining value was multiplied by the confidence value and totaled. This adjustment is one way of reducing highly subjective estimates. The resulting tabulations yielded a total improvement of $990,125. The projected ROI, which was based on the feedback questionnaire at the beginning of the program, is

$$\text{ROI} = \frac{\$990,125 - \$358,900}{\$358,900} \times 100 = 176\%$$

Although these projected values are subjective, the results were generated by participants who should be aware of what they could accomplish. A follow-up study would determine the true results delivered by the group.

Caution is required when using a forecast ROI. The calculations are highly subjective and may not reflect the extent to which participants will achieve results. A variety of influences in the work environment and program setting can enhance or inhibit the attainment of performance goals. Having high expectations at the beginning of a program is no guarantee that they will be met.

Although the process is subjective and possibly unreliable, it does have some usefulness:

1. If the evaluation must stop at this point, this analysis provides more insight into the value of the project than data from typical

Table 6-2. Level 1 Data for ROI Forecast Calculations

Participant No.	Estimated Value (dollars)	Basis	Confidence Level (percent)	Adjusted Value (dollars)
1	80,000	Reduction in lost-time accidents	90	72,000
2	91,200	OSHA reportable injuries	80	72,960
3	55,000	Accident reduction	90	49,500
4	10,000	First-aid visits/visits to doctor	70	7,000
5	150,000	Reduction in lost-time injuries	95	142,500
6	Millions	Total accident cost	100	—
7	74,800	Workers' compensation	80	59,840
8	7,500	OSHA citations	75	5,625
9	50,000	Reduction in accidents	75	37,500
10	36,000	Workers' compensation	80	28,800
11	150,000	Reduction in total accident costs	90	135,000
12	22,000	OSHA fines/citations	70	15,400
13	140,000	Accident reductions	80	112,000
14	4 million	Total cost of safety	95	—
15	65,000	Total workers' compensation	50	32,500
16	Unlimited	Accidents	100	—
17	20,000	Visits to doctor	95	19,000
18	45,000	Injuries	90	40,500
19	200,000	Lost-time injuries	80	160,000
				Total: 990,125

reaction inputs, which report satisfaction feelings about the program. Executives usually find this information more useful than a report stating that "40 percent of participants rated the program above average."

2. These types of data can form a basis for comparing different programs of the same type (for example, safety). If one program

forecast results in an ROI of 300 percent and a similar program forecast results in a 30 percent ROI, it would appear that the first program might be more effective. The participants in the first program have more confidence in the planned implementation.

3. Collecting these types of data focuses increased attention on outcomes. Participants will understand that specific action is expected, which produces results for the program. The data collection helps participants plan the implementation of what they are learning. This issue becomes clear to participants as they anticipate results and convert them to monetary values. Even if the forecast is ignored, the exercise is productive because of the important message it sends to participants.

4. The data can be used to secure support for a follow-up evaluation. A skeptical executive may challenge the data, and this challenge can be converted into support for a follow-up evaluation to see whether the forecast holds true. The only way to know whether these results will materialize is to conduct a postprogram evaluation.

5. If a follow-up evaluation is planned, the postprogram results can be compared with the ROI forecast. Comparisons of forecast and follow-up data are helpful. If there is a defined relationship between the two, the less-expensive forecast can be substituted for the more-expensive follow-up. Also, when a follow-up evaluation is planned, participants are usually more conservative with their projected estimates.

The use of ROI forecasting with reaction data is increasing, and some organizations have based many of their ROI forecast calculations on this type of data.

◆ ◆ ◆

Final Thoughts

This chapter is the first of four chapters on measuring results. Measuring reaction is included for almost every learning and development program and is an important measure of the program's success. Although data is collected for many reasons, two important reasons stand out. The first is making adjustments and changes throughout the program as problems or barriers arise. The second is capturing the participants' level of satisfaction with the program as measured by its content relevance and having it included as one of the key types of data represented in the chain of impact.

This level of data is not without its share of critics. Many professionals in the learning and development field will find that at this level, which is often referred to as "happiness," the data is sometimes irrelevant and the subject of much misuse and abuse. Executives also are not fond of reaction data, although they see how it might be helpful to the learning and development team.

Learning Measurements

Still Perceived by Executives as Low Value

Measuring learning is a classic role for learning and development teams. Understanding how much learning has occurred is particularly important for programs in which skill building is the primary objective. The extent to which the participants learn new tasks and new processes may be one of the biggest determinants of the program's success.

Though important to the learning and development team, from the executive viewpoint, this information is perceived merely as operational data, from which to make program adjustments. Though most executives are not interested in learning data, this chapter explores several issues that confront the appropriate level of measurement activity at this level, and why this activity is necessary.

The Executive Viewpoint

"I've never understood what the learning measures on our scorecard really mean. When I see the percent of people who've passed the certification exams, for example, I don't know if that's good, or not so good. Also, when they tell me the differences in pretest and posttest scores, I'm not sure if that's important from our perspective."

Executives do not score the learning level of measurement very high. They see this type of data as important for the learning and development team, but not important enough to judge a program's success. The results of the CEO survey show that executives ranked learning measures fifth out of a ranking score of 1 to 8, where 1 is the most valuable. With regard to use, 32 percent indicated that it was reported to them now, and only 28 percent said that it should be reported. See appendix D for more details. Here are a few specifics.

It's What You Do

"Some learning measures are helpful, but that's the principal activity in this process. However, some type of contribution would be more important."

Obviously, for learning and development, measuring learning is important; it's the nature of the function. Unfortunately, learning measures are not necessarily connected to outcomes, which often leaves the executive asking "So what?" For example, within a sales department, what sales people *do* is *sell*. Obviously, the consequence of selling is sales. To executives, observing what people do and relating what they do to an intended outcome is straightforward. However, when observing what individuals are learning, the outcomes are not so clear; therefore, pressure is placed on the learning and development team to move the measurement process beyond focusing on learning measures.

It's Necessary

"I sometimes get frustrated with the learning and development function when they've told us how much people have learned. That's like the IT Department telling us that people know how to use the software. It just doesn't mean that much; what does matter is what they do with what they've learned."

No executive would say that learning is not important. It is; it must take place in every organization. People must know how to do their jobs and do them properly. Many executives are concerned about having an unprepared workforce. They want employees to know what to do in critical situations, particularly in terms of safety, customer service, production, and delivery. Measuring what individuals must know in those essential jobs is comforting to executives. No executive wants to face an unprepared workforce, and knowing that learning has occurred will provide some comfort. However, most CEOs want more data.

A Simple Measure Would Help

When it comes to measuring learning, consideration must be given to what are the appropriate measures and what learning measures are relevant to key stakeholders. Individual test scores measure only that participants pass a test based on some criterion, but lack clarity about a participant's ability to do a job. The percentage improvement in a pretest and posttest provides insight into the degree to which change in knowledge has occurred, but again, it adds little value if there is a concern with ability to perform. The percentages of passes and fails on demonstrations is not always helpful, especially if it is important to know what it is that those who failed missed from a content standpoint. With so many different types of learning measures, a summary of results either becomes too cumbersome due to the sheer number of data items or lacks relevance, or both. Executives need, perhaps, one or two measures that give them some comfort that participants have the requisite knowledge and skills to do their jobs well.

At the End of the Day, It's a Process

"This is more of an operational measure in the learning and development section. It certainly tells them when there's a problem, and then they can take action. At the top, there's not much that we can do but to ask them what they're going to do. Therefore, it doesn't belong in our reporting scheme."

Often, learning is part of a process to achieve something else, and perhaps it is not so important to measure the process, but, instead, the outcomes of that process. That's what executives say about this measurement category. Perhaps it should be on the learning and development scorecard for the department only, but not the executive scorecard.

Why Learning Is Important

Several key issues illustrate why learning is an important measure. Individually, each issue can justify the need to measure learning. Collectively, they provide motivation for taking a more rigorous approach for measuring the amount of knowledge, skills, information, and attitude change that is achieved during a program. These issues are

- Learning measures compliance, sometimes.
- Learning measures competencies, sometimes.
- Learning measures certification, sometimes.
- Learning is the solution—it must be measured.
- Learning is part of the chain of impact.
- There are consequences of an unprepared workforce.

Learning Measures Compliance, Sometimes

Executives are facing an increasing number of regulations with which they must comply. Regulations involve all aspects of business, and governing bodies consider them necessary to protect customers, investors, and the environment. Sometimes, programs are implemented to ensure that the organization is in compliance with these regulations. For some regulations, measuring learning becomes the most critical measure to ensure compliance. Employees must have a certain amount of knowledge about the regulation to comply. Sometimes, specific skills are needed. Consequently, knowledge and skills are measured to ensure compliance.

Learning Measures Competencies, Sometimes

The use of competencies and competency models has dramatically increased in recent years. In a struggle to have a competitive advantage, many organizations have focused on people as the key to success. Competency models are used to ensure that employees are doing the right things. They clarify and articulate what is required for effective performance. A competency model describes a particular combination of knowledge, skills, and characteristics needed to perform a role consistent with the organization's strategic direction.

With this increased focus on competencies, the issue of measuring learning surfaces. Behaviors are learned and knowledge is acquired directly from learning and development programs. Though some programs are implemented to develop new competencies, almost every major program enhances existing competencies. Consequently, the focus on competencies is causing increasing interest in measuring learning.

Learning Measures Certification, Sometimes

The concept of certification has seen phenomenal growth in the learning and development field. Employees are becoming certified in a variety of processes, ranging from Microsoft products to Six Sigma implementation. With this focus on certification comes increased emphasis on measuring learning. Almost every certification program requires an individual to demonstrate that he or she knows some content or knows how to put some theory to practical use. Achieving certification in a specific body of knowledge places more emphasis on measurement than typical learning and development programs.

Learning Is the Solution—It Must Be Measured

When new equipment, processes, and technology are implemented, the human factor is critical to success. Whether there is restructuring or the addition of new systems, employees must learn how to work in the new environment; this requires new knowledge and skills. Complex environments, multifarious processes, and difficult tools must be used in an intelligent way to reap the desired benefits for the organization. Employees must learn in different ways, not just in a formal classroom environment. Learning must incorporate technology-based study, on-the-job training, and informal methods.

Learning Is Part of the Chain of Impact

At times, participants don't fully understand what they must learn to make a program successful. Any link in the chain of impact, described in appendix A, can break. One such link is at Level 2, learning. (For the details on Level 0 through Level 5, see appendix A.) The break indicates that employees just don't know what to do or how to do it properly. When application and implementation are less than successful, the first questions to answer are: What went wrong? Where was the chain broken? What areas need to be adjusted? What needs to be altered? Did participants gain the knowledge necessary to be successful with application and implementation? When learning is measured, evaluators can determine whether a lack of learning is the cause of the breakdown. In most cases, they may be able to eliminate the problem if a lack of knowledge is the problem. Learning measurement is needed to explain why employees are, or are not, performing the way they should be.

There Are Consequences of an Unprepared Workforce

Perhaps the most important reason for the focus on measuring learning is to ensure that the workforce is prepared. There are many stories describing how employees are incapable of doing what is needed to perform their jobs. This issue is particularly important for safety and customer service issues. Because of this concern, many executives want to know if the workforce is prepared. The only way to ensure that employees have the knowledge and skills to perform their jobs successfully is to measure it with credible, valid, reliable processes.

Measures Defined

Most learning measures focus on knowledge and skills, as well as participant confidence to use the skills. Sometimes, learning measures are expanded to different, but overlapping, categories. Table 7-1 lists typical learning measures.

Knowledge often includes the assimilation of facts, figures, and concepts. Instead of "knowledge," the terms *awareness, understanding,* and *information* may be used. Sometimes, perceptions or attitudes may change

Table 7-1. Typical Learning Measurement Categories

Skills

Knowledge

Awareness

Understanding

Information

Perception

Attitudes

Capability

Capacity

Readiness

Confidence

Contacts

---

based on what a participant has learned. For example, as the result of being in a diversity program, participants' attitudes toward having a diverse work group often change. Sometimes, the desire is to build a reservoir of knowledge and skills and tap into it when developing capability, capacity, or readiness. Capability tends to be a reflection of job readiness.

When participants use skills for the first time, an appropriate measure might be their confidence to use those skills in their job settings. This is critical in job situations where accuracy and reliability are imperative. Sometimes, networking with others is part of a program. Contacts made through networking may be valuable later. These contacts may reside within the organization or be external to the organization. For example, a leadership development program may include participants from different functional parts of an organization. An expected outcome, from a learning perspective, is for participants to meet others with whom they will connect at particular times in the future.

What's Wrong with Learning Measures?

Measuring learning is not without its problems, which may inhibit a comprehensive approach. Like other measures, this one has been misused, abused, and misunderstood. Here are a few specific concerns with regard to learning measurement:

- fear of testing
- ethical and legal issues
- too many resources required
- formal versus informal measurement.

Fear of Testing

Measuring learning is sometimes equated with testing, and participants often have a fear of testing. Few people enjoy taking tests. Even if it is a simple test, individuals in a program may have a fear of failing the test. Others resent being tested. The challenge is to make testing (or learning measurement) less threatening, and to ensure that test scores rarely, if ever, affect a job situation.

A test may question the professional autonomy of many individuals. Occasionally, formal learning programs will involve engineers, scientists, accountants, physicians, lawyers, or other professional employee groups. These individuals often feel that, because of their professional status or credential requirements, they have all the knowledge and expertise necessary to succeed. In a formal learning program, testing may appear to question their professional competence, and thus may be resisted. Many professionals want exemption from any activity resembling a test. The challenge is to keep the testing processes at a low profile and show the importance of learning measurement to the program while at the same time keeping test results confidential.

Ethical and Legal Issues

Ethical and legal considerations are challenges for testing. When test scores affect participants and their job status, a test must be formally checked for validity and reliability. Although not an issue for all programs, test validity and reliability become concerns when the acquisition of certain skills or knowledge is important for participants' job success (for example, a promotion, salary increases, or job assignment). The challenge is to take a reasonable approach, allocating resources to formally check for validity or reliability, when necessary.

A related issue is testing with diverse groups. Test results may differ across diverse groups, sometimes having an adverse impact on a particular group that federal or local laws protect. Even if a group is not protected, ensuring that testing does not have a disparate impact is important. Because of legal and ethical issues that sometimes arise from testing, many learning and development professionals avoid formal testing, eliminating the requirement to defend the validity and reliability of a test.

Too Many Resources Required

Measuring learning can require too many resources. Budgets are often tight; spending excessive amounts of resources on developing and administering tests may be undesirable or unnecessary. There is always a trade-off between resources used and the accuracy of a measurement. The important point is to manage resources for measurement as they are managed for other processes. This management process often leads to informal measurement.

Formal versus Informal Measurement

Part of the problem with learning measurement is the confusion about informal and formal assessment, which is occasionally labeled "subjective versus objective" or "unstructured versus structured." Some measurements involve tests, role-plays, skill practices, performance demonstrations, and simulations. These formal (structured, objective) processes are often resource intensive to develop but more accurate in their assessment. Informal (subjective, unstructured) assessments are taken directly from participants, team members, or sometimes facilitators. They require fewer resources to administer but lack the accuracy of formal assessments.

The reality is that most programs have informal assessments. Although accuracy may suffer, these instruments serve as measures of learning. These instruments are important because adjustments are often made if they are inappropriate. Some CEOs think that their learning and development functions are not really measuring learning when they take informal assessments. But informal measures are necessary to ensure that individuals have the knowledge and skills offered in the program.

Though they are often a supplement to formal assessments, they may often be the only available method for measuring knowledge and skill acquisition.

How to Improve These Measures

To make learning measures more appropriate, relevant, efficient, and ex-ecutive friendly, several actions are possible. Making changes in learning measures is a challenging and perplexing issue. It often commands more resources and may create some resistance. There are several possible ways to improve learning measures, some formal and some informal.

Use Formal Measures Sparingly

This is a twofold issue. First, formal or structured measures are needed to ensure that participants know what's needed to do a particular job. For-mal measures are important in critical jobs involving safety and health, crucial operational issues, and customer-serving jobs. The dilemma of having more formal measures is that more resources are needed to ensure that a test is both valid and reliable. However, efficiencies can be gained by transferring validated measurement tools for standard programs sup-porting specific job situations to similar programs supporting comparable job situations.

Knowing when investment in rigorous test development is unnecessary is also an important issue. Checking a test for validity and reliability is necessary when a human resource action is planned as a result of the test score. For example, if a specific assignment, job promotion, movement on a career ladder, or even a salary increase is a consequence of success-ful program completion, then investment in validity and reliability testing is wise, if not imperative. However, human resource actions are often not a consequence of most learning and development programs; therefore, investing in validity and reliability is not as necessary, reducing the cost of learning measurement.

Developing formal testing and additional testing processes may require having expertise in this area. It may be important to have someone on the staff participate in formal learning programs, showing how to do this in a feasible, realistic way.

Use Informal Measures

Informal measures of learning are often acceptable. These may involve participant self-assessment, ideally done anonymously in a nonthreatening environment. This also may involve team assessments or, in some cases, facilitator assessments. These types of informal data can be collected on a routine basis and reported to executives. Technology has been devised to help develop tests, score them, and administer them efficiently, thereby reducing some of the costs. However, informal measures provide another view of learning success and often resonate with senior executives.

Innovative Approaches to Measure Learning

Some innovation opportunities exist for measuring learning, particularly as it relates to the needs of the executive group. Three specific ideas are to

- Build Level 2 into Level 1.
- Build a learning measure into the scorecard.
- Do an ROI forecast with learning data.

Building Level 2 into Level 1

It may be helpful to ask a few questions about the extent of learning, built into the reaction questionnaire. These are self-assessments, but they still may be important measures. This approach meets three goals for the learning and development team. First, there is pressure to measure a higher percentage of programs at the learning level. Ideally, learning should be measured in every program. Building one or two learning measures into a Level 1 questionnaire creates 100 percent coverage, dramatically increasing the percentage of programs evaluated. The second goal is to be efficient with additional measurements, thus conserving resources. The third goal is to provide a single measure for the management team, which is described next.

Building a Learning Measure into the Scorecard

Because executives need only one or two measures on learning, it may be helpful to capture this type of data on a self-assessment basis and roll it into the scorecard. For example, this question may be asked in every program: "To what extent have you learned the content of this program?"

The data could be captured on a scale of 1 to 5 and reported to the executive group. Although this information lacks specificity, it provides some assurance that learning is taking place—with this assurance coming from the people who know what they learned. As the data is reported routinely, the measure provides some evidence of less or more learning over time. This approach allows a high percentage of programs to be measured, using the same question each time. Collecting and reporting these types of data using technology makes the process smooth and efficient and allows results to be built right into the scorecard for the senior team.

Conducting an ROI Forecast with Learning Data

With formal testing, participants are required to demonstrate their knowledge or skills at the end of a program, and their performance is expressed as a numerical value. When this type of test is developed and used, it must be reliable and valid, as described above. A test should reflect the content of the program, and successful mastery of program content should be related to improved job performance. As a result, there should be a strong relationship between test scores and subsequent on-the-job performance. The strength of this relationship, expressed as a correlation coefficient, is a measure of test validity. Figure 7-1 illustrates a perfect correlation between test scores and job performance.

This testing situation provides an excellent opportunity for an ROI calculation with learning data. If there is a statistically significant relationship between test scores and on-the-job performance, and the performance can be converted to monetary value, then it is possible to use test scores to forecast the ROI from the program, using these steps:

1. Ensure that the program content reflects the desired on-the-job performance.
2. Develop an end-of-program test that reflects program content.

Figure 7-1. The Relationship between Test Scores and On-the-Job Performance

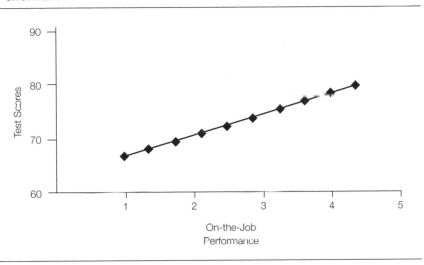

3. Establish a statistical relationship between the test data and the output performance of participants.
4. Predict performance levels for each participant, using their test scores.
5. Convert the performance data to monetary values.
6. Compare the net predicted value of the program with program costs.

Usually this forecast is not pursued unless the correlation has already been developed.

♦ ♦ ♦

Final Thoughts

This chapter has briefly discussed some of the key issues involved in measuring learning—an important ingredient in the success of learning and development programs. Even if done informally, learning must be assessed to determine how well the participants in a program have gained new knowledge and skills. Should any implementation problems arise later, understanding what went wrong would be difficult without having measured learning. Also, learning measurements provide an opportunity to make adjustments quickly to enhance learning and ensure proper program implementation. Sometimes, a formal, objective process is needed to accurately assess learning. However, informal assessments will be much more common because of the cost and convenience.

This data category creates some challenges for the learning and development team. Measuring learning is hard to manage on a routine basis because there are so many challenges involved. On top of that, executives see very little value in learning data, because it is perceived as an operational measure that must be properly resourced, measured, and acted upon. The next chapter moves on to a more valuable type of data: application.

Action, Behavior, and Application Measurements

An Executive "So What?"

Learning measures describe learning and development program participants' readiness to perform on the job, but program application measures tell you if success is on the horizon. Like a good map, the effective use of newly acquired knowledge will render your trip a success by ensuring that you arrive at the ultimate destination marked by the positive business improvements resulting from your program.

Therefore, it is obvious that measuring program application is necessary. For some learning and development programs, it is the most critical data set, because it provides an understanding of how much progress has been made with successful implementation. Application measures also describe barriers and enablers that are impeding or supporting success.

This level of measurement is not without its share of issues, however. Though it is important and necessary to show on-the-job success, application measures fall short of delivering data on the consequences (impact) of the effective use of knowledge, skills, and information. Executives have interest in this level of data as well as various concerns about it, as described in this chapter. This chapter offers ways to overcome concerns about this level of measurement as well as issues and approaches to ensure successful evaluation.

The Executive Viewpoint

"I'm pleased to see data reflecting on-the-job progress. Previously, our team only focused on the data in the classrooms. This is much more helpful."

Executives weighed in heavily on the issues of action, behavior, and application, offering a mix of both positive and negative positions. Our survey results show that the CEOs responded to rank application data fourth on a scale of 1 to 8, with 8 being the lowest. In terms of use, only 11 percent indicated that application data is now reported, with 61 percent suggesting that it should be reported. On the basis of these results, application is a measurement level that needs more focus. More detail is presented in appendix D.

Behavior Is Important

"I realize that the behavior is very important. Part of our job is to change behavior, and it's good to know we're making progress on this important issue."

Almost every executive would agree that a focus on behavior is important; after all, many of them are attempting to shape the behavior of people in their organization through development programs, change management programs, and leadership development efforts. They see the importance of 360-degree feedback, which is probably accepted by most executives as important behavioral input needed to change a manager's leadership approach. Many executives, especially those selling directly to consumers, also recognize the importance of mystery shoppers. After all, a mystery shopper is an observer capturing Level 3, behavioral change data. (For the details on Level 0 through Level 5, see appendix A.) Often many assessments, changes, initiatives, and learning and development programs are developed because an organization needs to make behavioral changes.

There's Action—Necessary for Results

"I know when there is action, there will probably be results. Execution is important."

Most executives appreciate measures that show action is being taken in an effort to achieve results. After all, if the applied actions are the right actions, positive results should follow. There's some comfort in knowing that on-the-job performance is being measured. With so much attention to execution, it is important to see participants following through on their intended actions after they have been involved in a learning program.

It's Not Results

"Although the activities are reported, I'd prefer to see the business results. To me, it's not so much what they're doing, but what they've achieved with what they're doing that makes a difference. I'd like to see a connection to our major business goals."

Most executives will quickly point out that activity does not always translate into results, underscoring the fact that application is only activity. Most want to see a connection to business unit measures or some connection to the business performance of the organization. Ideally, there should be a linkage to important business goals, because activity does not always mean that there is an immediate connection. There may be delayed connections. Still, there is a need to show the long-term consequences. In short, executives have a concern that this data set is short of what's needed in the organization.

I Need a Simple Measure

"Some of this data is very confusing. There seems to be some progress made in certain areas, but I wonder if that's the same across all of our programs."

Current reporting at this level can be quite cumbersome, because the measure varies from reporting 360-degree feedback to mystery shopper feedback to action plan implementation to questionnaire feedback to many other types of processes. Executives are left wondering "What does all of this mean?" It would be helpful for them to have a few simple measures that reflect on-the-job behavior or actions across programs that bring a sense of success to the entire organization.

Why Application Is Important

Many learning and development programs fail due to breakdowns in application. Participants don't use what they've learned when they should, or at the expected level of effectiveness. Measuring application, action, and behavior is critical to understanding a program's implementation. And without successful implementation, there will not be improvements in business impact—and benefits will not be gained from the program.

Valuable Information

The value of information increases as progress is made moving up the chain of impact—from reaction (Level 1) to ROI (Level 5). Thus, information concerning application (Level 3) is more valuable to clients than reaction and learning data. This does not discount the importance of the first two levels, but it emphasizes the importance of moving up the chain of impact. Measuring a program's application often provides critical data about not only its success but also the factors that can contribute to future programs' greater success.

A Critical Transition

The two previous measures, reaction (Level 1) and learning (Level 2), are collected during a program's operational phase, where more attention and focus are placed on the participants' direct involvement in the program. Because the participants are somewhat "captive," data is usually easier to collect. Measuring application occurs later and captures the participants' use of knowledge and skills on the job. Essentially, measures at this level reflect the degree of initial postprogram success. This is a key transition period, which means that measuring application is a critical issue, although data collection is often more difficult.

In Many Cases, It's All That's Needed

Because many programs focus directly on the need to change behavior or processes, the program sponsor often speaks in these terms and has concerns about these measures of success. Major programs designed to empower employees, create self-directed teams, or build a loyal customer base will concentrate on the application of learned skills. Many compliance programs only need to be measured at this level because compliance is defined based on what employees do on the job.

The Greatest Opportunity for Process Improvement

For a program to add business value, the chain of impact must remain intact. Unfortunately, measurement at the application level is often the weakest link, for research shows that 60 to 80 percent of the knowledge skills acquired in a learning program are never applied. Individuals' failure to do what is expected is the most common reason for a break in the chain of impact, leaving little or no corresponding business impact data, resulting in a less-than-desired (and often negative) ROI. This breakdown most often occurs because participants encounter barriers, inhibitors, or obstacles that may deter their implementation of the program. Although the reaction may be favorable and participants do learn what they must, barriers prevent them from applying their new skills and knowledge to their jobs.

Often, when a program is unsuccessful, the first question asked is "What happened?" When a program fails to add value, the first question should be "What can we do to improve the program?" In either scenario, it is important to identify barriers to success; problems encountered during implementation; and obstacles to the actual application of the knowledge, skills, and information. At this level of evaluation, these problems must always be examined. In many cases, the participants can provide important recommendations for making improvements.

When a program is successful, the obvious question is "How can we repeat this, or even improve on it, in the future?" The answer to this question is usually found at this level of evaluation, as enablers are identified. Identifying the factors that directly contribute to program success is always necessary. These same items can be used to replicate the process to produce new or improved results in the future. And when participants identify these issues, they provide an important prescription for success.

Success Stories

Measuring application allows the sponsor and the learning and development leader to reward those who do the best job of applying the skills and knowledge. Measures taken at this level identify clear evidence of success and achievement, providing a basis for performance reviews or special recognition. Rewards often reinforce value, keep participants on track, and communicate a strong message for future participants. Care must be taken, however. If Level 3 data is used for performance reviews, then the Level 3 data collected from participants via self-administered questionnaires may be perceived as biased.

Measures Defined

This level of measurement focuses on activity or action, not the consequences of those actions (which is Level 4, impact). The number of activities to measure can be mind-boggling. Table 8-1 shows some coverage areas for application. These examples can vary; however, these action items are included in most programs. Essentially, application may mean applying skills, using skills, performing tasks, following procedures, completing steps, taking action, using technology, or many other possibilities.

What's Wrong with Application Measures?

Although important and necessary, application measures have their share of problems. Collectively, they represent serious challenges at this level of evaluation. The most common ones are

- ◆ Not enough.
- ◆ Much of it is perception.

◆ Accuracy versus cost.

◆ Low response rate.

◆ No standards.

◆ It's only activity.

Not Enough

This is the first level of data taken from the workplace, showing what individuals have accomplished (or not accomplished) as a result of the learning and development program. These important data items are

Table 8-1. Examples of Coverage Areas for Application

Action	Explanation	Example
Increase	Increase a particular activity or action.	Increase the frequency of the use of a particular skill.
Decrease	Decrease a particular activity or action.	Decrease the number of times a particular process has to be checked.
Eliminate	Stop or remove a particular task or activity.	Eliminate the formal follow-up meeting, and replace it with a virtual meeting.
Maintain	Keep the same level of activity for a particular process.	Continue to monitor the process with the same schedule as previously used.
Create	Design, build, or implement a new procedure, process, or activity.	Create a procedure for resolving the differences between two divisions.
Use	Use a particular process, procedure, or activity.	Use the new skill in situations for which it was designed to be used.
Perform	Conduct or do a particular task, process, or procedure.	Perform a postaudit review at the end of each activity.
Participate	Become involved in various activities, projects, or programs.	Each associate should submit a suggestion for reducing costs.
Enroll	Sign up for a particular process, program, or project.	Each associate should enroll in the career advancement program.
Respond	React to groups, individuals, or systems.	Each participant in the project should respond to customer inquiries within 15 minutes.
Network	Facilitate relationships with others who are involved or have been affected by the project.	Each project participant should continue networking with contacts on, at least, a quarterly basis.

essential to understanding on-the-job behavior. However, not enough of this is accomplished. In the best practice organizations, only about 30 percent of learning and development programs have any type of follow-up at Level 3 each year. For most organizations, it's much lower, often around 5 to 10 percent. Still, far too many organizations do not collect any data at this level, leaving the learning and development budget at risk of being adjusted, reduced, or even eliminated. Without the level of data, there is no evidence that learning and development is making a difference in the organization. More evaluation is needed at this level.

Much of It Is Perception

Because this evaluation often involves behavioral change, the data is based on perception. Behavioral change doesn't necessarily appear in the records, where it becomes a verifiable fact, but it's based on what someone has observed or a self-evaluation. Even an observation made by others is subject to error and misinterpretation. Self-assessment may even be more suspect. Still, there is certainly some importance in perception data. After all, job satisfaction, employee engagement, and customer satisfaction are extremely important measures, and all rely on perception data.

Not all the data at this level, however, has to be perception based. For example, when individuals learn how to use software, many of the current software packages provide a user performance profile, detailing how the participant is using what he or she has learned.

Accuracy versus Cost

Because much of this data is based on perception, there is a problem with accuracy, leaving some learning and development team members to avoid this type of data altogether. Self-assessment data, taken directly from participants, is perceived to be inaccurate because of potential error or bias. When more objective methods are considered—such as observation, which must be invisible or unnoticeable—bias is removed, but accuracy can still be an issue. Unfortunately, there is a payoff between accuracy and costs. The more accuracy that is needed at this level, the more it will cost to obtain it.

Low Response Rate

Because individuals are no longer held captive in an audience, in a classroom, or at the keyboard, this data is subject to the whims, desires, and attitudes of the individuals. Notoriously, most learning and development teams experience a low response rate at this level, diminishing the quality of the results. These low response rates are usually due to the lack of discipline and use of specific tactics on the part of the evaluator. This topic will be discussed in more detail below.

No Standards

Unlike some of the other levels, there are no standards at this level, at least none that are accepted in the industry. Knowing what to ask and how to ask it is not standard, which makes it impossible to compare data across programs, even with other organizations. This situation will change as more Level 3 evaluations are conducted and technology suppliers adopt consistent questions.

It's Only Activity

Although this type of data is important, it's only activity data with actions, behavior, or application, and thus it's a matter of someone doing something, not necessarily accomplishing something. Therefore, this data set often leads to many questions, including "So what?" "What have they accomplished?" "What's the impact?" "What's the consequence?" "What's the business value?" and "Do they help achieve our goals?" When application data is presented to executives, the questions often follow, based on a desire to know what difference the use of knowledge and skills actually makes.

How to Improve These Measures

Application measures focus on the use of knowledge, skills, and information—not the ability of participants to use their knowledge. Measures of "ability" demonstrate a person's capability—but they do not demonstrate the routine application or use of knowledge, skills, and/or information. The application measures must be relevant to the job behavior needed to achieve desired business results. To put it another way, measures of application may indicate that participants are routinely applying the knowledge and skills, but if they are not the right set of knowledge and skills, the intended business results will not improve. In addition, there must be ample data so that good decisions can be made with regard to application and the organization's effect on learning transfers.

Connect to Needs Assessment

During the needs assessment process, this question should be asked: "What is being done, or not being done, on the job that is inhibiting the business measures that need to improve?" When this question is answered adequately, a connection is made between application measures and business measures. When this is addressed, the activities or behaviors that need to change are identified, and they serve as the basis for data collection. In essence, application measures are identified in the needs assessment, making it much easier to conduct an evaluation at this level.

Too many initial analyses focus on either impact measures, which define the business measures that need to be improved, or learning, which uncovers what people do not know. More focus is needed on performance needs, which involve the tasks, processes, procedures, and behaviors that must be in place or change for successful implementation.

Develop Objectives at This Level

As with the other levels, data collection at the application level begins with objectives. Without clear objectives, collecting data is difficult. Objectives define expected activity, action, application, or behavior. Application objectives are powerful because they provide participants and other stakeholders with clear direction as to what action is desired, needed, or expected from the program. The basic principles for developing these objectives are similar to those for developing learning objectives. A performance statement with a condition and criteria is developed. This statement ultimately evolves into the questions asked during the evaluation process.

Link with Learning

Application data should be linked closely with the learning data discussed in chapter 7. Program evaluators seek success by applying knowledge and skills, which logically must reflect the knowledge and skills acquired during program implementation. During the program, participants learn information and develop skills to perform tasks on the job. Application data measure the extent to which participants are applying what they have learned on their jobs. Sometimes, the objectives measured at the application level are the same as those measured at the learning level, but in the context of use in the work environment.

Build Data Collection into Programs

Application data is collected after program completion. Because of the time lag between program and routine use, securing the appropriate quality and quantity of data is difficult. Consequently, designing data collection into the program from the beginning is one of the most effective ways to secure data. Data collection tools, positioned as application tools, provide a rich source of data. These tools are built in as part of the implementation process. For example, action plans can be designed into a leadership development program and positioned as an application tool that also shows the impact of applying the leadership skills. When the process is completed, a credible data set can be captured, but only because data collection was built into the process from the beginning. Table 8-2 shows how to use an action plan.

Address the Barriers to and Enablers for Transferring Learning

One of the important reasons for collecting data at this level is to uncover the barriers to, and enablers of, the use of knowledge, skills, and information. Although both groups are important, barriers can impede an otherwise successful program. The barriers must be identified and actions must be taken to minimize, remove, or go around the barrier. This problem is serious, because every program entails barriers to learning transfer. When these barriers can be removed or minimized, the program has a much better chance of success.

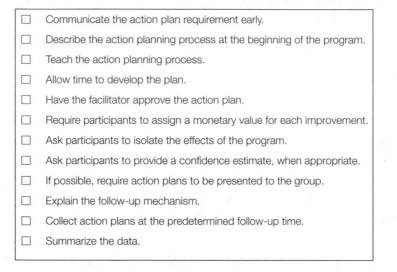

Table 8-2. Checklist for Action Planning

☐   Communicate the action plan requirement early.

☐   Describe the action planning process at the beginning of the program.

☐   Teach the action planning process.

☐   Allow time to develop the plan.

☐   Have the facilitator approve the action plan.

☐   Require participants to assign a monetary value for each improvement.

☐   Ask participants to isolate the effects of the program.

☐   Ask participants to provide a confidence estimate, when appropriate.

☐   If possible, require action plans to be presented to the group.

☐   Explain the follow-up mechanism.

☐   Collect action plans at the predetermined follow-up time.

☐   Summarize the data.

Although a variety of data collection methods can be used, in each method, a step, process, or effort should be made to identify these barriers. When they are identified, they become important reference points for changes and improvements. Table 8-3 shows the typical barriers that will stifle the success of programs. These are almost universal with any type of program, but others may be specific to the particular setting and program. The important point is to identify them and then use the data in meaningful ways to try to make them less of a problem.

Along with barriers, there are enablers, which support or enhance the transfer of learning. Working with enablers provides an opportunity to make improvements beyond the success that has already been achieved. They provide prescriptions for other programs as well and are very powerful. Enablers may be a direct reflection of a barrier—the only difference being that the phenomena are actually supporting the transfer of learning.

For example, a manager's lack of support for the transfer of learning is one of the barriers identified most often. On the other hand, a manager's

Table 8-3. Typical Barriers to Successful Implementation

- My immediate manager does not support the learning.
- The culture in our work group does not support the learning.
- No opportunity to use the skills, knowledge, and information from the program.
- No time to implement the skills.
- Didn't learn anything that could be applied to the job.
- Our systems and processes did not support the use of the skills.
- The resources are not available to implement the skills.
- Changed job and the skills no longer apply.
- The project is not appropriate for our work unit.
- Didn't see a need to implement the project.
- Could not change old habits.

support for transfer is also an enabling factor. When a manager asks about a program, gives participants opportunities to apply what they learn, and also offers them opportunities to share what they learn with the team, he or she is enabling transfer.

Another example of factors that support the transfer of learning is when other departments supporting program implementation in some way come through with their tasks. For example, we have heard countless times that the IT Department will often not have a system ready for the application of new technology when participants have completed a training program for that system. When IT understands its role and the timing of the training and has all systems ready for application, it has enabled participants to apply what they have learned.

Removing barriers and replicating the approaches used by enablers ensures a systemic learning process. Managers' lack of support for the application of knowledge, skills, and/or information impedes the success of a program. But when managers systematically enable learners to apply newly acquired knowledge and skills, they perpetuate program success, thereby contributing to the organization's overall success.

Improve Response Rates

For most evaluations, questionnaires and surveys will be used to collect application data. When a follow-up evaluation is planned, a wide range of data on issues and details will be collected in the questionnaire. However, asking for too much detail can have a negative impact on the response rate. The challenge, therefore, is to approach questionnaire and survey design and administration with the goal of achieving the maximum response rate. The actions listed in table 8-4 can be taken to ensure a successful response rate. Although the term "questionnaire" is used, the discussion that follows also applies to surveys, interviews, focus groups, and action plans.

Share Responsibilities

Measuring application involves the responsibility and work of others. Because these measures are made after the program's operation, an important question may surface in terms of who is responsible for this follow-up. Many possibilities exist, from learning and development staff to the client's staff, as well as the possibility of external, independent consultants. This matter should be addressed at the planning stage so that there are no misunderstandings about the division of responsibilities. More important, those who are responsible must understand the nature and scope of their roles and what is needed to collect the data.

Use the Data

Data becomes meaningless if not used properly. As we move up the chain, the data becomes more valuable in the minds of the sponsors, key executives, and other stakeholders who have a strong interest in the program. Though data can be used in dozens of ways, these are the principal uses for data after it is collected:

- Report and review results.
- Adjust design and implementation.
- Identify and remove barriers.
- Identify and enhance enablers.
- Recognize successful individuals.
- Reinforce desired actions.
- Improve management support.
- Market future programs.

Table 8-4. Improving Response Rates

- Provide advance communication about the questionnaire.
- Clearly communicate the reason for the questionnaire.
- Indicate who will see the results of the questionnaire.
- Show how the data will be integrated with other data.
- Keep the questionnaire simple and as brief as possible.
- Keep questionnaire responses anonymous or at least confidential.
- Make it easy to respond; include a self-addressed, stamped envelope or email address.
- Use the local manager to distribute the questionnaires, show support, and encourage response.
- If appropriate, let the target audience know that they are part of a carefully selected sample.
- Use one or two follow-up reminders.
- Have the introduction letter signed by a top executive.
- Enclose a giveaway item with the questionnaire (pen, money, and so on).
- Provide an incentive (or change of incentive) for quick response.
- Send a summary of results to target audience.
- Distribute questionnaire to a captive audience.
- Consider an alternative distribution channel, such as email.
- Have a third party gather and analyze data.
- Communicate the time limit for submitting responses.
- Consider paying for the time it takes to complete the questionnaire.
- Review the questionnaire at the end of the formal session
- Carefully select the survey sample.
- Allow completion of the survey during work hours.
- Add emotional appeal.
- Design questionnaire to attract attention, with a professional format.
- Let participants know what actions will be taken with the data.
- Provide options to respond (paper, email, Website).
- Use a local coordinator to help distribute and collect questionnaires.
- Frame questions so participants can respond appropriately and make the questions relevant.

Use Sampling

To minimize resources and tackle this level of evaluation, sampling is necessary. Sampling is used in two ways. First, only a certain percentage of programs are evaluated at this level. For best practice, this is usually 30 percent. In addition, not all the participants are evaluated. Often, one or two groups can represent a small number of participants, perhaps ranging from 25 to 100. The small sample keeps the resource requirements to a minimum, while at the same time providing some insight into the progress being made, along with the barriers and enablers to success.

Keep It Simple

Evaluation at this level can become complex. It is not unusual for Level 3 follow-up studies to use questionnaires that are five or six pages long, delving into all types of issues about the success of the program and what caused the lack of success. Though a comprehensive follow-up should be conducted when appropriate, a few simple measures can suffice in many situations. In essence, five issues are essential at this level:

1. the extent of use of skills and knowledge
2. the frequency of use of skills and knowledge
3. the success of use of skills and knowledge
4. the barriers to success
5. the enablers to success.

These issues can be explained in simple, follow-up questionnaires, emails, or phone interviews. The complexity can thus be significantly minimized.

Innovative Approaches to Measuring Application

Four main innovative measuring approaches available at this level of evaluation add value to the process:

- ◆ Use performance contracts.
- ◆ Develop ROI for Level 3.
- ◆ Use technology.
- ◆ Build application data into the scorecard.

Using Performance Contracts

A performance contract is essentially a slight variation of the action planning process. Based on the principle of mutual goal setting, this contract is a written agreement between a participant and his or her manager. The participant agrees to improve performance in an area of mutual concern related to the specific learning and development program. The agreement is in the form of a program to be completed or a goal to be accomplished soon after the program's completion. The agreement details what is to be accomplished, at what time, and with what results.

Although the steps can vary according to the specific kind of contract and the organization, a common sequence of events is as follows:

1. The participant becomes involved in a specific program.
2. The participant and his or her manager mutually agree on a topic for improvement related to the program.
3. Specific, measurable goals are set.
4. In the early stages of the program, the contract is discussed and plans are developed to accomplish the goals.
5. After the program is conducted, the participant works on the contract against a specific deadline.
6. The participant reports the results of the effort to his or her manager.
7. The manager and participant document the results and forward a copy to the learning and development team, along with appropriate comments.

The process of selecting the area for improvement is simple. The topic can include one or more of these areas:

+ *Routine performance*—includes specific improvements in routine performance measures, such as production, efficiency, and error rates.
+ *Problem solving*—focuses on specific problems, such as an unexpected increase in accidents, a decrease in efficiency, or a loss of morale.

- *Innovative or creative applications*—includes initiating changes or improvements in work practices, methods, procedures, techniques, and processes.
- *Personal development*—involves learning new information or acquiring new skills to increase individual effectiveness.

The topic selected should be stated in terms of one or more objectives. The objectives should state what will have been accomplished when the contract has been completed. The objectives should be

- written
- understandable by all involved
- challenging (requiring an unusual effort to achieve)
- achievable (something that can be accomplished)
- largely under the control of the participant
- measurable and dated.

The details required to accomplish the performance contract's objectives are developed following the guidelines for action plans presented above.

Developing ROI for Level 3

In almost every program, participants are expected to change their on-the-job behavior by applying what they learned in a program. On-the-job application is critical to program success, particularly when the focus is on competencies. Although the use of skills on the job is no guarantee that results will follow, it is an underlying assumption for most programs that, if the knowledge and skills are applied, there will be positive results. A few organizations attempt to take this process a step further and measure the value of on-the-job behavioral changes and calculate the ROI. In these situations, estimates are taken from participants, their supervisors, the management group, or experts in the field.

These six steps are used to develop a Level 3 ROI:

1. Develop the competencies for the target job.
2. Indicate the percentage of job success that is represented by the competencies included in the program.

3. Determine the monetary values of competencies using average salaries and the employee benefits of the participants.
4. Compute the worth of the preprogram and postprogram skill levels.
5. Subtract the postprogram values from the preprogram values.
6. Compare the total added benefits with the program costs.

Here's an example of one technique for measuring the value of on-the-job application. The U.S. government redesigned its introduction to a supervision course, a five-day learning solution for newly appointed supervisors. The program focused on eight competencies:

1. role and responsibilities of the supervisor
2. communications
3. planning, assigning, controlling, and evaluating work
4. ethics
5. leadership
6. analyzing performance problems
7. customer service
8. managing diversity.

The immediate managers of the new supervisors indicated that these eight competencies accounted for 81 percent of first-level supervisors' jobs. For the target group being evaluated, the average annual salary plus benefits for the newly appointed supervisors was $42,202. Thus, multiplying this figure by the amount of job success accounted for by the competencies (81 percent) yielded a dollar value of $34,184 per participant. If a person performed successfully in these eight competencies for one year, the value to the agency would be $34,184. Of course, this assumes that the employees were paid an amount equal to their contribution when they were fully competent.

Using a scale of 0 to 9, managers rated the skills for each of the competencies before the program was conducted. The average level of skills required for job success was determined to be 6.44. The skill rating prior to the job was 4.96, which represented 77 percent of the 6.44 (that is, participants were performing at 77 percent of the level required to be successful in the competencies). After the program, the skill rating was 5.59, representing 87 percent of the level necessary to be successful.

Monetary values were assigned based on the participants' salaries. Performance at the required level was worth $34,184. At a 77 percent proficiency level, the new supervisors were performing at a contribution value of $26,322. After the application of the learning, this value reached 87 percent, representing a contribution value of $29,740. The difference in these values, $3,418, represents the gain per participant attributable to the course. The program cost was $1,368 per participant. Thus, the ROI is:

$$ROI = \frac{\$3,418 - \$1,368}{\$1,368} = \frac{\$2,050}{\$1,368} \times 100 = 150\%$$

As with other estimates, a word of caution is needed. These results are subjective because the rating systems used are subjective and may not reflect an accurate assessment of the value of the program. Also, because a program is usually implemented to help the organization achieve its objectives, some managers insist on tangible changes in hard data, such as quantity, quality, cost, and time. For them, a Level 3 evaluation is not always a good substitute for Level 4 data, if Level 4 data is available. In this example, an assumption is made that the competencies acquired and applied will influence Level 4 business measures.

Although this process is subjective, it has several useful advantages. First, if there are no plans to track the actual impact of the program in terms of specific, measurable business results (Level 4), then this approach represents a credible substitute. In many programs, particularly with skill building for supervisors, identifying tangible changes on the job is difficult. Therefore, alternate approaches to determining the worth of a program are needed. Second, this approach results in data that is usually credible with the management group if its members understand how the data has been developed and the assumptions behind it. An important point regarding the projected ROI for the U.S. government course is that the data on the changes in competence level came from the managers who rated their supervisors. In this specific program, the numbers were large enough to make the process statistically significant.

Using Technology

Although technology is typically used at Levels 1 and 2 to measure reaction and learning, it can also be extremely helpful to facilitate data collection and analysis at Level 3. Automated surveys make it convenient for participants to provide data, and when combined with some of the techniques to increase response rate, data collection can be very powerful, expedient, and low cost.

Also, using social network technology can help facilitate discussions about the success of learning and development. Special forums, groups, and networks can be formed to evaluate the success of major programs. This is a great way to capture not only specific improvements and actions taken but also important success stories.

Finally, cellphone technology has made tremendous progress. It is possible to use cellphones or text-messaging devices to capture simple follow-up questions. When planned properly and executed precisely, the response rates for these techniques are quite high, making them very inexpensive and convenient for the learning and development team.

Building Application Data into the Scorecard

As with the previous level, it is necessary to capture application data to use on the macro-level scorecard. Specific questions must be identified at this level of evaluation, whether the data collection is by survey, questionnaire, interview, focus group, or action plan. These questions are then transferred to the macro scorecard, essentially rolling up all the follow-up evaluations into the scorecard. These questions have to be very simple and few in number. More important, they should attract executive interest. Typical candidates are the five simple measures described above, collected at a scale of 1 to 5.

The barriers and enablers can be forced-choice options in the questionnaires, and they can be translated into the top 5 or top 10 barriers and enablers. These simple measures can provide the executive team with some sense of the usefulness of learning and development across all programs. Of course, more detailed data is often collected in individual programs.

◆ ◆ ◆

Final Thoughts

An open door for success is every executive's ambition. This chapter has explored issues for measuring action, behavior, and application—which are critical in determining a learning and development program's success. This essential level of measurement determines not only the success achieved but also areas where improvement is needed and where success can be replicated. CEOs ranked this type of data fourth out of eight in terms of importance. Though 11 percent indicated that this type of data is being communicated, 61 percent say it should be.

This type of data does have problems that need immediate attention. Admittedly, these problems are fixable in an organization with its current resources and staff—it's a matter of having the discipline and assigning priority. Executives have very positive things to say at this level, but they also have concerns. These concerns can easily be addressed by dealing with the issues that must be resolved to make programs more successful, along with undertaking several innovative approaches.

Impact, Results, and ROI Measurements

Executives Want Them

Executives weighed in on the issue of impact, results, and ROI measurements because the relationship to learning and development is often one of mystery. Some executives think it's difficult to make the connection at this level, partly because many learning and development professionals have told them just that. Some executives would like to see the measurement, think it may be possible, and would appreciate the team giving it a try. And finally, still another group of executives knows it can be done and is requesting that this type of data be part of the measurement next time.

The Executive View

In the CEO survey results shown in table 9-1, business impact was ranked number 1 on a scale of 1 to 8, where 1 is the highest ranking. ROI was ranked number 2. More dramatically, only 8 percent of CEOs indicated that business impact was reported, while 96 percent suggest that it should be. Similarly, 4 percent had reports of ROI data, while 74 percent desired ROI data.

Table 9-1. CEOs' Perception of Learning and Development Measures (*N* = 96 large public and private companies)

Below is a list of measures. For each measure, an example is provided to help you understand the type of data captured with the measure. Please check if you are measuring this now (check all that apply). Next, indicate if the measure should be included in the future (check all that apply). Finally, rank the importance of the measure to you, with "1" as the most important and "2" as the second most important and so on, with "8" as the least important.

Measure	We Currently Measure This (percent)	We Should Measure This in the Future (percent)	My Ranking of the Importance of This Measure	
			Average	Rank
Impact: "Our programs are driving our top five business measures in the organization."	8	96	1.45	1
ROI: "Five ROI studies were conducted on major programs yielding an average of 68% ROI."	4	74	2.31	2

This chapter first summarizes the input from the executive group, with six categories:

- ◆ This data connects to the business.
- ◆ It's on my scorecard.
- ◆ Show me how it's connected.
- ◆ Show me the money!
- ◆ Is this credible?
- ◆ Show me a little effort.

"This type of data is what I want to see; however, I don't see this from my team at all."

This Data Connects to the Business

This category of data makes the business connection. The business measures reported clearly represent the executive's key performance indicators and thus illustrate business alignment. However, many executives rarely see this being done—and more often, not at all, which leaves them quite confused and frustrated.

"I have seen some connections to major projects, and this is encouraging. I would like to see more."

It's on My Scorecard

One reason this category of data resonates so well with executives is that business impact is built into their scorecard as key performance indicators. These measures are the most important data set for the executive group, and if they see any function or part of the organization driving these measures, they get excited, are encouraged, and feel very supported. But they rarely get to see this, and they get frustrated with a data set that's elusive.

"These are the basic measures that are essential to the business. This is the data set that we report to our board. Our learning and development team must connect to this on a routine basis."

"The data category is completely missing from any reporting I see from learning and development. I assume it's impossible to make the connection."

Show Me How It's Connected

"On rare occasions, I've seen a direct linkage between a learning program and business success. But it's rare. I'd like to see more."

When business data is reported, the executives are the first to raise the question of the linkage to specific programs. Many factors are involved, often even dozens that are driving specific business measures, particularly if they are not performing as they should. When the data is reported, there must be a linkage to the business. Otherwise, much credibility is lost.

*"Our team reports business data influenced by learning and development,
I see connections between the two. I'd like to believe that there is a
connection, but I need more evidence."*

Show Me the Money!

As mentioned in the beginning of this book, the messages of executives and administrators have evolved from "Show me something" to "Show me the money." Executives want to see the financial contribution; otherwise, they are stuck with only knowing the cost of learning and development. Presenting costs without showing the corresponding monetary contribution is dangerous.

*"When it comes to money and costs, all I see is what it's costing us.
I don't see any monetary contribution. In my ideal world, I'd like to see
the return on investment of the entire learning and development function,
but I realize that's probably not possible. But something short of that is
better than nothing."*

Is This Credible?

Some learning and development teams have tried to present ROI as return on expectations (ROE) or return on anticipation (ROA). Some have even presented data as return on training (ROT). This often leaves executives confused, because they want financial data for learning activities to follow the same standards and rules as that for other functions. However, most CLOs are not clear in their assumptions and have no standards with their data. Making decisions about which costs to include in an ROI calculation, for example, is a huge issue that can cause the ROI to vary considerably. Also, considering the number of years or months to include in the monetary benefits can vary the ROI significantly. A set of rules and standards is needed to make it work.

*"ROI data that's presented to me sounds a little fishy, often too inflated.
I don't fully understand the assumptions."*

Show Me a Little Effort

Some executives want to see progress. They want to see the learning and development team take on this challenge of connecting its activities to the business and even venturing out onto the ROI level. Doing this routinely will be difficult, but major projects and programs need this level of accountability. And when this is done, a surprising attitude seems to evolve among the executives, because they appreciate the effort. The fact is, they are not looking for perfection but just progress.

> *"Our team is tackling the ROI issue, and I'm very proud of them. Although it's not perfect, it's getting us further down the road."*

> *"I'm not looking for perfection here; I would like to see a little closer connection to the business and maybe even a casual look at ROI. A little bit of effort certainly would be welcomed."*

Why Is Measuring Business Impact, Results, and ROI Important?

Although there are obvious reasons for measuring business impact, results, and ROI, several specific issues support the rationale for making this effort. It's helpful to review some of the key issues.

The Highest Level of Data

Following the assumption that higher-level data creates more value for executives, business impact measures and ROI offer the most valuable data. Impact data represents the consequences of the application and implementation of a program—the bottom-line measures that are positively affected when a program is successful. Though almost all executives see this as the most valuable data, some executives want this data to be converted to monetary value so that they can clearly see the contribution in financial terms. Others want to see the next level of evaluation—the ROI. Essentially, this grouping of data (impact, results, and ROI) represents both the highest value of data and the top two levels in the five-level framework.

A Business Driver for Many Programs

For most programs, business impact data is the initial driver. The problem of deteriorating (or less-than-desired) performance or the opportunity for improvement in a business measure usually leads to a new program. If the business needs defined by these measures are the drivers, then the keys for evaluating the program are these same measures. The extent to which these measures have changed is the principal determinant of the program's success.

These are the measures often desired by the sponsor and the ones that the sponsor wants to see changed or improved. They often represent hard, indisputable facts reflecting performance that is critical to the business and operating-unit level of the organization.

Show Me the Money Data

Using this level of data, the actual amount of money gained can be determined. Impact data, as affected by the program, can be converted to monetary value to show the program's financial contribution. Although this conversion is actually a separate step, it is based on the business impact data collected in this step. Without credible impact data linked directly to the program, determining a credible monetary value for the program would not be possible. Thus, this type of data is one of the most critical results.

Easy to Measure

One unique feature of business impact data is that it is often easy to gather. Hard and soft measures at this level often reflect key measures that are plentiful throughout an organization. It is not unusual for an organization to have hundreds or even thousands of measures reflecting specific business impact items. The challenge is to connect a program's objectives to the appropriate measures. This is more easily accomplished at the beginning of the program's implementation due to the ease with which many of the data items can be located.

Common Data Types

The irony of this level of data collection is that these data types are the most common. When measuring reaction, learning, or application, the measures must be created, at least for many programs. However, at the business impact level, the data has been created, except for rare exceptions when it may have to be developed. Thus, the good news here is that these are common data items already being tracked and monitored by someone.

ROI: The Ultimate Level of Evaluation

The most compelling reason to calculate ROI is inherent in the advantages of using the ROI methodology. Many benefits have been achieved in the three thousand organizations using this methodology. These benefits are captured in follow-up benchmarking and in surveys with these groups. The payoffs are not just calculating the ROI but also radically changing how the stakeholders perceive the program's value and also bringing respect and a change of image to those who implement programs. Here are the key benefits of using ROI:

- ◆ Align programs to business needs.
- ◆ Show the contributions of selected programs.
- ◆ Earn the respect of senior managers and administrators.
- ◆ Build staff morale.
- ◆ Justify and defend budgets.
- ◆ Improve support for programs.
- ◆ Enhance the design and implementation processes.
- ◆ Identify inefficient projects or programs that need to be redesigned or eliminated.
- ◆ Identify successful projects or programs that can be implemented in other areas.

Measures Defined

The types of data in the category of measures are common and straightforward. Here is a brief summary of the most accepted terms.

Hard versus Soft Data

To help focus on the desired measures, a distinction is made for two general categories of data: hard and soft. Hard data is the primary measurement of improvement, presented through rational, undisputed facts that are easily gathered. It is the most desirable type of data to collect. The ultimate criteria for measuring the effectiveness of management rest on hard data items, such as productivity, profitability, cost control, and quality control. Table 9-2 provides examples of hard data grouped into categories of output, quality, costs, and time.

Hard data measures are often supplemented with interim assessments of soft data, such as brand awareness, satisfaction, loyalty, and leadership. Although a program designed to enhance competencies or manage change should ultimately have an impact on hard data items, measuring soft data items may be more efficient. Soft data is more difficult to collect and analyze but is used when hard data is unavailable. Soft data is difficult to convert to monetary values; is subjectively based, in many cases; and is less credible as a performance measurement. Table 9-3 provides a list of typical soft data items grouped into common categories.

The preference for hard data on programs does not reduce the value of soft data. Soft data is essential for a complete evaluation of a program; success may rest on soft data measurements. For example, in an empowerment program at a chemical plant, three key measures of success were identified: employee stress, job satisfaction, and teamwork—all soft data items.

Most programs use a combination of hard and soft data items in the evaluation. For example, an operator-training program in a manufacturing plant had these impact measures of success:

- reduction of production costs
- improvement in production schedules
- reduction in inventory shortages
- improvement in production capability
- reduction in stress.

These changes included both hard data (production costs) and soft data (capability, stress). The important point is that both hard and soft data have a place in evaluation, and thus most programs use both types.

Table 9-2. Examples of Types of Hard Data

Output	Time
Sales	Cycle time
Completion rate	Equipment downtime
Units produced	Overtime
Tons manufactured	Delivery time
Items assembled	Time to project completion
Money collected	Processing time
Items sold	Employee time
New accounts generated	Time to proficiency
Forms processed	Response time
Loans approved	Meeting time
Inventory turnover	Repair time
Patients discharged	Efficiency
Applications processed	Recruiting time
Students graduated	Average delay time
Projects completed	Late reporting
Output per hour	Lost time days
Productivity	
Work backlog	**Quality**
Incentive bonus	
Shipments	Failure rates
	Dropout rates
Costs	Scrap
	Waste
Shelter costs	Rejects
Treatment costs	Reject rates
Budget variances	Error rates
Unit costs	Rework
Cost by account	Shortages
Variable costs	Product defects
Fixed costs	Deviation from standard
Overhead cost	Product failures
Operating costs	Inventory adjustments
Project cost savings	Accidents
Accident costs	Incidents
Program costs	Compliance discrepancies
Sales expense	Agency fines
Participant costs	Penalties

Table 9-3. Examples of Types of Soft Data

Work Climate/Satisfaction	Customer Service
Job satisfaction	Customer complaints
Organization commitment	Customer satisfaction
Employee engagement	Customer dissatisfaction
Employee loyalty	Customer impressions
Tardiness	Customer loyalty
Grievances	Customer retention
Discrimination charges	Customer value
Employee complaints	Lost customers
Intent to leave	
Stress	**Employee Development/Advancement**
Teamwork	Promotions
Communication	Capability
Cooperation	Intellectual capital
Conflicts	Requests for transfer
	Performance appraisal ratings
Initiative/Innovation	Readiness
Creativity	Networking
Innovation	
New ideas	**Image**
Suggestions	Brand awareness
New products	Reputation
New services	Leadership
Trademarks	Social responsibility
Copyrights	Environmental friendliness
Patents process	Social consciousness
Patents improvements	Diversity
Partnerships	External awards
Alliances	

Tangible versus Intangible Data

Confusion often exists about the categories of soft data and the perceived lesser value placed on it. This leads to a critical definition in this book. Though the terms *hard data* and *soft data* can be used to discuss impact data, the terms *tangible data* and *intangible data* can also be used. Tangible data represents a category that has been converted to monetary value. Intangibles are defined as data purposely not converted to monetary value—that is, if data cannot be converted to monetary value credibly with a reasonable amount of resources, then it is left as an intangible.

This approach has several advantages. First, it avoids the sometimes-confusing labels of *soft* and *hard*. Second, it avoids the image that being soft equates to little or no value. Third, it brings definition to the situation. In some organizations, a particular data item may have already been converted to money and the conversion is credible because it actually becomes tangible. However, in another organization, the same measure has not been converted and cannot be converted with a reasonable amount of resources. Therefore, it is left as intangible. Fourth, it provides a rule that enhances the consistency of the process. This is one of the standards in the ROI methodology. Having this rule ensures that if two people conducted the same evaluation, they would get the same or similar results.

Specific Measures Linked to Programs

An important issue that often surfaces when considering ROI applications is the understanding of specific measures that are often driven by specific programs. Though there are no standard answers, table 9-4 summarizes typical impact measurements for various types of programs.

The measurements are quite broad for some programs. For example, leadership development may pay off in a variety of measures, such as improved productivity, enhanced sales and revenues, improved quality, cycle-time reduction, direct cost savings, and employee job satisfaction. In other programs, the influenced measures are quite narrow. For example, labor-management cooperation programs typically influence grievances, stoppages, and employee satisfaction. Orientation programs typically influence measures of early turnover (that is, turnover in the first 90 days of employment), initial job performance, and productivity. The measures that are influenced depend on the objectives and design of the program. The table also illustrates the immense number of measures that can be driven or influenced.

A word of caution is needed here. Presenting specific measures linked to a typical program may give the impression that these are the only measures influenced. In practice, a particular program can have many

Table 9-4. Typical Impact Measurements for Programs

Type of Program	Key Impact Measurements
Absenteeism control/ reduction	Absenteeism, customer satisfaction, job satisfaction, stress
Business coaching	Productivity/output, quality, time savings, efficiency, costs, employee satisfaction, customer satisfaction
Career development / career management	Turnover, promotions, recruiting expenses, job satisfaction
Communications training	Errors, stress, conflicts, productivity, job satisfaction
Compensation plans	Costs, productivity, quality, job satisfaction
Compliance programs	Penalties/fines, charges, settlements, losses
Diversity	Turnover, absenteeism, complaints, charges, settlements, losses
E-learning	Cost savings, productivity improvement, quality improvement, cycle times, error reductions, job satisfaction
Executive education	Productivity, sales, quality, time, costs, customer service, turnover, absenteeism, job satisfaction
Labor-Management cooperation programs	Work stoppages, grievances, absenteeism, job satisfaction
Leadership development	Productivity/output, quality, efficiency, cost/time savings, employee satisfaction, engagement
Management development	Productivity, sales, quality, time, costs, customer service, turnover, absenteeism, job satisfaction
Orientation, onboarding (revised)	Early turnover, training time, productivity, performance
Personal productivity / time management	Time savings, productivity, stress reduction, job satisfaction
Project management	Time savings, quality improvement, budgets
Retention management	Turnover, engagement, job satisfaction
Safety training	Accident frequency rates, accident severity rates, first aid treatments
Sales training	Sales, market share, customer loyalty, new accounts
Self-directed teams	Productivity/output, quality, customer satisfaction, turnover, absenteeism, job satisfaction

Type of Program	Key Impact Measurements
Sexual harassment prevention	Complaints, turnover, absenteeism, employee satisfaction
Six Sigma training	Defects, rework, response times, cycle times, costs
Stress management	Medical costs, turnover, absenteeism, job satisfaction
Software support	Productivity, sales, quality, time, costs, customer service, turnover, absenteeism, job satisfaction
Team building	Productivity, sales, quality, time, costs, customer service, turnover, absenteeism, job satisfaction
Supervisor training	Productivity, sales, quality, time, costs, customer service, turnover, absenteeism, job satisfaction
Wellness/fitness training	Turnover, medical costs, accidents, absenteeism

outcomes. Table 9-4 shows the most likely measures that arise from the studies that the ROI Institute has reviewed. In the course of a decade, we have been involved in over two thousand studies, and common threads exist among particular programs.

The good news is that most programs are driving business measures. These measures are based on what is being changed in various business units, divisions, regions, and individual workplaces. And these measures are the ones that matter to senior executives. The difficulty often comes in ensuring that the connection to the program exists. This is accomplished through a variety of techniques to isolate the effects of the program on the particular business measures, which are discussed below.

The Definition of ROI

The term *return on investment* is occasionally misused, sometimes intentionally. In this misuse, a very broad definition for ROI is offered that includes any benefit from a program. With this definition, ROI becomes a vague concept in which even subjective data linked to a program is included. The return on investment should be more precise and is meant to represent an actual value determined by comparing a program's costs with its benefits. The two most common measures are the BCR and the ROI formula.

For many years, learning and development leaders sought to calculate the actual return on investment for programs. If the program is considered an investment and not an expense, then it is appropriate to place it in the same funding process as other investments, such as the investment in equipment and facilities. Although the other investments may be quite different, executives and administrators often view them in the same way. Developing specific values that reflect the ROI is critical for the success of programs.

When selecting the approach to measuring ROI, it is important to communicate to the executives the formula that is being used and the assumptions made in arriving at the decision to use it. This helps avoid misunderstandings and confusion about how the ROI value was actually developed.

The Benefit/Cost Ratio

One of the oldest methods for evaluating programs is the benefit/cost ratio. The BCR compares the benefits of a program with its costs, using a simple ratio. In formula form, the ratio is

$$BCR = \frac{Program\ Benefits}{Program\ Costs}$$

In simple terms, the BCR compares the annual economic benefits of a program with its costs. Thus, a BCR of 1 means that the benefits equal the costs. A BCR of 2, usually written as 2:1, indicates that for each dollar spent on the program, two dollars are returned in benefits.

The principal advantage of using the BCR is that it avoids traditional financial measures that can lead to confusion when comparing program investments with other investments in the company. Investments in plants, equipment, or subsidiaries, for example, are not usually evaluated using the BCR. Some program leaders prefer not to use the same formula to compare the return on program investments with the return on other investments. In these situations, the ROI for programs stands alone as a unique type of evaluation.

Unfortunately, no standards exist that constitute an acceptable BCR from the client's perspective. A standard should be established within the organization, perhaps even for a specific type of program. However, a 1:1 ratio (break-even status) is unacceptable for many programs. In others, a 1.25:1 ratio is required, where the benefits are 1.25 times the cost of the program.

The ROI Formula

Perhaps the most appropriate formula for evaluating program investments is a program's net benefits divided by its costs. This is the traditional financial ROI and is directly related to the BCR. The ratio is usually expressed as a percentage, when the fractional values are multiplied by 100. In formula form, the ROI becomes:

$$\text{ROI \%} = \frac{\text{Net Program Benefits}}{\text{Program Costs}} \times 100$$

Net benefits are program benefits minus costs. The ROI value is related to the BCR by a factor of 1. Subtract 1 from the BCR and multiply by 100 to get the ROI percentage. For example, a BCR of 2.45 is the same as an ROI value of 145 percent (1.45 × 100 percent). This formula is essentially the same as the ROI for capital investments. For example, when a firm builds a new plant, dividing annual earnings by the investment yields the ROI. The annual earnings are comparable to net benefits (annual benefits minus costs). The investment is comparable to fully loaded program costs, which represent the investment in the program.

An ROI for a program of 50 percent means that the costs have been recovered and an additional 50 percent of the costs is reported as "earnings." A program ROI of 150 percent indicates that the costs have been recovered and that an additional 1.5 times the costs is captured as "earnings."

Using the ROI formula essentially places program investments on a level playing field with other investments using the same formula and similar concepts. Key managers and financial executives who regularly use ROI with other investments easily understand the ROI calculation.

What's Wrong with Data for Impact and ROI?

Obviously, this level of evaluation has the highest resonance with the executive group. In exploring what's wrong with these levels of measurement, the focus is not on the measures themselves but on the credibility of the data and the issues concerning collection and presentation.

Not Enough of It!

Unfortunately, this level of evaluation commands very little time and effort on the agenda of most learning and development professionals. For a variety of reasons, it is not a common process to connect major learning and development programs to business measures, and even less common to show the ROI. Best practice benchmarking data shows that only about 10 percent of these programs are linked to business impact; of these, fewer than 5 percent measure at the ROI level. And these are best practices; the average is unfortunately much less, about 5 percent for business impact and 2 percent for ROI. Obviously, this area needs improvement.

It's Out of Our Control

When connecting learning and development activities to business impact, there is a perception that this issue is out of the control of the learning and development team. However, this perception is only that—not the reality. True, the business data is not housed and reported by the team. But many, if not most, programs are initiated because of a business issue. Key sponsors are trying to improve profits, efficiencies, cost savings, cycle time, employee turnover, safety cycle time, project management time, and many other possibilities. All these are business measured and are usually housed in some other area. The perception is that because they are in other areas, away from the classroom and keyboard, a program cannot be connected to them. Obviously, this thinking is shortsighted and represents another area for improvement and change.

Is It Connected?

Perhaps the most critical credibility issue is the direct linkage of a business measure to the actual program. When data is reported, showing that a particular learning and development project has had a specific impact on a business measure (for example, sales training has influenced sales), the obvious question surfaces: "How much of the improvement, if any, is connected to this program?" Therefore, presenting this data without in some way isolating how the facts of the program are related to the data brings many skeptical concerns and questions.

Money Is Needed

In some results, it's not the actual measure that's vital but the benefits in monetary terms that the measure delivers. "So the program has actually reduced the call escalation in the call center. How did it affect the cost of operations in monetary terms?" These kinds of questions often surface when impact data is reported, leaving some learning and development leaders and staff to take the next step, which is converting the data to money.

Is the ROI Credible?

There's an old saying among executives that they can make the ROI come out to whatever they want it to be. Unfortunately, this is considered "Enron accounting"—attempting to change the assumptions to make the data look much better than it is. Here is where learning and development professionals have missed the mark when attempting to report ROI data. The assumptions underlying the ROI calculation must be totally understood by the audience. Otherwise, credibility is lost. In essence, there must be standardized assumptions with a conservative flair to make the ROI data credible for, and ultimately believable by, the audience. This is another important opportunity for improvement. Fortunately, the ROI methodology contains a proven, conservative set of standards (Phillips and Phillips 2007a).

How to Fix the Problems of Measuring Impact, Results, and ROI

Facing the giants can be, at the least, intimidating. Sometimes—given the issues of how to measure impact, results, and ROI—you may feel like all you have is a slingshot to your name and the faith that you can overcome your learning and development challenges. But slingshot or not, the right tools are essential to your success.

Almost all executives regard business impact data as the most important data type because of its connection to business success. Ideally, the connection to business measures starts at the conception of the program. For many learning and development programs, a less-than-desired performance in one or more business measures (representing the business need) initiated the need for the program.

For some executives, the most important value is money, as the economic benefits of programs are developed. Executives, sponsors, clients, administrators, and top leaders are concerned about the allocation of funds and want to see the contribution of a program in monetary values. Today, a growing number of executives are seeking, requesting, and requiring ROI.

In terms of program evaluation, ROI is the ultimate level of evaluation, showing the actual payoff from a program, expressed as a percentage and based on the same formula as the evaluation for capital investment. Because of its perceived value and familiarity to senior management, it is now becoming a common requirement for key programs. When ROI is required or needed, it must be calculated. Otherwise, it may be optional unless some compelling reason exists to take the evaluation to this level.

When a significant increase in business performance is noted after a program has been implemented, it is often linked to the program. Though the change in performance may be linked to the program, other factors may also have contributed to the improvement. If this issue is not addressed, the link to business impact is not credible.

Collectively, these issues concerning the measurement of impact, results, and ROI are perhaps the most serious for learning and development professionals. The irony is that this most valuable set of data for the members of the executive team commands the least amount of their attention in terms of measurement, resources, and effort.

Several actions are necessary to fix the problems of measuring impact, results, and ROI. The bad news is that this seems to be a daunting task, with many challenges for the learning and development team. The good news is that, though it takes some effort, many CLOs are meeting the challenge with excellent results. Here are a few specific ways to address these problems.

Improving the Front-End Analysis

Though this may appear to be an odd place to deal with the measurement piece, the problems are sometimes tracked back to the beginning of this process. As described above, a business need should drive many programs (that is, a new program should start with the end result in mind). The specified business need can be met only if there is a connection to it and the selected solution. This requirement shifts traditional front-end analyses away from classic skills and knowledge assessments and toward starting with the business problem and then linking it to job performance needs and, finally, to learning needs.

This shift is being accomplished by many organizations using many popular front-end models that identify the problems in terms of business needs and connects the solution to those needs, even if it's not a learning solution. What this means is that the need to show impact and ROI is essentially requiring organizations to focus more on energy, efforts, and resources in the front-end analysis, at least for the requests for major programs.

Using Higher Levels of Objectives

One of the most important ways to address the issues involved with impact and ROI measurement is by using program objectives. The learning and development team is very capable of developing appropriate learning objectives in the classic way of stating the objective in a performance content, followed by a condition and criteria. But learning objectives are not enough. These days, higher levels of objectives, including application and impact objectives, are now required to give proper focus to a learning program. Application objectives detail specifically what must be accomplished on the job, and impact objectives define specific business measures that must change. Just adding application and impact objectives often boosts the results significantly. With impact objectives, the business measures, defined in the objective, are monitored and reported as a connection to business impact (Phillips and Phillips 2008a).

Capacity Building

Pursuing these higher levels of measurement evaluation often requires skills and capabilities beyond what many learning and development professionals possess. Thus, they must learn how to change the dynamics of the learning and development process to focus on results from the beginning to the end. They must learn how to collect business impact data and, more important, how to isolate the effects of a program on data. Occasionally, they must be willing and able to tackle the issue of converting data to money. And yes, when an ROI needs to be calculated, it must follow a consistent approach with conservative standards to build the needed credibility. Achieving this type of routine in a sustainable way will require having staff with impact and ROI experience in the organization. These experts often are certified ROI professionals, and, in turn, they will brief and train other members of the team so that everyone understands their role in the process and what they must do to make it successful.

Overcoming Resistance and Fear

Because these levels of evaluation—impact and ROI—represent the ultimate in accountability, reporting them often stirs up fears among the members of the learning and development team. And these fears can translate into resistance to pursue new paths that will cause an effort to fail. After all, who wants to be held to this level of accountability, particularly if there's a risk that the results will reflect unfavorably on you? The logic works this way: "We're not sure that my program is adding value and contributing to the organization. If I measure the success of the program, up to and including impact, and maybe even ROI, I may find out that it's not working. And this will reflect unfavorably on my team (and me). After all, it's my program. I think I'd prefer to stay in the fog and not know."

Unfortunately, this logic is flawed and represents a tremendous barrier. To overcome this, organizations must implement this level of evaluation with the understanding that it's designed for process improvement and not for evaluating the team's performance. In essence, no member of the team will be criticized or punished for less-than-desirable results. Instead, the data will be used to drive improvement.

The sequence should work like this: If a program is designed to add business value, then it should be evaluated at the appropriate level. If it does not deliver the business value expected, a study will show why—the barriers to success will always be identified. The barriers and enablers will point to specific actions that can be taken to enable the program to deliver the desired value. Further adjustments will make it even more successful. Only on rare occasions will the evaluation result in discontinuing the program. Such an action would be taken only if it has been decided that the proposed solutions will never work.

Resistance and fear are minimized when the learning and development team understands impact and ROI analysis. Awareness of data analysis, the credibility of the measurement and evaluation process, and the use of data help minimize resistance and reduce the fears. When those involved see how the process works and the positive benefits to be gained by using this level of analysis, then they will be more inclined to embrace it. Also, if the team can become involved in making decisions about the use of the process, help select the programs for this level of analysis, and drive the use of the data, this can help reduce the fear and resistance. Additionally, other actions can be taken to overcome resistance and fear (see Phillips and others 2006).

Increasing Resources

Unfortunately, more resources are often required to enhance the measurement and evaluation process, at least for most organizations. In our work at the ROI Institute, we estimate that the investment in measurement and evaluation as a proportion of the learning and development budget is about 1 percent, or slightly less. Such a low investment level is inadequate. Our best practice investment is at the level of 3 to 5 percent. So, logically and rationally, learning and development teams must start committing more resources to this area. Otherwise, we will continue to suffer through the ups and downs of budgetary constraints as the economy goes through cycles.

Creating a Discipline and Culture for Sustainability

As this level of evaluation is pursued, a routine develops. A culture of accountability is created, whereby results are expected from programs and actions must be taken throughout the process with a results-based focus. Measurement and evaluation are systematic, routine, and not necessarily an add-on process. They are considered early and often. Collecting and analyzing data and using the results become systematic. This creates, essentially, a culture of measurement and accountability.

This accountability shift should not to be seen as a passing fad. And for it to work, it must be implemented gradually and slowly to become a culture of accountability. Efforts must be made to sustain it for long periods. The focus and discipline that are required must be driven by the learning and development executive. Proactive CLOs have made a difference in these levels of evaluations. They are determined to show the connection to the business, not only this year and next year but also in subsequent years. And for many progressive organizations, routine impact and ROI analysis has now been sustained for more than a dozen years. This can be done if the team is disciplined and focused, and if systems are in place to achieve and support the process.

Collectively, these issues must be tackled in addressing the issues of how to measure impact and ROI. Next, let's consider several additional innovative approaches.

Innovative Approaches to Measuring Impact and ROI

A variety of interesting and innovative approaches have been developed by organizations that have successfully tackled the issues of how to measure impact and ROI. Here's a sampling.

Start Simple and Make Progress

When the scope of the evaluation challenges is examined and the needs are clearly defined, the task often seems very daunting. Just from the typical investment level of less than 1 percent, moving to 3 to 5 percent illustrates the magnitude of the effort. This can appear to be impossible to achieve, causing learning leaders and staff to regard this level of analysis as too complex, expensive, and confusing.

Fortunately, many proactive learning and development functions are meeting this challenge. They start simple and make incremental progress, pushing more evaluations to the next level. They tighten up their current measurement at Level 1, to focus more on evaluating content. At Level 2, they seek simple learning measures. At Level 3, measurement is increased to add more follow-ups and, occasionally, pushing it up to impact data. (For the details on Level 0 through Level 5, see appendix A.) They even connect some programs to their impact—in some cases, by asking participants to simply indicate the extent to which the program has influenced certain measures. They focus on front-end analysis to ensure that new programs are connected to a business need. And they develop more application and impact objectives. These simple changes begin to connect to the business with small, incremental steps.

Using Success to Increase Resources

Because of the challenge of increasing the resources required for measurement and evaluation, one common innovative approach is to use the success of a current evaluation to make the business case for more evaluation. The approach proceeds like this. A major program is evaluated at the impact, and possibly at the ROI, level. This evaluation shows what is working and not working with the program. The "not working" portion shows what needs to be changed to make the program more successful. Likewise, the "working" portion shows what must change to make it even more successful, to add more value. Sometimes the changes are on the efficiency side, and the program can be delivered with less cost because of less time needed or an alternative delivery method.

In essence, this first evaluation shows that we've added value or reduced costs, or both. This conclusion is then presented to the senior team, along with a request that the value added or cost saved be considered in increasing resources for the measurement and evaluation process. Most executives can see value in this process and may free up resources to move more programs to this level of analysis. Some CLOs have taken this approach: "I would like to take our most ineffective, inefficient, or unnecessary program and eliminate it. Then, I would like to take that money, or a portion of it, to fund additional resources for this important process." This approach is very logical and often captures the support of executives.

Using Cost-Saving Approaches

As programs are routinely evaluated at the business impact and ROI levels, learning and development teams learn to make the process work efficiently, using several cost-saving approaches. Table 9-5 shows a variety of cost-saving approaches used by these progressive and cost-conscious learning and development functions to measure impact and ROI.

Isolating the Effects of Programs

An issue that is overlooked in most business impact evaluations is how to isolate a program's effects on impact data. In this step of the evaluation process, evaluators explore specific techniques for determining the amount of impact directly related to the program. Because many factors will affect performance data, this step is essential for increasing the accuracy and credibility of the impact measurement. These techniques have been used by organizations to address this important issue:

- ◆ A *control group* arrangement is often used to isolate the impact of a specific program. One group participates in the program, while another similar group—the control group—does not participate. The difference in performance between the two groups is attributed to the program. When properly set up and implemented, the control group arrangement is the most effective way to isolate the effects of a program.
- ◆ *Trend lines* can be used to project the values of specific impact measures before a program is undertaken. The projection is compared with the actual data after the program is conducted,

Table 9-5. Cost-Saving Approaches to Measure Impact and ROI

Approach 1: Plan for evaluation early in the process.
Guidelines: Define business needs, establish evaluation purposes, determine evaluation levels, develop project objectives, and determine evaluation timing.
Tools: Data collection plan, ROI analysis plan

Approach 2: Build evaluation into the process.
Guidelines: Link business needs, program objectives, and evaluation targets throughout the entire cycle of the needs assessment, instructional design, program delivery, and evaluation. Establish an infrastructure of evaluation policies, procedures, guidelines, and operating standards.
Tools: Linking needs to objectives and evaluation, policies, and procedures

Approach 3: Share responsibilities for evaluation.
Guidelines: Invite managers and employees to provide input on performance and skill deficits; ask stakeholders to review and approve evaluation plans; collect feedback data from participants and key stakeholders after the program.
Tools: Transfer approach matrix, management involvement checklist

Approach 4: Require participants to conduct major steps.
Guideline: Hold participants accountable for learning, applying new skills and knowledge, and identifying enablers and barriers to planned application of learning.
Tool: Action plan

Approach 5: Use shortcut methods for major steps.
Guidelines: Use just-in-time solutions for gap analysis, solution design, and data collection. Caution against an overreliance on shortcut methods and a quick-fix mentality.
Tool: Impact questionnaire

Approach 6: Use sampling to select the most appropriate programs for analysis.
Guidelines: Specific types of programs should be selected for a comprehensive, detailed analysis. Set targets for the number of programs to be evaluated at each level.
Tool: Matrix of selection criteria

Approach 7: Use estimates in data collection and data analysis.
Guidelines: Using estimates can save a great deal of time and money in the isolation and data conversion steps. Use the most credible and reliable sources for estimates, take a conservative approach, and develop a culture that accepts the estimation process.
Tools: Reaction and impact questionnaires, action plans

Approach 8: Develop internal capability in impact and ROI analysis.
Guidelines: Communicate the purpose and scope of the evaluation as a continuous improvement tool that will help assess program priorities and areas of impact. Develop staff capability and shared ownership through education and training and targeted development plans.
Tools: Management briefing outline, individual development plan

Approach 9: Streamline the reporting process.
Guideline: When management is comfortable with ROI evaluations and a results-based measurement focus has been integrated into the organization, a streamlined approach to reporting results may be more appropriate and cost-effective.
Tool: Streamlined impact study template

Approach 10: Use technology.
Guidelines: Use suitable software packages to speed up various aspects of ROI analysis, design, evaluation, and reporting. Use technology to increase internal capability by offering online needs assessments, self-assessments, or evaluation templates for key stakeholders.
Source: Phillips and Phillips 2008b.

and the difference represents an estimate of its impact. Under certain conditions, this technique can accurately isolate this impact.

- ◆ When the mathematical relationships between input and output measures are known, a *forecasting model* can be used to isolate a program's effects. The impact measure is predicted by using the forecasting model with preprogram data. The actual performance of the measure, weeks or months after the program, is compared with the forecasted value. The results give an estimate of the impact.

- ◆ *Participants* may be asked to estimate the amount of improvement that is related to a program. Participants are provided with the total amount of improvement, based on a comparison of preprogram and postprogram measurements, and they are asked to indicate the percentage of the improvement that is related to the program.

- ◆ *Participants' supervisors* may be asked to estimate the effect of a program on the impact measures. The supervisors are given the total amount of improvement and are asked to indicate the percentage that can be directly attributed to the program.

- ◆ *Senior management* may be asked to estimate the impact of a program. In such cases, managers provide an estimate of how much of the improvement is related to the program. Although it may be inaccurate, having senior management involved in the process has some advantages.

- ◆ *Experts* may be asked to provide estimates of a program's impact on performance measures. Because these estimates are based on previous experience, the experts must be familiar with the specific type of program and situation.

- ◆ When feasible, *all other influencing factors* for a program can be identified and their impact can be estimated or calculated; the remaining unexplained improvement is attributed to the program.

- ◆ In some situations, *customers* may be asked to provide input on the extent to which a program has influenced their decisions to use a product or service. Although this strategy has limited applications, it can be quite useful for isolating the effects of customer service and sales programs.

Collectively, these techniques provide a comprehensive set of tools for addressing the critical issue of isolating the effects of a program.

Converting Data to Money

To calculate the return on investment, the impact data for a program is converted to monetary values and compared with the program's costs. This step requires that a value be assigned to each unit of data connected with the program. Even if ROI is not pursued, monetary values are sometimes needed. For some programs, the impact is more understandable when the monetary value is estimated. For example, consider the impact of a leadership development program aimed at all the middle managers in an organization. As part of the program, the managers were asked to address at least two measures that matter to them and that must improve for them to meet their specific goals. These measures could represent dozens, if not hundreds, of different measures.

Many techniques for converting data to monetary values are available; which technique is appropriate depends on the type of data and the situation:

- *Output data* can be converted to data on profit contributions or cost savings. When using this technique, output increases are converted to monetary values based on their unit contribution to profit or the unit of cost reduction. Standard values for these items are readily available in most organizations.
- The *cost of quality* can be calculated, and quality improvements can be converted directly to data on cost savings. Standard values for these items are available in many organizations.
- For programs in which employee time is saved, *the participants' wages and employee benefits* can be used to develop a value for the time saved. Because a variety of programs focus on improving the time required to complete projects, processes, or daily activities, the value of time is an important issue. This is a standard formula in most organizations.

- *Historical costs*, developed from cost statements, can be used when they are available for a specific measure. Organizational cost data thus establishes the specific monetary costs saved or avoided by an improvement.
- When available, *internal and external experts* may be used to estimate the value of an improvement. In this situation, the credibility of the estimate hinges on the expertise and reputation of the experts themselves.
- *External databases* are sometimes available to estimate the value or cost of data items. Research, government, and industry databases can provide important information on these values. Although these types of data are plentiful, the difficulty of this technique lies in finding a specific database related to the program or situation.
- *Participants* can estimate the value of the data item. For this approach to be effective, the participants must be capable of providing a value for the improvement.
- *Supervisors or managers* can provide estimates if they are both willing and able to assign values to the improvement. This approach is especially useful when the participants are not fully capable of providing this input or in situations where the supervisors need to confirm or adjust the participants' estimates. This approach is particularly helpful in establishing values for performance measures that are important to senior management.
- *Soft measures* can be linked mathematically to other measures that are easier to measure and value. This approach is particularly helpful in establishing values for measures that are very difficult to convert to monetary values—for example, data related to intangibles such as customer satisfaction, employee satisfaction, conflict, and employee complaints.
- *Staff estimates* may be used to determine a value for an output data item. These estimates must be provided on an unbiased basis.

The data conversion step is absolutely necessary to determine a program's monetary benefits. The process is challenging, particularly when soft types of data are involved, but it can be accomplished by methodically using one or more of the techniques listed here.

Working with Intangibles

In addition to their tangible monetary benefits, most programs will have intangible, nonmonetary benefits. The ROI calculation is based on converting both hard and soft data to monetary values. Intangible benefits are program benefits that individuals choose not to convert to monetary values. These intangible benefits often include such measures as those listed in table 9-6.

One of the most popular intangibles is the award that the learning and development team receives. On the CEO survey, surprisingly, awards ranked number 3 on a scale of 1 to 8. In terms of use, 40 percent of respondents said that awards are reported and 44 percent stated that they should be reported.

During data analysis, every attempt is made to convert all data items to monetary values. All hard data items, such as those related to output,

Table 9-6. Intangible Program Benefits

Job satisfaction

Employee engagement

Reputation/Image

Awards

Workforce stability

Customer service

Complaints

Capability

Innovation and creativity

Conflicts

Partnerships

Corporate social responsibility

Networking

Communication

Stress

Team effectiveness

Leadership

Intellectual capital

quality, and time, are converted to monetary values. The conversion of each soft data item is also attempted. However, if the process used for conversion is too subjective or inaccurate, the resulting values lose credibility; in such cases, the data is listed as an intangible benefit, with an appropriate explanation. For some programs, intangible nonmonetary benefits are extremely valuable, and thus carry as much influence as the hard data items.

Using Forecasts

When considering impact and ROI, it may be helpful to use a forecasting process. Forecasts can be conducted before a program is developed to anticipate what impact may occur, or what ROI can be generated. Also, the forecast can be conducted when the program is implemented with data collected at the end of the program, essentially using only the reaction data. These time frames are very helpful for seeing the value of projects before they are developed, or at least in the initial stages of implementation.

In a preprogram forecast, the experts involved with a program estimate that improvement in a business impact measure will be generated if the program is effectively designed, developed, and delivered. Obviously, the quality of this forecast hinges on the quality of the experts—and the program. Several experts are used, and their various data items are combined in a convenient way to show a range of possible forecasts, including the most likely. If an ROI forecast is needed, the process works the same way, except that business impact data is converted to money. The forecasted monetary value is compared with the program's projected cost to develop a forecasted ROI. Several ROI forecast values are developed based on input data items from a variety of credible resources. The break-even point is also developed, along with the average forecast.

For instance, for the forecast at the end of a corresponding program using reaction data, the participants detailed the specific application and corresponding impact that would be generated by the program. These data sets were then adjusted using very conservative standards, and the impact was estimated. The ROI forecast could then be conducted by converting the impact data to a monetary value and comparing it with the program's projected cost. In such a situation, a Level 1 forecast can be helpful for seeing the power of a program as it is presented, and it also generates interest in doing a follow-up evaluation. Overall, impact and ROI forecasting is a very powerful tool used by many progressive learning and development functions. More detail can be found in other resources (see Phillips and Phillips 2007a)

◆ ◆ ◆

Final Thoughts

The good news is that business impact data is readily available and very credible. Connecting learning and development programs to these types of data is feasible and realistic. Unfortunately, this analysis takes the learning and development team out of their comfort zone.

After describing the types of data that reflect business impact, this chapter has provided an overview of the issues with business data. Where impact and ROI analysis is needed and sometimes required, there are many challenges to making it a reality. The credibility of data will always be an issue, and several strategies have been offered to enhance the credibility of data analysis. Too often, results are reported and linked with the program without any attempt to isolate the portion that can be attributed to it. If learning and development professionals are committed to improving the images of their functions as well as achieving desired results, this issue must be addressed early in the process for all major programs.

Executives are very interested in impact and ROI analysis, particularly for large-scale programs that are very expensive and strategic. Because of the costs, in both time and money, and their perceived connection to results, executives often want to see the ultimate level of accountability. When such is the case, this task must be pursued, and it is a challenge for many learning and development teams. Fortunately, some progressive organizations are accomplishing this work.

The Learning Scorecard

Executives Will Pay Attention If It's Relevant and Insightful

Developing a comprehensive learning and development function and process is a strategic decision, and top executives understand the need to bring a strategic focus to learning. They see learning as a driver to reach strategic goals and objectives. Though some learning and development functions are flourishing and achieving the desired results, others are perceived as being disconnected from business strategies and operating in a world unrelated to the work of the organization. They sometimes stray from the original goal and fail to demonstrate the actual contribution to the organization. They lack a process to show the management team the measurable value of learning and development and how programs and solutions are linked to strategy, influencing important business measures.

In the CEO survey, 22 percent of respondents said they have a learning scorecard. Our composite research with executives reveals six major concerns about a macro-level scorecard for learning and development. These translate into these specific types of information needed by the executives:

1. The impact of learning and development at the macro level, across all programs and other learning solutions.

2. Brief reports rather than detailed impact studies, at least for a few major programs. Executives want information they can quickly understand and digest.

3 The connection to business objectives and data to show that learning and development is making a contribution and driving certain business improvement measures.

4. The overall contribution of the process, but not necessarily the ROI analysis, for the entire learning and development function. Executives need some indication that the function is adding value, and that every program is evaluated at some level.

5. Different types of data are needed, both tangible and intangible, gathered in different time frames, and often from different sources.

6. The alignment between the major learning and development programs, strategic objectives, and operating goals.

These important needs of senior executives can be met with the learning scorecard.

For the learning and development team, additional data is often needed to ensure that processes are efficient and effective. Improvements are often identified to enhance future results. Thus, process improvement is a key focus of the evaluation data. In addition, the learning and development team needs data on application, impact, and ROI to:

1. Enhance the perception of the learning and development so that the key stakeholders (including executives) have positive impressions about the contribution and usefulness of major initiatives.

2. Build credibility for learning and development with all stakeholders. Data must provide convincing evidence from a realistic, valid, and reliable approach to show that the comprehensive measurement and evaluation process is credible.

3. Justify future expenditures. Executives who need to see that the contribution is significant and the payoff is appropriate approve most learning and development growth. An absence of this type of data may result in budget decreases instead of increases.

4. Enhance management support. Evaluation data should convince management that their support is important, necessary, and a critical part of learning and development success.
5. Provide information for benchmarking with other learning and development functions so that best practice comparisons are possible.

Collectively, these drivers and needs from different target audiences create an unprecedented demand for a measurement system that will collect, distribute, and interpret the necessary data on a routine basis.

Why a Scorecard?

In the past several years, a shift to results-based processes has been evolving in the learning and development function. Initially, learning and development reporting was activity based and not necessarily connected directly to many of the business strategies. The reports from functional specialists lacked accountability and the processes needed to show the value of their contribution. Overall, efforts to measure the impact of learning and development were nonexistent.

Today, things have changed. Many learning and development processes are linked to business strategies, and there is a more comprehensive approach to measurement and evaluation. Table 10-1 depicts this paradigm shift from activity-based to results-based programs. Though the last item on the list is the focus of this chapter—the method of communicating progress and reporting results—the issue involves many of the topics in the results-based approach discussed throughout this book. In the traditional, activity-based mode, the learning and development team would report results from an input perspective, where investment and commitment are emphasized, such as the number of hours consumed in learning activities, the number of participants involved in programs, and the amount of money invested in the process. Today, progressive learning and development functions present a complete scorecard that shows the impact of learning, revealing eight types of data, from input to ROI.

Table 10-1. The Paradigm Shift in Learning and Development	
Activity-Based	**Results-Based**
No business need for the program	Program linked to specific business
No assessment of performance issues	Assessment of performance effectiveness
No specific measurable objectives	Specific objectives for behavior and business impact
No effort to prepare participants to achieve results	Results expectations communicated to participants
No effort to prepare the work environment to support transfer	Environment prepared to support application
No effort to build partnerships with key managers	Partnerships established with key managers and clients
No measurement of results or ROI analysis	Measurement of results and ROI analysis
Reporting on programs is input focused	Reporting on programs is output focused

This learning scorecard primarily provides information to the client group, including top executives. However, it also provides useful measures for the learning and development team. Multiple customer demands are at the core of the scorecard's development. Although there are many stakeholders, two broad groups of customers are served by the learning and development function: the *consumers* and the *clients*. The consumers are the participants involved in the process. The clients are the executives who fund, support, request, or approve programs.

The learning and development team needs immediate information from the consumers in the form of feedback about its processes and programs. The staff must know the extent to which participants are learning new skills and knowledge from the processes in which they participate. The client group, on the other hand, is more interested in application, impact, and ROI. This group is interested in obtaining significant behavioral change from employees as they interact with customers, suppliers, and team members. They are also interested in the actual linkage to business impact—to have some assurance that the programs are helping the operating units achieve their goals. Some executives want the actual ROI, to ensure that major learning and development programs represent an important payoff for the organization. The demands of these two groups create the need for a balanced approach to measurement, reporting a variety of data, both qualitative and quantitative, collected in different time frames from different individuals.

Shifting to Output-Focused Reporting

Most traditional reporting is focused on the actual investment in, and activities about, learning—the input side of the statistics. CLOs use a variety of statistics, such as number of hours of learning programs, number of people involved, number of programs, number of multiple enrollments, and investment per associate. Though these statistics are useful in providing an indication of the level of support, scope, and investment, they do not reflect outcomes, such as application or business impact.

Most evaluation processes typically concentrate on micro-level activities, measuring one program at a time and reporting the results. But for a learning and development function with several hundred learning programs, it is practically impossible to measure every program at every level of evaluation; nor is it desirable. For some programs, however, it is extremely important to show business impact and ROI.

The challenge is to measure as many programs as possible at the higher levels (application, impact, and ROI) and to integrate the data in a meaningful way to show the overall contribution of the learning and development function. In essence, this process takes a micro-level activity (evaluation of a specific learning program) and presents a macro-level view (evaluation of all learning programs) of this function.

Figure 10-1 illustrates the concept. Though each program is evaluated on the micro level, only a few selected measures in each of the micro evaluations are captured for the macro evaluation. In essence, it takes the most critical, important, and executive-friendly measures to go on the learning scorecard. Building a macro report requires several important steps that address a variety of issues.

Figure 10-1. Micro-Level versus Macro-Level Scorecards

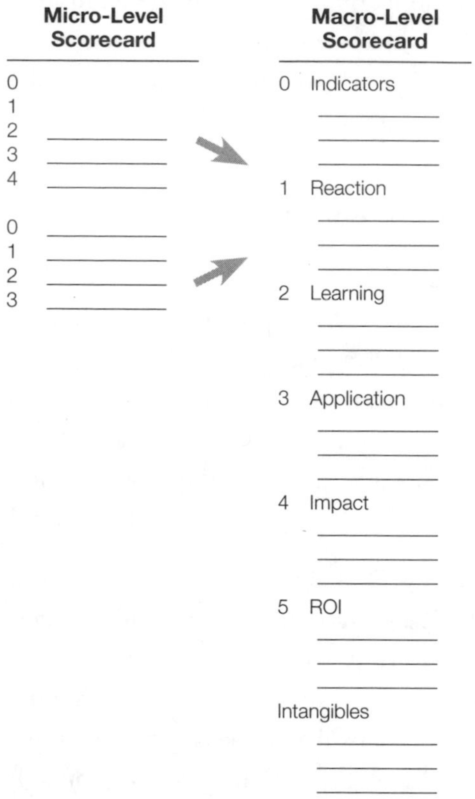

Beginning with the end in mind and picturing the fully developed score-card may be helpful in progressing with the steps to develop this type of reporting process. Figure 10-2 shows an outline of a comprehensive learning scorecard. This figure shows categories only and does not reveal the actual data. About 40 measures are included in the complete report. Eight major categories of data are presented, including:

0. Inputs and indicators showing the commitment of resources, including volume and efficiencies.
1. Reaction and planned action as participants are involved in learning solutions.
2. Skill and knowledge acquisition as participants are involved in learning solutions.

Figure 10-2. Sample Outline of Reporting for a Learning and Development Function

0. Inputs/indicators
    1. Number of employees involved
    2. Total hours of involvement
    3. Hours per employee
    4. Investment as a percent of payroll
    5. Cost per participant
    6. Delivery mechanisms

I. Reaction and planned action
    1. Percent of programs evaluated at this level
    2. Ratings on 3 items vs. target
    3. Percent with action plans
    4. Percent with ROI forecast

II. Learning
    1. Percent of programs evaluated at this level
    2. Types of measurements
    3. Self-assessment ratings on 3 items vs. targets
    4. Pre/post-average differences
    5. Percent receiving certification

III. Application
    1. Percent of programs evaluated at this level
    2. Ratings on 3 items vs. targets
    3. Percent of action plans complete
    4. Barriers (list of top 10)
    5. Enablers (list of top 10)
    6. Management support profile

IV. Business impact
    1. Percent of programs evaluated at this level
    2. Linkage with business measures (list of top 10)
    3. Types of measurement techniques
    4. Types of methods to isolate the effects of programs

V. ROI
    1. Percent of programs evaluated at this level
    2. ROI summary for each study
    3. Methods of converting data to monetary values
    4. Fully loaded cost per participant and comparison

Intangibles
    1. List of intangibles (top 10)
    2. How intangibles were captured

Awards
    1. Learning and development professional awards
    2. Industry awards

3. Behavior change and actions taken as participants apply on the job what they have learned.

4. Business impact driven from the application of learning—which may use individual, team, or organizational measures.

5. ROI for selected programs showing the actual return from specific learning solutions.

6. Intangible measures that are not converted to monetary values but represent important measures.

7. Awards received by the learning and development team.

Collectively, these categories satisfy executive needs and learning and development team needs, using the classic five levels of evaluation:

1. Reaction
2. Learning
3. Application
4. Business impact
5. ROI.

The Foundation for the Scorecard

The learning scorecard is built on a foundation that includes several important principles necessary for the development of a comprehensive measurement and evaluation process, which is referred to as the ROI methodology. The part of this process is the framework for evaluation, which represents different types of data collected at different time frames, as described in chapter 2.

A step-by-step process model is needed to plan and implement the evaluation, especially when programs are evaluated in a postprogram time frame. Whenever there is an attempt to measure application or impact, a process model is needed to ensure that the data is collected, analyzed, and reported in logical and sequential steps. Figure 10-3 shows the ROI process model used by thousands of organizations to develop impact studies on different types of learning solutions. It represents the most frequently utilized process model in the world to measure the impact of learning. Hundreds of case studies have been published on the process,

Figure 10-3. Model of the ROI Process: Calculating the ROI of a Business Performance Solution

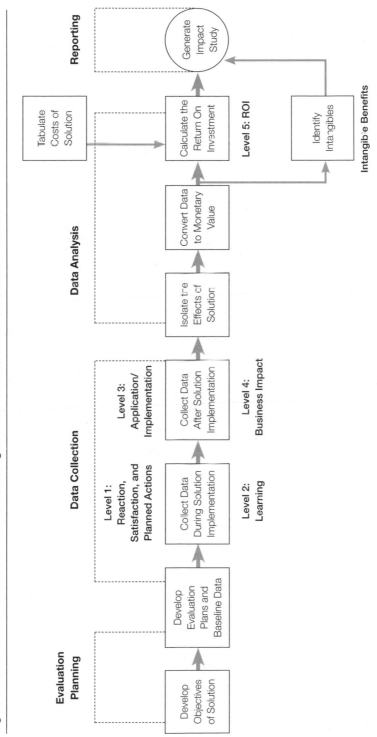

and almost four thousand individuals have been certified to implement this process within their organization.

An important feature of this model is the number of techniques available to isolate the effects of the learning solution from other influences. In almost any setting, there will be multiple influences on output data, and the process model must utilize several techniques to measure or isolate the effects of learning from the other influences. An important part of the process model is the multiple ways in which to convert data to monetary values. As more situations require ROI analysis, this step becomes essential. Data, driven by the program, is converted to monetary values and compared with the actual cost of the program to yield the actual ROI. The results, representing six types of measures, are reported to specified target audiences.

Operating standards are necessary, ensuring consistency in utilizing the approach. These standards ensure that the results of an impact study conducted by one individual can be replicated if compared with the same study conducted by another individual. Table 10-2 shows the operating standards for the ROI process model described here. These "guiding principles" provide basic philosophies and operating rules that not only ensure consistency but also offer a conservative approach to analysis. These principles also provide the rationale for several cost-saving approaches in the analysis, while maintaining process credibility.

Selecting the appropriate programs for impact and ROI evaluation can often be a tedious process in and of itself. But it is necessary to ensure the successful implementation of a comprehensive measurement and evaluation process. When the wrong programs are selected, the evaluation is not only costly but can also be frustrating if the process and results are ineffective—or worse, completely ignored by key stakeholders.

The selection process begins with a review of the learning and development budget. To ensure that evaluation up to such a comprehensive level is feasible within the constraints of the learning and development measurement and evaluation budget (usually 3 to 5 percent of the

Table 10-2. ROI Methodology Guiding Principles: The Standards

1. When a higher-level evaluation is conducted, data must be collected at lower levels.
2. When an evaluation is planned for a higher level, the previous level of evaluation does not have to be comprehensive.
3. When collecting and analyzing data, use only the most credible sources.
4. When analyzing data, select the most conservative alternative for calculations.
5. At least one method must be used to isolate the effects of the solution/program.
6. If no improvement data is available for a population or from a specific source, the assumption is that no improvement has occurred.
7. Estimates of improvements should be adjusted for the potential error of the estimate.
8. Extreme data items and unsupported claims should not be used in ROI calculations.
9. Only the first year of benefits (annual) should be used in the ROI analysis of short-term solutions.
10. Costs of a solution, project, or program should be fully loaded for ROI analysis.
11. Intangible measures are defined as measures that are purposely not converted to monetary values.
12. Communicate the results of the ROI methodology to all key stakeholders.

total learning and development expenditures), a target-setting process is developed to reflect the actual percentage of programs evaluated at each level. This procedure often begins with 100 percent of all programs evaluated at Level 1. (For the details on Level 0 through Level 5, see appendix A.) These evaluations are usually automated, easy to accomplish, and contain very important information needed to make adjustments quickly. As measurement moves up the chain of impact, the evaluation process becomes more difficult and expensive; thus, a declining percentage of programs is evaluated at higher levels to make evaluation economically feasible. Figure 10-4 shows sample evaluation targets for a large telecommunication company. This distribution is typical of what many learning and development functions are pursuing.

Although these percentages can vary with a particular organization, they almost always reflect declining percentages, often leaving a question about the appropriateness of evaluating so few programs at Levels 4 and 5. However, if those programs are carefully selected following predetermined criteria developed with input from the management team, the necessity for

Figure 10-4. Sample Evaluation Targets for a Large Telecommunications Company

Level	Target (percent of programs evaluated at this level)
1 Reaction	100
2 Learning	70
3 Application	30
4 Business impact	10
5 ROI	5

having a greater number of evaluations is often precluded. The typical criteria utilized for selecting programs at these levels are

- ◆ the life cycle of the program
- ◆ the linkage of the program to operational goals and issues
- ◆ the importance of the program to strategic objectives
- ◆ the cost of the program
- ◆ the visibility of the program
- ◆ the size of the target audience
- ◆ the investment of time
- ◆ top executives are interested in the evaluation.

Though these criteria are common, the list can be expanded or modified for a particular learning and development function. Because impact studies are expensive and difficult, it is necessary to focus evaluations at this level only on the programs designed to make a significant difference, those that drive business value, or those that are important to the management group. This keeps the measurement and evaluation process reasonable and feasible within economic parameters.

Collectively, these building blocks provide the foundation and rationale needed to develop a comprehensive measurement system.

The Scorecard

The data reported in the scorecard (figure 10-2) is derived from the measurements captured from the processes described in the above sections. This section provides more detail on building the blocks of the scorecard itself.

Inputs and Indicators

The traditional approach to measuring the learning and development function is to report on inputs and indicators. Though these measures are important, they do not reflect the results, only the level of commitment, volume, efficiencies, and trends in processes. And though the number of indicators is vast, it is important to also include measures of interest to top managers. Ideally, the management group should approve the indicators, and the inputs reported should stimulate interest with executives. Here are a few possibilities:

1. The number of employees participating in learning programs.
2. The number of hours of learning activity per employee.
3. Various enrollment statistics, including the demographics of participants, participation rates, completion rates, and so on.
4. Investment in learning reported in a variety of ways (total costs, cost per employee, direct cost per participant, and cost as a percentage of payroll are common ways).
5. Cost recovery, if there is a charge-back system. (Some learning and development functions operate in a charge-back or profit-center mode.)
6. Status of alternative delivery of learning.

Several other statistics can be reported on issues such as technology, on-the-job learning, trends, volume, and efficiencies. Any mix is appropriate to highlight and monitor an important trend. The indicators show the degree of management's commitment to the learning process and provide a brief view of the mix of programs offered.

Reaction (Level 1)

The first outcome level, reaction, represents an important area of measurement. This is the most popular level of measurement, often used in measuring almost 100 percent of programs. The 100 percent coverage does not necessarily reflect importance as much as it does the ease of measuring and the cost-efficient way in which the data can be tabulated. Some argue that 100 percent is not needed; a sampling is sufficient. However, other factors may drive the 100 percent coverage. If planned action is a part of the data collection at this level, it is important to capture planned action from all the participants. Also, some participants want to provide feedback data, particularly if they had an exceptionally satisfying or extremely disappointing learning event.

To enable a comparison of one program with another, it is necessary to capture input for several specific reaction measures. Though specific items can vary with the learning and development function, seven items are suggested:

- relevance to the job*
- amount of new information
- recommendation to others*
- importance of the information*
- intention to use skills and knowledge*
- effectiveness of the facilitator
- effectiveness of the delivery system.

These items represent some of the most useful reactions. Also, four of the seven (followed with an asterisk) have been found to have a significant correlation with application and serve as predictors of actual applications. These items can be easily compared from one program to another, thus enabling the interaction of data across programs.

Another potential Level 1 measure is the percentage of the participants with action plans. Because of the interest in participants applying what they learn, this has become an important measure. Also, because there is some concern that transfer will not take place, the presence of an action plan enhances the possibility of the actual application. This measure will usually correlate with the extent of the actual application.

The next set of potential measures focuses on the forecasting capability of several learning and development functions. Data can be collected with the reaction questionnaire to forecast application, impact, and ROI. Additional questions can be added to the standard reaction questionnaire to generate the information. Figure 10-5 shows the types of questions necessary to develop projections for Levels 3, 4, and 5. The form can vary and be expanded and is often included as a supplemental form. When a significant number of forecasted ROI calculations are developed, the average forecasted ROI with an additional adjustment is sometimes reported. This adjustment represents an additional reduction factor other than the confidence factor from the individuals providing input. This adjustment represents the unknown barriers that will inhibit the transfer of the skill to the work setting. Sometimes this factor can be as high as 60 percent and is usually based on experience within the organization.

Learning (Level 2)

The measurement of learning presents a challenge for many comprehensive learning and development functions, because they attempt to determine the extent to which participants acquire skills and knowledge in learning solutions. A first step in this category is to report the percentage of programs evaluated at this level. This percentage often ranges from 40 to 80, depending on the definition of a learning measure. Some learning

Figure 10-5. Sample of the Types of Questions Necessary to Develop Projections for Levels 3, 4, and 5

Planned Improvements

- As a result of this program, what specific actions will you attempt as you apply what you have learned?
- Please indicate what specific measures, outcomes, or projects will change as a result of your actions.
- As a result of the anticipated changes in the above, please estimate (in monetary values) the benefits to your organization over a period of one year.
- What is the basis of this estimate?
- What confidence, expressed as a percentage, can you put in your estimate? (0% = No confidence; 100% = Certainty) _____%

measurements are very formal, such as objective tests, simulations, and structured skill demonstrations. Others are less structured and informal, such as self-assessments, facilitator assessments, and team assessments. Learning measurements should be defined in this context and reported appropriately. Some learning and development functions define a learning measure as any type of measurement, whether formal or informal. Others make a distinction between the types of measurement, and this is often reported on the scorecard. Table 10-3 provides a simple breakdown of the different types of measurement processes that can provide insight into the extent of formal versus informal assessments.

To compare learning changes from one program to another and integrate the data into a macro view on the scorecard, it is essential to have only a few identical measures. Typical issues addressed in a self-assessment of learning change are

- ♦ acquisition of the skills and knowledge
- ♦ ability to use the skills and knowledge
- ♦ confidence in the use of skills and knowledge.

The scale is adjusted for each program so that exceptional ratings (that is, 5) are the same across programs.

Two other possibilities sometimes surface that can be included in this section of the scorecard. When available, pretest and posttest differences can be reported to show the percentage of improvement. Because this is a percentage improvement, an average measure for similar programs

Table 10-3. Types of Measurement Processes for Formal versus Informal Assessments

Formal Measures	Informal Measures
Objective tests	Self-assessments
Performance testing	Team assessments
Simulations	Facilitator assessments

provides insight into the extent of learning change for all those programs. Also, when some programs are designed to lead to a certification or qualification, the percentage of participants actually meeting requirements is often reported.

Application (Level 3)

To measure the actual change in behavior on the job and progress with application, measurements must be taken after the program is completed. The first in this category of measures is the percentage of the programs evaluated at this level (3). This percentage often ranges from 20 to 50, depending on the resources available and the types of follow-up evaluations planned. Three issues are recommended as standard follow-up items when assessing changes in skills and knowledge:

- the extent of use of the skill or knowledge on the job
- the frequency of use of new skill or knowledge (on the job)
- the effectiveness of the skill or knowledge (as applied on the job).

Essentially, these items can be collected on every program to show the extent to which the skills and knowledge are applied on the job. With this approach, exceptional performance (again, a rating of 5) is the same across programs, although what constitutes exceptional performance would vary with the program. For example, for some programs, exceptional performance may be defined as using the skill several times every day. For other programs, exceptional performance may require the use of the skills once a month. The important point is that the scale is adjusted with the program so that ratings can be compared across programs.

The next recommended measures can be very critical to the success of the learning and development function. The first of the four measures is to capture the percentage of the action plans completed by the desired follow-up time. This provides data on the extent to which participants apply and complete their assignments from the program. When compared with baseline data, this measure shows changes in transfer of learning to the job. The next measure captures the barriers to skill and knowledge application on the job. Forced-choice options for anticipated barriers are usually offered, along with space for additional barriers. Forced choices for typical barriers allow for integration across programs and can be arranged as a "top 10" list.

Table 10-4 shows the typical barriers. The enablers are those processes that enhance the transfer of learned skills and knowledge. The enablers provide insight into the reasons for success and sometimes mirror the barriers. A similar forced-choice option can be utilized with the enablers. The same process can be used to capture, tabulate, and integrate data on enablers as used with data on barriers.

A management support profile reveals the extent to which immediate managers support the programs. A management support profile taken from both the manager and the participant provides interesting information about the quality of support. Table 10-5 shows a range of follow-up questions on management support from the participants' perspective. Participants and managers are asked to check the appropriate statement that best describes the level of management support provided. Managers have their statements worded slightly different. When data is collected across programs and ranked, much can be revealed about the level of management support. Disconnects can be quickly revealed and converted into actions for improvement.

By listing the top 10 barriers, enablers, and management support issues, useful indices and trends are provided for management to see what helps

Table 10-4. Typical Barriers Listed on Follow-Up

The immediate manager does not support the skills/knowledge.

The culture in the work group does not support the skills/knowledge.

There is no opportunity to use the skills/knowledge.

There is no time to use the skills/knowledge.

The skills/knowledge could not be applied to the job.

The systems and processes did not support the use of the skills/knowledge.

Changed job and the skills/knowledge no longer apply.

The skills/knowledge taught are not appropriate in our work unit.

There is no need to apply what was learned.

Could not change old habits.

Table 10-5. Management Support Response: Options for Follow-Up Questions

> My manager asked me to forget these skills—we operate differently here.
>
> My manager questioned the appropriateness of the skills/knowledge.
>
> My manager complained about my absence and expressed concern about the program.
>
> My manager made no comment about the program.
>
> My manager asked about my reaction about the program.
>
> My manager encouraged my use of the skills/knowledge.
>
> My manager coached my use of the skills/knowledge.

or hinders the implementation of training. Trends are monitored and the data is turned into action plans to reduce or remove impediments to success and to enhance the enablers of application.

The next measure in this category is the data collection technique. This item provides input into the different methods utilized to capture both application and business impact data. Objective versus subjective processes can be emphasized. Some organizations are moving from the subjective to the objective, while others are moving in the other direction. Either way, the tracking of techniques shows the data collection trends in learning and development. Table 10-6 shows the typical options available for postprogram data collection.

Business Impact (Level 4)

The connection to business measures can be captured when studies are conducted to show business impact or when follow-up questionnaires are utilized to capture application data. In this category of measures, the first measure is the percentage of programs evaluated at this level. The percentage is usually around 10 to 20 when all the processes are in place to produce an impact study. However, this percentage can increase significantly if questionnaires, interviews, and focus groups are modified to capture business impact data, in addition to application data. When summarized and reported, this becomes important data.

Method	Level 3	Level 4
Surveys	✔	
Questionnaires	✔	✔
Observation on the job	✔	
Interviews	✔	
Focus groups	✔	
Action planning	✔	✔
Performance contracting	✔	✔
Performance monitoring		✔

Table 10-6. Methods of Collecting Postprogram Data

As shown in figure 10-6, the linkage of the program to business measures can be captured on a follow-up questionnaire. Only responses where there is a significant and very significant influence are tabulated. Impact study data, showing the movement of business impact measures, is reported on a different line of the report. Either way, the connection between the program and the business measure is reported. When presented as the top 10 list, it is possible to quickly examine disconnects or alignment issues. For example, if the most important business strategy is to improve customer satisfaction, then the program's connection to customer satisfaction measures should surface at the top of the list. If it does not, disconnects may be occurring or there could be misalignment.

Another measure reported on the learning scorecard is the method used to isolate the effects of the program. A variety of ways is available, and some organizations are moving to more research and analytical methods while others are using subjective estimations to save time and costs. Changes in the use of methods are identified as the different techniques are highlighted. Table 10-7 shows the possible techniques for isolating the effects of a program.

Return on Investment (Level 5)

From the viewpoint of many executives, the ultimate level of evaluation is the actual return on investment, where the monetary benefits are

Figure 10-6. Sample Follow-Up Questionnaire on Linkages to Business Impact Measures

Indicate the extent to which you think this program has influenced each of these measures in your work unit, department, or business unit:

	No Influence	Some Influence	Moderate Influence	Significant Influence	Very Significant Influence
Productivity					
Quality					
Response time					
Cost control					
Employee satisfaction					
Customer satisfaction					
Other (please specify)					

compared with the cost of the program. The first measure in this ROI category is the percentage of programs evaluated at this level. This number is usually quite low, usually in the 5 to 10 percent range. Not much additional information is needed on the learning scorecard for the ROI studies, because the number of studies is quite small.

The results of ROI studies are typically reported to target audiences, and only summary data is needed on the scorecard. A brief paragraph showing the nature of the study and the actual results, including the

Table 10-7. Techniques to Isolate the Effects of the Programs

Use of a control group arrangement

Trend line analysis of performance data

Use of forecasting methods of performance data

Participants' estimate of programs impact (percent)

Supervisors' estimate of programs impact (percent)

Management's estimate of programs impact (percent)

Use of previous studies and experts

Calculating or estimating the impact of other factors

Use of customer input

ROI percentage, is appropriate, along with the information on how to obtain additional details. This category includes two other measures: the method used to convert data to monetary values, and the cost per participant. Because the data conversion methods can vary, it is important to show the methods utilized so that trends can be tracked. Many organizations are moving toward the use of standard values and the use of estimates so that the cost to develop values can be minimized. The different approaches to convert data to monetary values are

- Convert output to profit or cost savings.
- Convert the cost of quality to money saved.
- Convert employees' time to compensation.
- Use historical costs.
- Use internal and external experts.
- Use data from external databases.
- Link with other measures.
- Use participants' estimates.
- Use supervisors' and managers' estimates.
- Use learning and development teams' estimates.

The cost per participant can be as important a measure for the learning scorecard as it is for the ROI studies. This value represents a fully loaded cost and is different from the cost per employee for training reported in the indicator category, which is usually a direct cost. The total program costs categories are

- needs assessment (prorated)
- development costs (prorated)
- program materials
- instructor/facilitator costs
- facilities cost
- travel/lodging/meals
- participant salaries (and benefits) for time away from work
- administrative/overhead costs
- evaluation costs.

This total cost is then divided by the number of participants in the program. The program cost per participant is reported on the scorecard and can be compared with the direct cost of the program.

Intangible Measures

An additional category of important data is intangible measures. These measures may be included in the business impact category of a report or mentioned in a separate section, particularly if there are significant numbers of impact studies. Intangibles are defined as the measures that are purposefully not converted to monetary values, although they are very important to the organization and there is evidence of linkage to the learning and development programs.

The top 10 intangibles are sometimes reported, providing an opportunity to check for alignment and disconnects with organizational strategy. The most important intangibles in the organization—ranging from teamwork to networking to brand awareness to customer satisfaction—are listed as questions for participants to complete. On the follow-up evaluation on Level 3, this question may appear listed this way: "To what extent did this program influence this measure?" The reaction could be on a scale from 1 to 5, where 1 is no influence and 5 is a very significant influence. When these questions are combined on all of the follow-ups, a profile is revealed of the intangibles driven by the programs. The intangible driven most becomes the most important and influential for the programs, and so forth. This approach is easy to do and provides some insightful information about how the programs are linked to these important measures.

Awards

Today, many awards are made available to learning and development functions and provide recognition for some of the best functions. Some are professional awards provided by professional organizations, such as the American Society for Training and Development. Magazines, such as *Training* and *Chief Learning Officer*, provide others. Still others are through conference organizers, such as the Corporate University Best in Class Awards. In addition, the industry in which an organization operates sometimes provides awards.

Achieving awards and listing them on the learning scorecard can be helpful, but particularly for executives who want external recognition. As you recall, our survey shows that "awards" was ranked 3 out of 8 by those responding. After all, it's usually hard work and excellent progress that brings this type of recognition. And when the award is obtained consistently, it shows a sustained best practice approach. The downside of awards is that the basis for achieving them is sometimes not very objective. Unfortunately, many awards are given based on the quality of the entry or nomination. Some heads of learning and development functions have boasted about being able to win any award that's available (as he or she has) because of the appropriate resources behind the awards. Still, they are worth pursuing and should be considered for the overall scorecard.

The Learning Scorecard—Short Version

Some senior executives are frightened to see the comprehensive nature of the learning scorecard presented in this chapter. This is particularly true when previous scorecards or attempts to develop a scorecard have been dominated by input measures, as many of them are. When this is the case, perhaps moving to the shorter version would be a first step. Figure 10-7 shows a short version of the comprehensive scorecard described in this chapter and contains only 15 measures, but all are very powerful and important to the executive group. Most of the measures are self-explanatory and reflect the measures presented in this chapter; however, a few deserve some explanation.

In the area of reaction, the perceived value of the program can be captured, even as an index, which is an average of several questions that might always be asked, and presented to your team as one measure. Also, the business impact linkage can be obtained during the program, instead of waiting until the follow-up. In this case, a question is added in the

Figure 10-7. Short Version of the Learning Scorecard

0 Inputs/indicators
1. Number of programs
2. Hours per employee
3. Cost per employee

1 Reaction
1. Perceived value (index)
2. Business impact linkage

2 Learning
1. Percent of programs evaluated at this level
2. Learning (index)

3 Application
1. Percent of programs evaluated at this level
2. Application index
3. Top barriers to learning transfer

4 Business impact
1. Percent of programs evaluated at this level
2. Business impact linkage

5 ROI
1. Percent of programs evaluated at this level

Intangibles
1. Top intangibles

Awards
1. Industry and professional awards

reaction questionnaire that lists all the key business impact measures in the organization with a statement that says, "Please provide the extent to which this program will influence this measure." A scale of 1 to 5 is used, with 1 being no influence and 5 being very significant influence. In essence, this is the very same question asked on the follow-up, but here it's collected almost 100 percent of the time and shows perceived linkage immediately.

Under learning, the index can be constructed using one or two measures but presented as an average. It could be an average of the three presented in this chapter, or it could be a single measure. On number three, the application index is an average of the three suggested in this chapter. The rest of the measures are self-explanatory.

Reporting Data

Although simple and straightforward, the data outlined in the learning scorecard can be quite cumbersome when several hundred programs involving thousands of participants are conducted each quarter. An important issue is to use consistent rating scales and consistent questions and statements. Also, the only way that complete data can be accumulated and reported economically is through the use of technology. If reaction and learning data is collected with a questionnaire during or at the end of a learning program, the data can be quickly integrated and available instantaneously.

In addition, when a standard follow-up questionnaire is utilized to capture application and impact data, most of the data items at these levels can be integrated. For higher levels of evaluation (3, 4, and 5), data volume may become smaller because convenience sampling is utilized and the task should be feasible and reasonable. Ideally, if data is collected online, it can be rolled up into an online reporting format. In the short version of the learning scorecard, the report can be developed showing only one or two measures for each of the seven categories. The fully loaded scorecard, presented in figure 10-2, can be developed over time as resources are available and data collection instruments are revised. The key is to begin with the end in mind with a mockup of the report, presented to the executive group. Both reports provide a tremendous amount of data that shift reporting from being input focused to output focused. The frequency of reporting can be monthly, quarterly, or annually—the more frequent, the better. Online reporting should be an ultimate goal.

Challenges

Three main challenges must be addressed as CLOs move from the traditional activity-based reporting focused on input to a comprehensive scorecard of successes based on output. Because a macro view of learning and development is needed, this shift is long overdue and can be accomplished with a reasonable amount of resources. The first challenge is to allocate additional resources for measurement and evaluation. The learning scorecard can be developed, including all the measurement and evaluation processes for about 3 to 5 percent of the total learning and development budget. This is not an unreasonable amount when the value of the process is considered. Also, this additional investment can pay off in significant cost savings.

The second challenge is to approach the task in a disciplined, methodical manner. This is particularly difficult when it is not required (directly) by executives. Waiting for the executive request for more of a contribution on the scorecard (and less input data) may be too late. The best time to pursue this is when it is not mandated by executives.

The third important challenge is the actual use of the data. Not only does this reporting reveal success in terms of the contribution, but it also provides a tremendous amount of process improvement data that enables the learning and development team to make adjustments throughout the learning cycle. All the data should be collected with its ultimate use in mind. If it is generated only to fill up boxes in a chart or lines on a report, it will become worthless. Because of the possibilities, the executive group and the learning and development team need to decide how the data can best be used and interpreted.

◆ ◆ ◆

Final Thoughts

The good news is that the challenge of reporting useful data that measures learning and development success and contribution is feasible. Success is possible in almost any setting, but it is most likely with careful planning, a framework that focuses on results, a determination to make it work, and perhaps a few additional resources. Most CEOs report that they don't see a learning and development scorecard. This is a great opportunity to develop a learning scorecard for the executives—but only if it contains data the executives want to see.

 Chapter 11

Partnering with Business Executives

Connecting Lessons Learned to Successful Practices

Developing a productive relationship with business leaders is a win-win situation. A productive relationship creates value by helping the business achieve goals while providing direction and guidance for the learning and development team. When operating effectively, business impact can be significant and enables CLOs to have a seat at the table.

Establishing an effective collaborative relationship with management is the best route to success with learning and development programs. Input from the management team is an integral part of the process. Managers' involvement is sometimes critical to successful implementation of a program. An effective relationship can help guarantee success with high-quality input and helpful cooperation.

This chapter explores six key strategies for building relationships and learning and development success:

- increasing commitment from top executives
- improving support from managers
- enhancing the reinforcement of learning
- increasing management involvement
- developing partnerships with key managers
- focusing programs on results.

As explained in more detail just below, these strategies and the actions they engender can overlap. Suffice it to say, they are all important in ways that positively interlock.

The partnership relationship is an outgrowth of the learning organization movement. Most major organizations have been transformed (or are in the process of being transformed) into learning organizations. In the classic definition of the learning organization, the management team takes a more active role in the learning process and partners with learning providers to ensure that employees acquire the skills and knowledge necessary for success. In essence, management becomes a willing partner in the process. On the other hand, sometimes executives and managers fail to support learning.

Why Executives and Managers Fail to Support Learning

It is helpful to review why managers don't support learning. Their reluctance can be linked to a variety of reasons. Some are valid, while others are based on misunderstandings about the learning and development function and its impact in the organization. The early chapters revealed the most common problems:

- ◆ *Questionable results:* Executives and managers aren't convinced that learning and development adds value. They don't see programs producing useful results. Middle managers are rarely asked, "Is this learning program helping you reach your objectives?" Learning professionals deserve much of the blame for this. A program's perceived learning effectiveness all too often is determined by participants' reactions and measures made during the program. Managers need more understandable and useful application and impact data.
- ◆ *Very expensive:* Managers have the mistaken perception that a formal learning and development program has a double or triple cost, because the direct cost is ultimately taken from

operating profits and sometimes charged to their department. And an employee's salary is paid while he or she is in the program, which takes the employee away from his or her job, which must still get done—cutting productivity.

◆ *Lack of input:* Managers don't support learning because their input is not part the process. They are not asked for their views about the content or focus of a program during needs assessment and program development. They are rarely given objectives linking learning to business results. Thus, they don't develop a sense of ownership.

◆ *Not enough relevance:* Managers have little reason to believe that learning programs are relevant to a particular job or will help their work units. They see content descriptions that bear little resemblance to work issues. They hear comments about programs unrelated to current challenges and discussions of rats, penguins, and fish. They have many demands for resources and thus must quickly eliminate frills and perceived busywork. No relevance equals no need—equaling no priority and leading to no support.

◆ *Lack of involvement:* Managers don't support learning because they aren't actively involved in the process. Even in the best organizations, the manager's role is severely limited—sometimes by design and other times by default. To gain respect for the learning and development function, managers need to be actively involved in it.

◆ *No time for learning and development:* When setting priorities, managers are facing ever-increasing demands on their time and don't feel they can support learning, so it doesn't make it to the top and nothing happens. And they often feel that requests for support will always take more time, but many actions *don't* require much time.

◆ *No preparation:* Sometimes, managers lack the skills to reinforce participants after a program. They may not know how to offer feedback, answer questions, facilitate dealing with issues, or help achieve results. To effectively reinforce participants, they need specific skills—just as they do for planning and budgeting.

◆ *Lack of knowledge:* Executives aren't always aware of the scope of the learning and development process—from needs assessment to development, delivery, and evaluation. They may see bits and pieces but not how together they create an effective process. Perhaps they know it's a legitimate function to equip new employees with required skills and knowledge; but beyond that, they aren't fully aware of how the process can improve the organization— and it's difficult to support when they don't understand it.

Collectively, these reasons for not supporting learning and evaluation equate to challenges for the CLO and represent opportunities for managers. If the issues are not addressed effectively, management support will not exist, the transfer of learning will be diminished, and business results will be severely limited or nonexistent.

The Executive's Role

Executives' actions and attitudes have a significant influence on the impact and success of learning and development programs. This influence, and the environment external to program development and delivery, is the focus of this chapter. Although the members of the learning and development team may have no direct control over some of these factors, they can exert a tremendous amount of influence on them.

Several overlapping, sometimes-confusing terms used in relation to the six key management actions identified above can have similar meanings and thus need additional explanation:

◆ *Executive commitment* usually refers to the members of the top management group and includes their pledge or promise to allocate resources and support to the learning and development effort.

◆ *Management support* refers to the actions of the entire management team, which reflects its attitude toward the learning and development process and team. The major emphasis is on middle and first-line management. Their supportive actions can have a tremendous impact on the success of learning programs.

- *Management involvement* refers to the extent to which managers and executives outside the Learning and Development Department are actively engaged in the learning process in addition to participating in—sponsoring—programs. Because "commitment," "support," and "involvement" have similar meanings, they are used interchangeably in the current literature.
- *Management reinforcement* refers to actions designed to reward or encourage a desired behavior. The goal is to increase the probability of the behavior occurring after a participant attends a learning program.
- *Maintenance of behavior* refers to the actions needed to maintain a change in behavior on the job after the program is completed—primarily accomplished by developing partnerships.
- *Transfer of learning* refers to the extent to which the learned behavior from the program is used on the job—primarily accomplished by focusing on results. In this regard, the term *operating manager* is used to represent the key managers involved in producing, selling, or delivering the products and services.

Table 11-1 summarizes the key management actions related to these six concepts with the target group, scope, and payoff.

Table 11-1. Comparison of Key Executive and Management Actions

Management Action	Target Group	Scope	Payoff
Executive commitment	Top executives	All programs	Very high
Management support	Middle managers, first-level supervisors	Usually several programs	High
Management involvement	All levels of managers	Specific programs	Moderate
Management reinforcement	First-level managers	Specific programs	Moderate
Developing partnerships	All levels	All programs	High
Focusing on results	All levels	Specific programs	High

Increasing Commitment from Top Executives

Commitment is necessary to secure the resources for a viable learning and development effort. Ten general areas of emphasis for strong top management commitment are shown in table 11-2, with the positive response percentages from 22 CEO interviews (described in detail in appendix E). These 10 areas need little additional explanation and are necessary for a successful learning effort.

Table 11-2. Areas of Emphasis for Strong Top Management Commitment from CEO Interviews (*N* = 22)

For the following actions, check all that apply to you and your learning and development team:

	Action	Percent Responding Positively
1.	Develop or approve a mission for the learning and development function. Provide input and perspective.	73
2.	Allocate the necessary funds for successful learning and development programs. Initial funding may be based on benchmarking. Later, it is based on value added.	95
3.	Allow employees time to participate in learning and development programs. Encourage, but don't require, a minimum level of participation.	73
4.	Be actively involved in learning and development programs and require others to do the same. This includes conducting parts of formal programs and coaching or mentoring others.	45
5.	Support the learning and development effort and ask other managers to do the same. Define and communicate ideal support.	59
6.	Position the CLO in a visible and high-level place on the organization chart, ideally reporting directly to the CEO or other top executive.	23
7.	Require that each learning and development program be evaluated in some way, recognizing that most evaluations will include reaction and learning data only.	64
8.	Insist that learning and development programs add business value and require supporting data, including a few ROI studies each year.	77
9.	Set an example for self-development. Show that continuous improvement is necessary in a learning organization.	59
10.	Create an atmosphere of open communication with the CLO. Schedule quarterly reviews with the CLO to discuss progress, opportunities, and issues.	14

Now for the big question: How can top management's commitment to the learning and development function be increased? Quite often, the extent of commitment is fixed in the organization before the CLO becomes involved with the function. The amount of commitment varies with the organization's size, nature, and scope. Mostly, it depends on how the function has evolved, the top management group's attitude and philosophy toward learning, and how the function is managed. The particularly operational aspect lies in how the effort is managed. The team can have a significant effect on top management's commitment in the future by focusing on six important areas:

- delivering business results
- encouraging management involvement
- exhibiting professionalism
- communicating needs
- showing resourcefulness
- taking a practical approach.

Results

The commitment of top executives will usually increase when programs obtain the desired results. As illustrated in figure 11-1, this is a virtuous cycle, because commitment is necessary to create the effective programs that in turn obtain the desired results. When the results are obtained, commitment is increased. Nothing is more convincing to a group of top executives than programs with measurable results in terms they can understand. When a program is proposed, additional funding is usually based solely on the results the program is expected to produce.

Management Involvement

Commitment is increased when there is extensive involvement at all levels of management. This involvement, which can occur at almost every phase of the learning process, shows a strong cooperative effort toward developing employee potential within the organization. Chief executives want their managers to make a concerted effort to increase their teams' and departments' skills and knowledge. Specific techniques for increasing involvement are covered later in the chapter.

Figure 11-1. The Commitment-Results Cycle

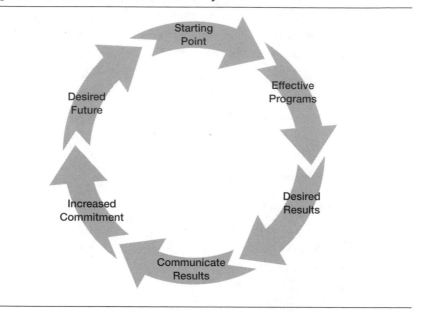

Professionalism

A highly professional learning and development group can help influence the strength of commitment from top management. Achieving excellence is the goal of many professional groups and should be the mandate of the CLO. The learning and development team must be perceived as professional in all actions, including being open to feedback and criticism, adjusting to the changing needs of the organization, maintaining productive relationships with other teams, setting examples throughout the company, and practicing what is taught in the learning and development programs. Professionalism appears in attention to detail in every program—detail that is often overlooked by nonprofessionals.

Communicating Needs

The CLO must be able to communicate development needs to top managers and enable them to realize that learning is an integral part of the organization's operation. This communication may be in the form of proposals or review sessions with the top management group. When chief executives understand the need, they will respond through additional commitment. CLOs must be advocates for learners from across the organization. The CLO's role is to translate learning needs and objectives into actions for the company. Management relies on CLOs to identify need and create solutions for improving individual and organizational performance.

Resourcefulness

The learning and development function should not be a narrowly focused group. Too often, learning and development teams are regarded as capable in technical training, team development, or sales training—but not problem solving or consulting. When the members of a learning and development team are viewed as versatile, flexible, and resourceful, they can be used to help solve organizational performance problems and not be confined to formal development activity. The result: additional commitment on the part of management. The members of the learning and development team define the function. Their willingness to develop capabilities and those of individuals across the organization is critical for business success.

Practical Approach

The CLO must take a practical approach. The members of a learning and development team who focus too much on theories and jargon may be regarded as noncontributors in the organization. Though there is a place for theoretical processes, learning solutions should be followed by practical application. Programs should be relevant and taught by experienced people who understand the content as well as the business. This practical approach will help ensure additional commitment.

Building Support from Managers

A familiar complaint from the learning and development team is that there is not enough support from managers. To improve support requires an understanding of ideal support, defining the gaps, and planning specific actions.

Ideal Support

In addition to executives, middle-level and first-level managers are also important for success. Before discussing the techniques involved in improving the support for learning and development programs, it is helpful to present the concept of ideal management support. Ideal support occurs when a manager reacts in these ways to a participant's involvement in a program:

- Encourages participants to be involved in programs.
- Volunteers personal services or resources to assist with learning and development.
- Makes an agreement with the participant before attending the program outlining the changes that should take place or tasks that should be accomplished after the program is completed.
- Reinforces the behavior change taught in the program; this reinforcement may be demonstrated in a variety of ways.
- Conducts a follow-up of the results achieved from the program.
- Rewards participants who have achieved outstanding accomplishments linked to the program.

This type of support for a program represents utopia for the CLO. Support is necessary both before and after the program is conducted. Actions before a program can have a tremendous impact on learning during the program and application on the job. Follow-up actions are also very important to drive results. Often, management actions do not follow this path. It is imperative that individuals in organizations take responsibility for their own development and make changes in their performance independent of management. People tend to manage as they are being managed, unless they learn different skills.

Degrees of Support

A key area of support involves postprogram activities. In this context, the terms *support* and *reinforcement* are almost synonymous, because when support is exhibited, it helps reinforce what the participants have learned. Before pursuing specific techniques for improving postprogram support and reinforcement, it is useful to classify managers into four different types according to their degree of support:

- supportive
- responsive
- nonsupportive
- destructive.

But before we look briefly at these four types, a caveat is needed: The simple term *manager* can be used to represent the manager of a participant in a program. This same analysis can apply to other managers above that level. A label has been attached to each of the four types of managers that best describes their attitude and actions toward learning and development.

Now back to the four types. A *supportive* manager is a strong, active supporter of all learning efforts, is involved in programs, and is anxious to have his or her employees take advantage of every appropriate opportunity. This manager vigorously reinforces the material presented in programs and requires participants to apply it. He or she will publicly voice approval for learning and development; provides positive feedback to the CLO and other team members; and frequently calls on the team for assistance, advice, and counsel. This manager is an ally and a valuable asset.

A *responsive* manager supports learning and development, but not as strongly as the supportive manager. He or she allows employees to participate in learning and development programs and encourages them to get the most out of the activities. This manager usually voices support for programs, realizing that it is part of his or her responsibility, but usually does not go out of his or her way to aggressively promote learning programs or activities. This manager will reinforce the material presented in the program, probably at the prodding of the learning and development team. This manager views the support for formal learning programs no differently than the support for budgeting—it is something that must be done, but he or she is not excited about it.

A *nonsupportive* manager will privately voice displeasure with formal learning programs. He or she reluctantly sends participants to programs, doing so only because everyone else does or because it is required. This manager thinks the organization spends too much time on learning and development activities and does not hesitate to explain how he or she achieved success without any such formal programs. When participants return from a program, there is very little, if any, reinforcement from this manager. This manager's actions may destroy the value of the program. A typical comment after a program will be, "Now that the program is completed, let's get back to work."

A *destructive* manager works actively to keep participants from being involved in learning and development programs. This manager openly criticizes the CLO and the learning and development programs, believing that all such activities should be accomplished on the job in the "real world," not in a formal classroom setting. He or she requires that all e-learning programs be taken at night or on the weekends. When participants return from a program, there is usually negative reinforcement, with typical comments such as "Forget what was discussed in that program and get back to work." Fortunately, this type of manager is rare in today's setting; however, there may be enough of these individuals to cause some concern.

When development is a key area of accountability for a company's managers or executives, management support is much easier to obtain. Businesses today realize that an educated staff is a competitive advantage and the cost of not learning is too great. Managers have begun to take the impact of learning seriously, and in many cases those who refuse to support learning are not going to be successful—and neither will their businesses.

Improving Support

The degree of managers' support is based on the value they place on learning, the function and role of learning, and, in some cases, the actions of learning and development team members. To improve management support, the CLO and the team should carefully analyze each situation and work to improve relationships with individual managers or the management group. This requires four critical steps.

First, key managers—those whose support is necessary—must be identified. The target group may be the decision makers, the entire middle-management group, or all senior managers.

These managers are analyzed and classified, based on their degree of support, in the four categories given just above—supportive, responsive, nonsupportive, or destructive. Input from the entire team may be helpful in classifying all the key managers. As shown in figure 11-2, manager support follows a normal distribution curve. The percentages in the figure represent the allocation in one organization—a construction materials firm—not known for having strong supporters of learning. The goal is to shift the curve to the right—the responsive to the supportive and the nonsupportive to the responsive. In addition, the destructive managers need to be shifted to nonsupportive, if possible (or neutralized).

Second, the reasons for support or nonsupport are analyzed. Managers will usually show support (or nonsupport) for learning and development based on a series of facts, beliefs, and values related to learning and development.

Third, the best approach for each manager is selected. The strategy for improving a relationship with a particular manager depends on his or her degree of support.

Fourth, the approach may need to be adjusted. Managers are individuals, and what works for one may not work for another. If an attempt to change a manager's supportive behavior does not work, possibly another approach will succeed. Typical actions to enhance support are:

♦ Utilize preprogram agreements and commitments to determine specific goals and objectives for participants in the program.

Figure 11-2. Classification of Managers in a Construction Materials Firm

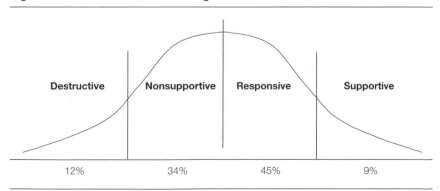

Destructive	Nonsupportive	Responsive	Supportive
12%	34%	45%	9%

- Clearly define responsibilities of managers in the learning and development process.
- Provide clear instructions and expectations to managers.
- Develop application and impact objectives for programs.
- Encourage managers to attend programs designed for their direct reports.
- Conduct follow-up discussions with managers to review the success of programs using application and impact data.
- Encourage managers to provide advice and counsel to the learning and development team on key issues, concerns, and business challenges.

Increasing the Reinforcement of Learning

With results-based learning, there must be an effective relationship between the facilitator, the participant, and the participant's immediate manager. This relationship can be viewed as part of a three-legged stool representing the major stakeholders. One leg is the discussion leader, who conducts the program. The next leg is the participant, who experiences the program. And the third leg is the participant's manager, who reinforces what is being taught. If any leg is missing, the application of learning collapses.

The importance of involving the participant's manager as an integral part of the process cannot be understated. Too often, participants return from a program to find roadblocks to successfully applying what they have learned. Faced with these obstacles, even some of the best participants revert to old habits and forget most of what was learned in the program. Regardless of how well the program is conducted in the classroom, unless it is reinforced on the job, most of its effectiveness is lost.

The reason for this lies in the nature of learning. In first learning a skill, participants go through a frustrating period when using the new skill feels uncomfortable and the desired results are not being produced. This period represents a decline in results and is difficult for most participants. However, those who persist gain the expected reward that is obtained from the new behavior. If the participant continues to exercise the new behavior or skill, it eventually feels more natural, and performance improves. However, without proper reinforcement, particularly during the time when results decline at first, participants may abandon the acquired skills. They may revert to the old, familiar way of behavior with no change.

Although self-reinforcement and peer reinforcement are helpful, the learner's immediate manager is the primary focus for reinforcement efforts. These managers exert significant influence on the participant's postprogram behavior by providing reinforcement in these ways:

- Help participants diagnose problems to determine if new skills are needed.
- Discuss possible alternatives for handling specific situations and act as a coach to help the participants apply the skills.
- Encourage participants to use the skills frequently.
- Serve as a role model for the proper use of the skills.
- Give positive rewards to participants when the skills are successfully used.

Each of these activities will reinforce what has been taught and can have a tremendous impact on participants' skills and knowledge.

Increasing Management Involvement

Management involvement in learning and development is not a new process; organizations have been practicing it successfully for many years. Although there are almost as many opportunities for management's involvement in the learning and development process as there are steps in a learning design model, management input and active participation will generally occur only in the most significant ones. Management should be involved in most of the key decisions of the Learning and Development Department. The primary vehicles for obtaining or soliciting management include

- program leaders
- advisory boards, committees, and councils
- task forces

- managers as experts
- managers as participants
- involving managers in analysis and evaluation
- new roles for managers
- linking pay to involvement.

Program Leaders

The key to involving management and professional personnel is to use them as course leaders or facilitators. The concept of leaders teaching leaders has become a very effective way to deliver customized leadership development. Jack Welch, former chairman of General Electric, was involved in management development programs regularly at GE's Management Development Center. He would allocate several days a month to teaching in certain programs. This approach presents some unique challenges to the Learning and Development Department. Not everyone has the flair for leading discussions in a development program. The extent to which managers are involved in programs can vary considerably. In some efforts, the learning and development team conducts the entire program. At the other extreme, some programs are conducted entirely by operating management. The right combination depends on these factors:

- the capability of the learning and development team
- the capability of operating management and other professional personnel
- the value placed on having operating management and other professional teams identified with the program
- the size and budget of the learning and development team
- the physical location of the program as compared to the location of operating managers.

There may also be other factors specific to the organization. The use of leaders to teach programs creates a strong atmosphere of commitment and support and can provide critical knowledge and information that cannot be achieved with external facilitators.

Advisory Boards, Committees, and Councils

Some organizations have developed boards, committees, or councils to enhance management involvement in the learning and development process. These committees, which act in an advisory capacity to the CLO, may have other names, such as councils or people development boards. As shown in table 11-3, committees can be developed for individual programs, specific functions, or multiple functions. They can be one-time committees or standing committees, depending on the program's duration. Committees can be used in many stages of the process, from needs analysis to communicating program results. The learning and development team benefits from management input and from its commitment as well, when the committee buys into a specific program. It is difficult for managers to criticize something destructively when they are a part of it.

Task Forces

Another potential area for management involvement is through the use of a task force. The task force consists of a group of employees—usually management—who are charged with the responsibility for developing a learning and development program. Task forces are particularly useful for programs beyond the scope of the learning and development team's capability. Also, a task force can help considerably in reducing the time required to develop a program.

Table 11-3. Types of Committees and Boards

Responsible for	Examples
Individual program	New Team Leader Development Committee Account Executives' Learning Committee Product Knowledge Course Committee Apprenticeship Training Advisory Board
Specific function	Sales Training Council Nurse Professional Development Committee IT Training Advisory Group Underwriting Training Committee
Multiple functions	Management Development Council Faculty Development Committee Skills Training Committee Compliance Board

A major difference between the function of a task force and that of a committee is that the task force is required to produce a deliverable. It must devote a considerable amount of time to a project or program. The time required may vary from a two-week assignment to a six-month, full-time project. This time span, of course, depends on the nature of the program being developed and the availability of assistance for the task force.

The task force approach is very economical. It relieves the learning and development team of time-consuming program development that may be an impossibility for a subject unfamiliar to the team. Additional involvement on the part of management and professional personnel can help improve the program's credibility and enhance the results.

Managers as Experts

Managers may provide expertise for program design, development, or implementation. Subject matter experts provide a valuable and necessary service while developing attachment to the program. For example, at a Whirlpool refrigerator manufacturing plant, managers served as experts in a major job-redesign project. The traditional assembly line was replaced with a work-cell arrangement. The expertise of the managers was critical to program success.

Managers as Participants

Managerial participation can range from attending an entire program to auditing a portion to examining its curriculum. However, participation may not be feasible for all types of programs, such as specialized courses designed for only a few individuals. This approach is best when one or more of these conditions exists:

- A high percentage of the manager's subordinates will attend the program.
- Support and reinforcement from the manager are essential to the program's success.
- It is essential for the manager to have the same knowledge or skills that the subordinates will learn from program attendance.

Involving Managers in Analysis and Evaluation

Another area where managers can be involved is analysis and evaluation. In analysis, managers review needs assessment data and confirm the learning needs to approve a solution. Sometimes, managers are directly involved in assessment and analysis. Manager involvement in evaluation is usually through a team or committee arrangement. One approach requires managers to collectively examine the application and business impact of learning. Some possibilities are

- Invite managers to participate in focus groups about a program's success.
- Ask managers to collect a program's application and impact data.
- Ask managers to review a program's success data.
- Ask participants to interpret a program's results.
- Convene managers to share a program's overall results.
- Ask managers to communicate program data to their teams.

Thus, involving managers and showing them how evaluation can work increases commitment and support. Sometimes executives are involved in planning annual learning initiatives. At Qualcomm, the learning and development team conducts an annual needs assessment with division executive teams and their team. The annual learning needs are compiled into a learning plan, which is reviewed and approved by the division president and the senior team. This has proved to be an excellent way of obtaining management support across the organization.

New Roles for Managers

The approaches described just above are traditional ways to involve managers in the learning and development process when the focus is on achieving results. But there are also many other ways available to increase their involvement in learning and development programs—including these kinds of new roles:

- Coordinate or organize programs.
- Participate in needs assessments.

- Provide expertise in program design.
- Facilitate programs.
- Reinforce learning.
- Evaluate program learning, application, and impact.
- Drive actions for program improvement based on evaluation data.

Table 11-4 summarizes the opportunities for managers' involvement along the traditional steps in the learning and development cycle. The potential strategy for involvement is identified. The CEO's role is more limited. In the CEO survey in large organizations, 78 percent approved the budget, 73 percent reviewed requests to major programs, and 61 percent reviewed the results of major programs. Only 18 percent actually taught segments or programs. Table 11-5 shows the results.

Linking Pay to Involvement

A great way to get a manager's attention on an issue is to link it to compensation. Therefore, an effective strategy for some companies is to link manager bonuses to involvement in learning and development efforts. A difficulty of this approach is selecting the proper measures. Though managers might not agree with the construction of the metrics or the measures as targets, they will become more aware of the organization's people development goals. Survey data from the Conference Board suggests that putting employee development measures in bonus plans correlates with successful links between business strategies and certain people measures.

Summarizing the Benefits of Management Involvement

In summary, there are six major benefits from involving management and professionals in the learning and development process:

1. Program credibility is enhanced.
2. Managers' ownership of programs increases because they have been involved in the process of developing, conducting, or evaluating them.
3. Participants and the learning and development team have more interaction with management, which enhances relationships and improves needs assessment.

Table 11-4. Manager Involvement Opportunities

Step in the Results-Based Process	Opportunity for Manager Involvement	Most Appropriate Technique
Conduct analysis	High	Task force
Develop measurement and evaluation system	Moderate	Advisory committee
Establish program objectives	High	Advisory committee
Develop program	Moderate	Task force
Implement program	High	Program leader
Monitor costs	Low	Expert input
Collect and analyze data	Moderate	Expert input
Interpret data and draw conclusions	High	Expert input
Communicate results	Moderate	Manager as participant

Table 11-5. The Executive View: CEO Involvement in Learning and Development (*N* = 96 CEOs of *Fortune* 500 and Large Public Organizations)

In what ways are you personally involved in learning and development (check all that apply)?

Action	Percent Checking
I introduce / close out major programs.	29
I actually teach segments of major programs.	18
I review requests for major programs.	73
I review results for major programs.	61
I use the learning and development scorecard to monitor progress and make adjustments.	34
I conduct/host periodic review meetings to examine the success of learning and development.	22
I personally approve the learning and development budget with input from others.	78
Other.	18

4. The skills of managers involved are enhanced.
5. Internal leaders teaching classes can lower the cost of external facilitation.
6. Managers are rewarded for their contributions to learning.

These advantages should encourage more CLOs to use the skills and expertise of managers in the learning and development process. The influence of the management group—especially key operating and support managers—should not be ignored, but instead it should be utilized to improve the quality and image of learning and development initiatives.

Developing Partnerships with Key Managers

The CLO must create effective partnerships with key business leaders. A partnership relationship can take on several different formats and descriptions. In some situations, it is very informal, loosely defined, and ill structured. If this is the case, the CLO may not want to develop partnering relationships to a formal level but instead continue to refine them informally. In other situations, the CLO formalizes the process to the extent that particular activities are planned with specific individuals, all for the purpose of improving relationships. The quality of the relationships is a major goal, and assessments are sometimes done to gauge progress. Still other CLOs make the process very formal: Individuals are discretely identified, and a written plan is developed to improve the partnership. Sometimes a contract is developed with a particular manager. In these situations, assessments are routinely done and progress is reported formally. Though these approaches represent three distinct levels of formality, it is possible for a CLO to move through these different levels as the partnering process matures and achieves success. Other sources provide more detail on this issue; see Elkeles and Phillips (2007) and Rothwell, Lindholm, and Wallick (2003).

Focusing Programs on Results with Higher Levels of Objectives

Objectives are powerful because they provide direction, focus, and guidance. They create interest, commitment, expectations, and satisfaction.

Their effect on different stakeholders varies; they are a necessity, not a luxury. Though the power of objectives at the reaction and learning levels is evident, the importance of objectives at higher levels, at application and impact, requires additional explanation.

Application and Impact Objectives Drive Programs

Objectives at the levels of application and impact are routinely omitted from programs. Ironically, they are the most powerful levels because they focus on an organization's needs. They

- provide focus and meaning to the program
- provide direction to stakeholders
- define success.

Application and Impact Objectives Enhance Design and Development

A risk not worth taking is sending vague objectives to a program designer or developer. Designers are creative, using their imaginations to build program content. Without clear, specific direction, they will insert their own assumptions regarding the ultimate use of the project (application) and the impact to the organization (impact). These higher-level objectives

- define content issues
- help with designing exercises and activities
- make skill practice and role-plays more relevant
- facilitate action plans.

Application and Impact Objectives Improve Facilitation

Objectives are the first information reviewed before facilitating a meeting or learning session, and they define the facilitator's approach in teaching the project or program. They provide guidance for the facilitator to know how to present, what to present, and the context in which to present. These higher levels of objectives

- show the end result and provide the focus to achieve it
- focus the discussions to application and impact
- ensure that the facilitator has job-related experience.

Application and Impact Objectives Help Participants Understand What Is Expected

Participants need clear direction as to why they are involved in a program and what they are expected to do. Essentially, the role of a participant changes with higher levels of objectives. Of course, participants are expected to attend meetings and learning sessions, become involved and engaged, and learn. When application and impact objectives are communicated to them, they will realize that there is an expectation for them to apply what they learn and that the application of knowledge should reap some benefit. Again, application and impact objectives remove the mystery from the program and the roles within it. These higher-level objectives

- clarify expectations by detailing what the participant must do
- set clear expectations about what the participant must ultimately accomplish
- define "what's in it for me?"
- explain why the program is being conducted.

Impact Objectives Excite Executive Sponsors

The sponsors—those who fund a learning and development program—often request data showing how well the program has achieved its goal. Impact measures resonate with executives and program sponsors. It is no secret that executives do not get excited about reaction and learning objectives. They are not as concerned with reactions to a program, or even what is learned. Rather, their interest lies in what participants do with what they learn and the ultimate impact of this knowledge on the organization. Impact objectives

- connect the program to the business
- connect the program to key performance indicators
- show business value.

◆ ◆ ◆

Final Thoughts

Working constructively with executives and key managers can have a very positive impact on learning and development if the process is properly utilized and receives the appropriate emphasis. These efforts enhance the respect and credibility for the learning and development team, while helping to ensure success with programs and initiatives. Establishing effective relationships with executives is an important role for the CLO. Building relationships requires time, priority, focus, and planning.

This chapter has presented six specific strategies for building managerial and staff relationships and thereby achieving success in the learning and development function: increasing commitment from top executives, improving support from managers, enhancing the reinforcement of learning, increasing management involvement, developing partnerships with key managers, and focusing programs on results. Although these strategies sometimes overlap, they are complementary and are all necessary to enable the learning and development function to add the maximum value to an organization.

The driving forces creating the need for learning and development will continue, challenging the CLO to tap the influence of managers and executives and explore ways to make the process successful. Increasing executive commitment and support is a desired objective for most CLOs, and it is a natural evolution of organizations as they strive for continued success. Good luck!

◆ Epilogue

As we finish writing this book, the United States and other countries around the world are in a deep recession. Unfortunately, we've seen its effects on the learning and development community. Unique situations have occurred, with companies such as Citigroup announcing early in the recession that they were trimming their expenses and eliminating all internal and external training as well as other unnecessary expenses. Other *Fortune* 500 companies have completely dismantled their learning and development functions, though some of them are not losing money but merely trimming their expenses to remain lean and efficient. We have also seen learning and development functions in other companies go untouched during this recession. This action is encouraging because, although these firms have trimmed other expenses, they have not cut back on their investment in employees.

In an ideal world, the top executives of every company would view investments in learning and development as essential during tough economic times; and in most situations, they would demand more investment instead of less. In a downsized company, the combination of having only a few employees with the tension of trying to get business in this economy can be challenging, but an additional investment can make employees tougher in their approach and more skilled in their execution, and make the organization more effective and efficient. Fewer employees in many areas also may mean that the remaining employees have to take up the slack, so additional learning and development is needed for them as well.

Regrettably, however, most executives don't see it this way. For the most part, they view learning and development as something that is necessary, but not as a process yielding a return on investment. They have a desire to see more data, more value, and more connection to the business, but the majority of those responsible for the learning and development function have not stepped up to this challenge. It is vital that learning and development leaders set the right priorities, have the discipline to follow through on them, and tenaciously make them sustainable—and this book provides the how-to for doing this as it builds on executives' suggestions. The challenge is left up to the leaders of the learning and development community to position their function as a crucial, business-contributing process that helps drive organizations in good times and bad.

We encourage readers of this book to meet this challenge, because we believe it will pay handsome rewards in the future. If you need more dialogue on this issue, please contact us and join our network.

Jack J. Phillips (jack@roiinstitute.net)
Patti P. Phillips (patti@roiinstitute.net)

Appendix A

Definition of Terms

Within the learning and development field, there is a variety of frameworks, concepts, and terminology. This variety is often confusing to not only learning and development professionals but even more so to their critical clients. Thus, this appendix defines and explains

- measures, metrics, and analytics
- value
- types of data
- the chain of impact
- the levels of program objectives
- business alignment
- isolating impact
- data conversion
- return on investment
- learning scorecards
- stakeholders.

Measures, Metrics, and Analytics

According to *Webster's New Explorer Dictionary*, *The American Heritage Dictionary*, and the *The Oxford English Dictionary*, *measure* is the dimension, capacity, or amount of something ascertained by comparison with a standard through the act of measuring. Measures are units of measurement—for example, size, amount, degree.

This book uses the term *measure* to reflect the value of learning and development. Measures are grouped by broad categories. Business impact measures are classified as productivity, quality, time, cost, and a host of other categories. Application measures may be perceptions based on observation, measures of scale, or measures of actual activity using numerical measurement. Learning measures may be the knowledge, skills, or information captured in tests or role-plays. Reaction measures may be perceptions captured on a scale of 1 to 5.

The term *metric* is defined much like the term *measure*. A metric is a standard for measuring something, although this standard is often a composite of two or more measures. The term is derived from the metric system of measurement. Metrics are typically associated exclusively with quantitative units; whereas measures refer to both quantitative and qualitative units. "Measures" and "metrics" are often used interchangeably without much fanfare regarding differences.

The most current buzzword, and to some people the vaguest, is *analytics*. At its most basic level, analytics is defined as the science of analysis. Sometimes the term is interchanged with *metric*; however, the process of analysis is usually the intended meaning when referring to analytics. Thomas Davenport (2006) suggests that analytics includes the processes of data collection and analysis.

Measurement is defined as the act, or process, of measuring. The term is often used in the context of measurement and evaluation, where measurement represents data collection and evaluation means making sense of the data.

Evaluation is the understanding and interpretation of the data collected through the measurement process (also known as analytics). This often involves judgment from the observer or evaluator. This information is used to make decisions that will influence the status of the project or program being evaluated.

The terms *measure, measurement,* and *evaluation* are much the same as *metric* and *analytics*. Metrics are perceived to be more desirable than measures. Analytics seem to be more desirable than data analysis. New terms are used because the old ones have not delivered the perception of value that executives want. Unfortunately, terminology can't disguise bad information. So, for the purposes of this book, we primarily use the fundamental terms *measure*, *measurement*, and *evaluation*, and we focus on defining those measures that are meaningful to senior executives.

Value

The changing perspectives on value, as well as the shifts occurring in organizations, have led to a new definition. *Value* is not defined by a single number. Rather, its definition is a variety of measures that must be balanced with quantitative and qualitative data, as well as financial and nonfinancial perspectives. The data sometimes reflect tactical issues, such as activity, as well as strategic issues, such as ROI. Value must be derived using different time frames, not necessarily representing a single point in time. It must reflect the value systems that are important to stakeholders, who all have a different perspective on value. The data comprising value must be collected from credible sources, using cost-effective methods; and value must be action oriented, compelling individuals to make adjustments and changes.

Types of Data

It is helpful to examine measurement and evaluation of learning as a chain of impact, where data is collected at different times, sometimes from different sources. Figure A-1 shows this value chain—which is fundamental to much of the current work in evaluation of learning and development.

This concept shows how value is developed, often from different perspectives. Some stakeholders are interested in knowing about inputs so that they can be managed and made more efficient; others are interested in reaction; still others are interested in learning. More recently, clients and sponsors of learning and development activities have become more interested in actual behavior change (application) and the corresponding business impact. Many stakeholders are concerned about the actual return on investment.

Figure A-1. The Types and Levels of Data in the Chain of Impact

Level	Measurement Focus	Typical Measures
0—Inputs and indicators	Inputs into the program, including indicators representing scope, volumes, costs, and efficiencies	Types of topics, content Number of programs Number of people Hours of involvement Costs
1—Reaction and planned action	Reaction to the program, including the perceived value of the project	Relevance Importance Usefulness Appropriateness Intent to use Motivational
2—Learning and confidence	Learning how to use the content and materials, including the confidence to use what was learned	Skills Knowledge Capacity Competencies Confidences Contacts
3—Application and implementation	Use of content and materials in the work environment, including progress with implementation	Extent of use Task completion Frequency of use Actions completed Success with use Barriers to use Enablers to use
4—Impact and consequences	The consequences of the use of the content and materials expressed as business impact measures	Productivity Revenue Quality Time Efficiency Customer satisfaction Employee engagement
5—Return on investment (ROI)	Comparison of monetary benefits from the program to program costs	Benefit/cost ratio ROI (percent) Payback period
6—Intangible benefits	Measures purposely not connected to money	Customer satisfaction Employee engagement Teamwork Networking

The Chain of Impact

The data described in figure A-1 is arranged as a chain of impact. The chain must be evident if a particular learning program or performance improvement project is adding business value. All stakeholders involved in the program must understand this chain of impact. The sponsor must see how this chain generates business value. Participants must realize that they have a critical role and that their involvement and success are shown through the chain. Designers, developers, and facilitators must understand how the chain of impact works. This chain can be broken at any level, and the evaluation will indicate where it is broken. Was it broken because of adverse reaction, or no learning, or no application? Or was there no connection to a business measure? The information in this book will help you understand whether the chain of impact is intact and where it can be strengthened. When the chain of impact is considered throughout the process of evaluation, some interesting characteristics begin to evolve.

The types of data become more valuable as the process moves from reaction to ROI—at least from the client's perspective. The lower levels of data types—for example, reaction and learning—are primarily consumer oriented. Reaction data is essentially a consumer satisfaction index. Learning data is often provided to the consumer to build confidence. Impact data and ROI data are more client focused. These are the types of data that clients want to see from learning and development programs. However, though the power to show results increases as data moves through the chain, measuring and evaluating the data becomes more expensive and more difficult, reserving evaluation at these higher levels to the strategic, expensive, and high-profile programs. The reverse is true for usage. As expected, the highest level of data collection activity occurs at Level 1 due to the ease to gather data and the limited cost of data collection, while low levels of activity occur at Level 4 and Level 5.

The Levels of Program Objectives

In the learning and development field, program objectives have focused primarily on learning or instruction. However, for many if not most programs, objectives need to be expanded to include Level 3 and Level 4 objectives. One of the most important developments in measurement and evaluation is the creation of higher levels of program objectives. Program objectives correspond with the different levels of evaluation represented on the value chain:

- input objectives (number of programs, participants, hours, and the like)—Level 0
- reaction objectives—Level 1
- learning objectives—Level 2
- application objectives—Level 3
- impact objectives—Level 4
- ROI objectives—Level 5.

Ideally, the levels of objectives should be in place at the highest level desired for evaluation. This is determined by the need for the program. When the need, objectives, and evaluation are linked, there is business alignment.

Business Alignment

Business alignment is a critical issue for senior executives, who want learning and development programs to drive business outcomes. But what is business alignment, and how is it achieved? First, business alignment means that alignment is achieved at the very beginning of a learning and development initiative. That is, steps are taken to ensure that the learning solution is connected directly to a business need. Second, alignment occurs also during the implementation of a program. With specific impact objectives, participants achieve business objectives. With the objectives in place, expectations are communicated, and focus is maintained throughout the process. Third and finally, business alignment is achieved after a program has been implemented, through evaluation. Alignment at this phase is achieved when steps are taken to isolate the impact of the program.

Isolating Impact

An often-overlooked issue in some evaluations is the process of isolating the effects of learning on impact data. This step is important because many factors will usually influence business performance data after a learning program is conducted. Several techniques are available to determine the amount of output performance directly related to the program. These techniques will pinpoint the amount of improvement directly linked to the program, resulting in increased accuracy and credibility of the evaluation data. This issue is very important to executives.

Data Conversion

Data conversion refers to the process of converting business impact measures to monetary value. This concept is sometimes referred to as "monetizing" measures. To calculate the return on investment, business impact data collected in the evaluation is converted to monetary values and compared with program costs. This step requires that a value be placed on each unit of data connected with the program. Several techniques are available to convert data to monetary values. In many cases, standard values are available, because organizations have attempted to place value on measures they want to increase and develop costs for measures they want to avoid. When these are not available, the existing records (or a combination of records) may show the cost or value of the measure. Also, internal experts, external experts, or external databases can be sources of values.

Return on Investment

Many executives and managers have taken the "show me the money" approach. This requires that at least a few major programs be elevated to the ROI level. When the ROI is actually developed, it should be calculated systematically, using standard formulas. Two formulas are available. The benefit/cost ratio (BCR) is the program benefits divided by the costs.

In formula form, the BCR is

$$BCR = \frac{\text{Program Benefits}}{\text{Program Costs}}$$

The return on investment calculation uses the net benefits divided by program costs. The net benefits are the program benefits minus the costs, then multiplied by 100 to calculate the ROI percentage. In formula form, the ROI is

$$ROI\ \% = \frac{\text{Net Program Benefits}}{\text{Program Costs}} \times 100$$

This is the same basic formula used in evaluating other investments for which the ROI is traditionally used as earnings divided by investment.

Learning Scorecards

In recent years, there has been much interest in developing documents that reflect appropriate measures across the organization. Scorecards, such as those originally used in sporting events, provide a variety of measures for top executives. In Kaplan and Norton's (1996) landmark book *The Balanced Scorecard*, the concept was brought to the attention of organizations. Kaplan and Norton suggested that data be organized in four categories: financial, internal business processes, learning and growth, and customer.

But what exactly is a learning scorecard? *The American Heritage Dictionary* defines a scorecard from two perspectives:

1. A printed program or card enabling a spectator to identify players and record the progress of a game or competition.
2. A small card used to record one's own performance in sports such as golf.

Scorecards come in a variety of types, whether Kaplan and Norton's balanced scorecard, the scored set of data in the president's management agenda using the traffic light grading system (green for success, yellow for mixed results, red for unsatisfactory), or some other approach. Regardless of the type, top executives place great emphasis on the concept of scorecards. In some organizations, the scorecard concept has filtered down to various functional business units, and each part of the business is required to develop scorecards. A growing number of learning and development executives have developed scorecards to reflect the success of their activities.

Stakeholders

Many stakeholders are involved in comprehensive measurement and evaluation systems. A *stakeholder* is defined as any individual or group interested, or involved, in the learning program or project. Stakeholders may include the functional manager where the program is located, the participants, the organizer, the program leader, facilitators, and key clients, among others. These typical stakeholders are referred to routinely throughout the book:

- *Sponsor/clients:* These are individuals who fund, initiate, request, or support a particular project or program. Sometimes referred to as the sponsor, they form the key group—usually at the senior management level—whose members care about the program's success and are in a position to discontinue, maintain, or expand the program.
- *Participants:* These are the individuals who are directly involved in the program. The terms *employee, delegate, associate, user,* and *stakeholder* may represent these individuals. For most programs, the term *participant* appropriately reflects this group.
- *Immediate managers:* These are individuals who are one level above the participants involved in the program. For some programs, this is the team leader of the participants. Often they are middle managers, but, most important, these people have supervisory authority over the participants in the program.
- *The organization:* This is the entity within which the particular program or process is evaluated. Organizations may be companies (either privately held or publicly held); government organizations at the local, state, federal, and international levels; nonprofits; or nongovernmental organizations. They may also

include educational institutions, associations, networks, and other loosely organized bodies of individuals.

- *Program managers:* These individuals are responsible for a project, program, initiative, or process. This is the individual who manages the program and is interested in showing the value of the program before it is implemented, during its implementation, and after it is implemented.

- *Program team:* These individuals are involved in a program, helping to analyze and implement it. These are individual team members who may be full or part time on a particular program. For larger-scale programs, these individuals are often assigned full time, on a temporary basis, or, sometimes, on a permanent basis. For small programs, these may be part-time duties.

- *Evaluator:* This individual evaluates a specific program. This person is responsible for measurement and evaluation. If this is a member of the program team, extreme measures must be taken to ensure that this person remains objective. It may also be a person who is completely independent of the program. This individual performs these duties full time or part time.

- *Finance and accounting staff:* These individuals are concerned about the cost and impact of the program from a financial perspective. They provide valuable support. Their approval of processes, assumptions, and methodologies is important. Sometimes, they are involved in the program evaluation; at other times, they review the results.

- *Analysts:* These individuals collect the data to determine whether the program is needed. They are also involved in analyzing various parts of the program. Analysts are usually more important in the beginning, but they may provide helpful data throughout the program's operation.

- *Bystanders:* These are the individuals who observe the program, sometimes at a distance. They are not actively involved as stakeholders but are concerned about the outcomes, including the money. These bystanders are important because they can become cheerleaders or critics of the program.

- *C-suite executives:* These are critical to the material in this book. They represent major stakeholders or players to ensure the success of learning and development.

- *CEO / managing director / agency executive:* The top executive is the most important C-suite executive. The top executive could be a plant manager, division manager, regional executive, administrator, or agency head. The CEO is the top administrator or executive in the operating entity where the program is implemented. These executives are the most influential stakeholders. Their input provides much of the focus of this book.

- *Chief financial officer (CFO) / finance director / finance administrator:* This top financial executive has become a major player in the evaluation of all types of projects and programs. Traditionally, the CFO has been charged with the responsibility for evaluating capital expenditures in an organization. Now, the CEO is asking the CFO to ensure that other major investments are measured often in the same way, often using ROI. This person will be both a key influencer and stakeholder in measuring the success of learning and development programs.

- *Chief learning officer (CLO):* In many organizations, the title for the head of learning and development is now the CLO. This reflects a higher level of status and sometimes a higher reporting relationship. It also suggests the broadened responsibilities and importance of learning and development as a process. This title evolved from training director to manager of training and development to manager of learning and development to vice president of learning and development to chief training officer to senior vice president of learning and development to chief learning officer. This evolution reveals the importance, scope, and significance of the learning and development function.

The Survey

ROI INSTITUTE™

January 14, 2009
Company
CEO
Address
City, State Zip

Dear CEO:

There's no getting around it. As a top executive, investment is part of your job, especially investing in employees' professional growth and development. For today's organizations, some with more than $1 billion budgets for formal learning and development, executives are almost always faced with the mystery of the value received from that investment. But for some, measuring the success, including the return on investment, of learning and development is an attainable process when the learning leaders know how success is defined, particularly success according to *you,* the top executive.

To help learning leaders better achieve this understanding, we've enclosed a brief survey designed to capture how executives like you define measures of success in your learning and development investments. Please take 15 minutes to complete this survey and return it in the enclosed self-addressed stamped envelope no later than **January 30, 2009.** In return, we will provide you a copy of the complete study by **March 13, 2009.** These results will show how your measures of success compare with other *Fortune* 500 CEOs.

As experienced top executives who have served in major organizations, we realize the nature of your busy schedule and demanding pressures. But we also know that success for your learning and development team is essential, and your response will be of great benefit to them and others in their field. Your personal perspective is important to us, so we ask that you <u>not forward</u> this survey to the learning and development executive in your organization. We want to hear from you, and only you.

As a small token of our appreciation, enclosed is a copy of our book *Show Me the Money: How to Determine the ROI of People, Projects, and Programs.*

Thank you for your input into this important research project.

Sincerely,

Jack J. Phillips
Chairman
ROI Institute, Inc.

Patti Phillips
President & CEO
ROI Institute, Inc.

Enclosures

CEO Survey
Investing in Employee Learning and Development

Thank you for taking time to complete this survey. Your response will assist the learning and development industry as it strives to position the profession to better serve organizational needs. It should take about 15 minutes to complete. After completion, please return it in the enclosed self-addressed stamped envelope no later than **January 30, 2009**

I. What is your approximate annual learning and development direct budget?
$_____

II. How many organizational layers exist between you and the head of learning and development (if this person reports to you, place a "1" in the blank)? _____

III. Which of the following best describes your approach to investing in learning and development (check the <u>one</u> best answer):

☐ We try to avoid the investment if possible, hiring employees on a contract basis, hiring fully competent people who do not need training, and using temps when necessary.

☐ We invest only the minimum—what is absolutely necessary for job-skill training.

☐ We invest at levels consistent with our benchmarking studies, using measures such as amount of learning and development as percent of payroll.

☐ We invest heavily in learning and development, essentially meeting all needs that are identified in the organization.

☐ We invest when we can see some type of benefit for investing, essentially investing when we see a pay-off.

IV. To what extent are you satisfied with the measures (value) of learning and development?

☐ Very Satisfied

☐ Satisfied

☐ Dissatisfied

☐ Very Dissatisfied

V. Below is a list of eight categories of measures of success of learning and development. For each measure, an example is provided. Please check if you are measuring this now (check <u>all that apply</u>). Next, indicate if the measure should be included in the future (check <u>all that apply</u>). Finally, rank the importance of the measure to you, with "1" as the most important and "2" as the second most important and so on, with "8" as the least important.

Measure Category	We Currently Measure This	We Should Measure This in the Future	My Ranking of the Importance of This Measure
1. **Inputs:** "Last year, 78,000 employees received formal learning."	☐	☐	_____
Comment about this type of data:_____			
2. **Efficiency:** "Formal learning costs $2.15 per hour of learning consumed."	☐	☐	_____
Comment about this type of data:_____			
3. **Reaction:** "Employees rated our training very high, averaging 4.2 out of 5."	☐	☐	_____
Comment about this type of data:_____			
4. **Learning:** "92% of participants increased knowledge and skills."	☐	☐	_____
Comment about this type of data:_____			
5. **Application:** "At least 78% of employees are using the skills on the job."	☐	☐	_____
Comment about this type of data:_____			
6. **Impact:** "Our programs are driving our top 5 business measures in the organization."	☐	☐	_____
Comment about this type of data:_____			
7. **ROI:** "Five ROI studies were conducted on major programs yielding an average of 68% ROI."	☐	☐	_____
Comment about this type of data:_____			
8. **Awards:** "Our learning and development program won an award from the American Society of Training and Development."	☐	☐	_____
Comment about this type of data:_____			

Complete the following statements:

VI. What I like best about the information I receive regarding the success of learning and development is:

_____

_____

VII. What I like least about the information I receive regarding the success of learning and development is:

_____

_____

VIII. I wish I had more data regarding the contribution of learning and development such as:

_____

_____

IX. Do you have a learning and development scorecard in place?   Yes ☐   No ☐
Comments on the scorecard:

_____

_____

X. In what ways are you personally involved in learning and development (check all that apply):

☐ I introduce / close out major programs.

☐ I actually teach segments of major programs.

☐ I review requests for major programs.

☐ I review results for major programs.

☐ I use the learning and development scorecard to monitor progress and make adjustments.

☐ I conduct/host periodic review meetings to examine the success of learning and development.

☐ I personally approve the learning and development budget with input from others.

☐ Other:_____

Check here if you would like a copy of the results   ☐

Thank you for participating in this research to be used by the learning and development industry.

Name (optional): _____   **Title:** _____

Company: _____

Address: _____

City/State/Zip: _____

Additional Interview Questions

1. Do you have a Corporate University? Yes ☐   No ☐
   If yes, how's it working? _____
   _____
   _____

2. Do you consider your organization a "Learning Organization"? Yes ☐   No ☐
   If yes, how's it working? _____
   _____
   _____

3. Explain any disappointment in measuring the success of learning and development.
   _____
   _____
   _____

4. Explain any success in measuring the success of learning and development.
   _____
   _____
   _____

5. How would you characterize your commitment and support for learning and
   development? What would cause you to increase it?
   _____
   _____
   _____
   _____

6. For the following actions, check all that apply to you and your learning and development team:

   1. Develop or approve a mission for the learning and development function. Provide input and perspective. ☐

   2. Allocate the necessary funds for successful learning and development programs. Initial funding may be based on benchmarking. Later, it is based on value added. ☐

   3. Allow employees time to participate in learning and development programs. Encourage, but don't require, a minimum level of participation. ☐

   4. Get actively involved in learning and development programs and require others to do the same. This involves conducting parts of formal programs and getting involved in coaching or mentoring. ☐

   5. Support the learning and development effort and ask other managers to do the same. Define and communicate ideal support. ☐

   6. Position the CLO in a visible and high-level place on the organization chart, ideally reporting directly to the CEO or other chief executive. ☐

   7. Require that each learning and development program be evaluated in some way, recognizing that most evaluations should include reaction and learning data only. ☐

   8. Insist that the learning and development programs be cost effective and require supporting data, including a few ROI studies each year. ☐

   9. Set an example for self-development. Show that continuous improvement is necessary in a learning organization. ☐

   10. Create an atmosphere of open communication with the CLO. Schedule quarterly reviews with the CLO to discuss progress, opportunities, and issues. ☐

Analysis of the Survey Results

A ttempting to do the impossible, we conducted a CEO survey aimed at obtaining direct feedback about the success of learning and development from a significant number of CEOs in large organizations. To our knowledge, no significant data has come from these elusive groups, although many one-to-one interviews are presented in profiles in magazines, but rarely do they discuss specifics on results. Surveys of this nature are often directed to heads of learning and development, where they are asked about their impression of the results their executives want, instead of obtaining this information directly from the CEOs. A few surveys have been attempted at the top executive level, but, unfortunately, the survey is instead passed down to the CLO.

To obtain the executives' views on learning and development, we sent a survey and a letter with instructions that asked the CEO not to forward our survey to the Learning and Development Department, in hopes that we could hear directly from this important executive. The survey— which was brief and easy to complete, with a self-addressed, stamped envelope—was formatted and designed for the most optimal response rate possible, which for us was at least 10 percent, and an optimistic 30 percent. (Survey is presented in Appendix B.)

Techniques to Achieve a Higher Response Rate

Data was collected from October 2008 to February 2009, using an accurate CEO database from *Fortune* magazine. We discarded any firms on the list who were currently facing economic turmoil, such as AIG, Lehman Brothers, General Motors, Ford, Merrill Lynch, Morgan Stanley, Chrysler, or any company that reported a significant loss. This trimmed 99 companies from the *Fortune* 500, leaving 401 for this survey. We selected 50 large, private-sector employers, using Hoover's Website as a guide. Essentially, these companies would be listed in the *Fortune* 500 if they were publicly held companies. Together, these provided a total of 451 in the large company sector to receive this survey.

In our work at the ROI Institute, we teach our clients how to achieve a high response rate on questionnaires. In a well-executed ROI study, for example, it is not unusual to have 70 to 90 percent return rate. We applied the same discipline, determination, and techniques to this project, because this group was particularly difficult to reach. Their exclusivity is in part a result of their "gatekeepers" (assistants, vice presidents, and more), who protect them from tasks that may be deemed time consuming or not essential to their role. In many large organizations, dozens of gatekeepers may be assigned to filter merely one executive's requests and demands. Consequently, we knew that our approach for this survey had to be creative. We used 10 powerful techniques to achieve a higher response rate. Here are four of them:

1. Survey responses were anonymous, unless CEOs elected to provide contact data. (No one did!)
2. A copy of our book *Show Me the Money: How to Determine ROI in People, Projects, and Programs* was enclosed as a small token of appreciation for their participation in the survey; top executives, and CEOs, have reacted positively to this book. The mere title speaks to them, as they have been demanding "show me the money" for years.
3. We wrote personal notes on almost all the letters, based on our relationships with that organization. For many of them, we are shareholders and wrote a plea for results as an act of accountability. In other cases, we are customers and wrote that we were interested

from a customer viewpoint. We used this angle whenever it carried weight, such as for Charles Schwab, but not for Procter & Gamble. Sometimes we would mention our current relationship, with phrases such as "We have projects ongoing," "We serve as a regular consultant," or, as in the case of IBM Services, "We act as an official subcontractor." Other notes revolved around our love for the company and their products, when it was appropriate, such as, "We love FedEx Kinko's" or "Starbucks" or "Whole Foods," which are a part of our everyday lives. A personal approach helps to move the survey past the gatekeepers, and, perhaps, stand out along numerous other requests.

4. Perhaps our most powerful act was to use someone else in the company, who was not in the learning and development area. In approximately 20 percent of these firms, we knew someone, usually a middle manager. We asked them to deliver the book and survey directly to the CEO. Of course, we provided incentives, such as additional books or a great bottle of wine. These personal touches were deliberately designed to get our survey beyond the CEO's gatekeeper.

Response Rate

Ninety-six individuals responded, representing a 21.3 percent of the total. Executives chose to remain anonymous, some did not answer particular points or provide comments. A few executives gave us extensive comments and seemed to take a great interest in doing so. Some sent us thank-you notes for the book; others said they were not able to accept the book based on ethical reasons and returned it; and a few passed it along to others and let us know who received it.

This response is especially significant when considering the difficult economic circumstances during the time the survey was conducted. Trying to spend a few minutes on a survey addressing learning and development was not at the top of the agenda for most executives during this time frame. To our knowledge, all the returned surveys were actually completed by the CEO, which was our request. We suspect that if a CLO had completed it instead, he or she would have acknowledged it.

The Results

This section describes the results for investment in learning and development, reporting relationships, satisfaction with the current measures of success, coverage of measures, the learning scorecard, and executive involvement.

Investment in Learning and Development

Investments of these companies range from a low $10 million to a high $640 million. Sometimes executives scribbled notes about how they were not sure of the exact amount. The average number was $138 million, as shown in figure D-1.

Regarding the rationale for setting the investment level, CEOs selected a strategy from a list. Table D-1 shows the responses. Although these results confirmed what we expected to a certain extent, a few surprises surfaced.

Figure D-1. Investment Range

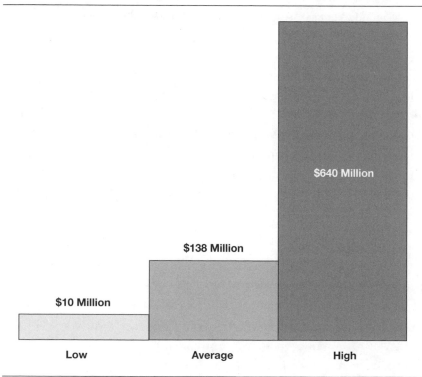

Only 4 percent acknowledged that they try to avoid these investments, but, based on what we have observed in our work, we suspect that this number may be a little higher. Twenty percent of CEOs said they invest only the minimum. In part, this may be due to the current economic times, where executives have had to trim activities that are perceived to be unnecessary. As expected, benchmarking was the highest (at 39 percent). Because we asked that only one strategy be checked, we suspect that a combination of benchmarking and other possibilities is being used. We limited the choice to only one in the survey to determine the dominant approach for setting the investment level.

Surprisingly, a significant number of CEOs (10 percent) mentioned that they invested in all learning and development needs. Although we worded this option so that they would feel comfortable with the choice, this is probably overinvesting. From our own experience, we see this routinely, and a few executives are proud that they can invest in practically any learning request.

Finally, it's quite refreshing to see that a significant number invest when they see value (18 percent). We assume, however, that there are many different definitions of the term "value" and that this does not always mean ROI calculations.

Table D-1. CEO Input on Investment (*N* = 96 large public and private firms)

Which of the following best describes your approach to investing in learning and development? Check the one best answer:

4%	We try to avoid the investment if possible, using contract workers, hiring fully competent employees who do not need training, and using temps when necessary.
20%	We invest only the minimum—what is absolutely necessary for job-skill training.
39%	We invest at levels consistent with our benchmarking studies, using measures such as the training cost per employee.
10%	We invest heavily in learning and development, essentially meeting all needs that are identified in the organization.
18%	We invest when we can see some type of benefit for investing, essentially investing when there is a pay-off.
9%	Don't know/Did not respond.

Reporting Relationships

An important factor in this study is to determine how close the CLO, the head of learning and development, is to the CEO. In this study, a 1 indicates that the CLOs report directly to the CEO. A 2 means that there are two levels between them, and a 3 means that there are three levels between them. The average was 3.2, which means that the CEO is at least three levels up. This distance is a little disturbing, considering so much effort has been focused on pushing this function to a higher level position within the company.

One challenge that has compounded accountability issues in learning and development is the lack of interaction between the learning and development professional and the senior executive team. In most organizations, this interaction is limited. Only in a few organizations does the top learning executive report to the CEO. Even in those organizations, the time spent with the CEO is not proportional to time the CEO spends with other direct reports. Senior executives have limited time, and they spend it in those areas they perceive to be critical, important, and central to the organization's success. Unfortunately, many executives do not see learning and development rising to this level of criticality, thus, allocating less time to engaging in it. The problem is compounded when the learning and development executive reports through one or more executives and only interacts with the CEO on special projects or an occasional review of the learning and development budget. Regrettably, these budget reviews are when senior executives hope to see a connection between learning outcomes and the business to justify increasing or sustaining budgets. It is no surprise, then, that there is confusion and misunderstanding of expectations with regard to requirements for measures of learning success.

Satisfaction with the Current Measures of Success

Limited interaction with executives often forces the learning and development leader to guess what the top executives want in terms of measures of success. This guesswork becomes more inaccurate when filtered through multiple layers of interpretation. Asking top executives outright what specific measures they want to improve often yields ineffective or misguided dialogue. After all, top executives do not see their responsibility as defining the measures of success. Essentially, they want the learning and development leaders to report improvement in measures of success that are meaningful to them in terms of business contribution.

We asked the executives a very general question regarding their level of satisfaction with the measures of success for learning and development. We created a 4-point scale to force the executives to take a stand. On a 4-point scale, a 1 would be very dissatisfied, and a 4 would be very satisfied. We were hoping to see at least a 3; unfortunately, the results were 2.52, indicating some dissatisfaction. Table D-2 shows the results.

Coverage of Measures

We knew it was easiest to have executives respond to particular checklists, and deciding which metrics to use was very critical. We provided eight categories and mapped them into the levels of evaluation. The first two categories were "inputs" and "efficiencies," which are process measures or inputs to the process, including volume, costs, and speed. The next two categories, "reaction" and "learning," are typical learning measures. "Application" is the extent of the use of knowledge and skills. "Impact," which is the business measure, and "ROI" created much interest. We included ROI because of the abundance of information about its use. Finally, we included "awards," which many CLOs are currently pursuing and reporting to the executives, particularly in large organizations.

Obviously, these map into the levels of evaluation described in the literature. The first two categories (inputs and efficiencies) is Level 0. Reaction is Level 1. Learning is Level 2. Application is Level 3. Impact and awards

Table D-2. Satisfaction with Measures of Success of Learning and Development (percent)

1—Very dissatisfied	8
2—Dissatisfied	45
3—Satisfied	41
4—Very satisfied	6

are Level 4, and ROI is Level 5. Although other specific measures may be identified, they all should fit into one of these eight categories.

Given this list, we wanted to know three things:

1. "What metrics are being reported to you now?"
2. "What should be reported that isn't being reported now?"
3. "How would you rank these in terms of value?"

Table D-3 shows the responses. In this table, the first column gives the percentage of CEOs who checked each item as a metric being reported; the second column gives the percentage indicating that it should be reported; and the third column gives the average ranking number for the group, recognizing that the lower the number, the higher the ranking. An 8 score would indicate 8 on the list, and a 1 score would indicate first on the list. Inputs and efficiencies were ranked 6 and 7, respectively; input shows the scope and volume, something executives need to know. These types of data are always being reported. Though most CEOs receive this type now, they quickly recognize its limited value. Reaction is ranked the lowest which may not be a surprise, although it's the number 1 outcome measure reported to executives. This particular measure could be improved with more focus on content.

The category of awards was rated higher than we expected. Both pessimists and optimists wrote comments. The optimists were proud of their awards and thought they reflected the quality and significance of the learning and development team. Others said that the awards mean very little and are often based on how much they're willing to spend on the award application.

The highest two areas were impact and ROI, which should come with little surprise, because the CEOs always want to see this kind of data, especially during these tough economic times. This reporting creates a very important dilemma for learning and development: These are the least-reported data sets, but yet are of the most valuable to executives. Therein lies the challenge and opportunity for the learning and development team.

Table D-3. The Results for Specific Measures

Measure	We Currently Measure This	We Should Measure This in the Future	My Ranking of the Importance of This Measure	
			Average	Rank
a. Inputs: "Last year, 78,000 employees received formal learning."	(90) 94%	(82) 86%	6.73	6
b. Efficiency: "Formal learning costs $2.15 per hour of learning consumed."	(75) 78%	(79) 82%	6.92	7
c. Reaction: "Employees rated our training very high, averaging 4.2 out of 5."	(51) 53%	(21) 22%	7.15	8
d. Learning: "Our programs reflect growth in knowledge and skills of our employees."	(31) 32%	(27) 28%	4.79	5
e. Application: "Our studies show that at least 78% of employees are using the skills on the job."	(11) 11%	(59) 61%	3.42	4
f. Impact: "Our programs are driving our top five business measures in the organization."	(8) 8%	(92) 96%	1.45	1
g. ROI: "Five ROI studies were conducted on major programs yielding an average of 68% ROI."	(4) 4%	(71) 74%	2.31	2
h. Awards: "Our learning and development program won an award from the American Society for Training & Development."	(38) 40%	(42) 44%	3.23	3

Note: The first column gives the percentage of CEOs who checked each item as a measure being reported; the second column gives the percentage indicating that it should be reported; and the third column gives the average ranking number for the group, recognizing that the lower the number, the higher the ranking.

Learning Scorecard

We asked about the learning and development scorecard, and we discovered that only 22 percent of the CEOs said that they had a learning and development scorecard. This is surprising, given the work to develop balanced scorecards in large organizations. Of course, a scorecard very well could be in place, but it does not make its way all the way to the CEO.

On the positive side, this result indicates some executives are reviewing scorecards on a routine basis. For the most part, the comments in the scorecard were either negative or constructive. Only one indicated that he or she was pleased with the scorecard that is in use. The other comments were referred to as "inadequate," "incomplete," "doesn't have all the data," and "doesn't really connect to the business." This leaves some great opportunities to make improvement in this area.

Executive Involvement

A critical issue for learning and development departments is the extent of the executive involvement. Most would argue that executives are taking a more active role or are more involved with the investment and, thus, more results will be achieved. Table D-4 shows the responses from CEOs regarding their level of involvement, given a list of possibilities. The CEOs could check all that apply. As expected, the top area is that the CEO personally approves the learning and development budget, which was indicated by 78 percent. Second on the list, indicated by 73 percent, was that they review requests for major programs, while 61 percent review the results of those programs. A total of 24 percent use a scorecard to monitor the progress and make adjustments. Next, 29 percent opened and closed major programs, while 22 percent host or conduct periodic review meetings, and only 18 percent teach segments of major programs. Disappointingly, the two lowest ones—holding periodic review meetings, and being involved by teaching segments—can have the most impact on learning and development success. Periodic review meetings represent an opportunity to review progress, make adjustments, and check results. This is a great way to stay connected and provide feedback to see the

Table D-4. CEO Involvement in Learning and Development

	In what ways are you personally involved in learning and development?
29%	I introduce / close out major programs.
18%	I actually teach segments of major programs.
73%	I review requests for major programs.
61%	I review results for major programs.
24%	I use the learning and development scorecard to monitor progress and make adjustments.
22%	I conduct/host periodic review meetings to examine the success of learning and development.
78%	I personally approve the learning and development budget with input from others.
18%	Other:_____

results to boost funding in the future. Getting involved in teaching is a powerful way to connect learning and development to the organization and deliver value. Jack Welch (General Electric) and Andy Grove (Intel) are two examples where this was extremely effective.

Summary

In summary, while the results are based only on data for 96 executives, the amount of information is significant. To our knowledge, the results may be the highest level of large company CEO involvement in research on measuring the success of learning and development ever assimilated. The results present some challenges for the CLO and the learning and development team.

♦ Appendix E

Analysis of the Interview Results

To obtain more insightful executive comments regarding the success of learning and development with specific measurement-related issues, we developed additional interview questions, as shown in appendix C. Ideally, we wanted approximately 30 minutes to pose questions face to face with the executives. As a substitute, we offered a telephone interview. The interview would allow for probing, clarifying understanding, and developing additional comments that could be helpful for learning and development leaders.

Sources and Response Rate

Several different sources were part of the interviews. At first, we asked for interviews from the *Fortune* 500 group. These individuals were involved in the CEO survey. In some cases, they agreed, but the number was very small, representing only 6. Also, we contacted a group of about 75 CLOs to explain our research and asked them if they would be interested in having their CEO involved in an interview. Much to our disappointment, the vast majority was not interested, nor in pursuing an interview. Only 5 agreed to have their CEO interviewed. For a third group, we worked directly with some of our clients, where we currently had projects under way and asked if we could take a few minutes to talk to their CEO. That generated another 8. Finally, we had 3 CEO interviews in medium organizations. Of these 22, 10 were conducted face to face and 11 by telephone.

Corporate University

The concept of adopting or developing the corporate university concept is an important issue among learning and development providers. We wanted to see if this concept is working for these executives. Of those interviewed, 23 percent (5) considered that they have a corporate university. In terms of its effectiveness, their answers were not very specific. Some commented, "It has a good reputation," "The image is appropriate," and "It's supported quite well"; others stated that it was delivering the value but with no specifics. Still others expressed concerns that it may be slightly removed from the organization, not clearly connected to the business, or not have the accountability for that level of expenditures.

Learning Organization

Because of the emphasis in recent years for creating a learning organization, we explored how well this concept is working. Twenty-seven percent (6) of the executives considered themselves to be a learning organization, and they admitted that they were not sure that it was working. Most view it as a necessity in today's complex organization with the pressure to provide continuous learning. Most were at loss about its value, and some were concerned that although they had spent a large amount on learning, they suspected that it might not be adding a significant business value.

Pluses and Minuses of Measuring Learning and Development

Two questions in the interview focused on the disappointments and successes of measuring the success of learning and development. Many of the executives' comments regarding these issues were included in various places in the book. A significant amount of disappointment was registered about lack of connection to the business or showing value in terms they appreciate and understand. Several of the successes were focused on particular learning and development projects, some of which they were involved in and were proud of their results.

Commitment

Executive commitment, particularly from the top, is an important ingredient to the success of any learning and development function. The extent to which executives are committed to learning and development was explored in two ways.

First, an open-ended question was asked to provide an opportunity for executives to characterize their commitment. For the most part, they felt that they were strongly committed to this process, which underscores why they were participating in the interview—to show their commitment in some way.

Next, the executives were provided a table to check the commitment actions they follow. In some cases, this part was read to them, and they either agreed or disagreed. Table E-1 shows their responses on a percentage basis. The highest-percentage item in the table is that they allocate funds. This task was expected; ultimately, they approve the learning and development budget.

As number two, executives insist that the learning and development function be cost-effective with supporting data. This item is not surprising in its importance, given the influence of the executive and the current economic climate.

The third item is a tie. Executives were involved in setting the mission and then allowing time to participate in programs.

Then, as number five, they required that each program be evaluated in some way. We expected that to be a little higher, when considering the current economy, but it may be a reflection of not understanding the evaluation methodology.

Table E-1. CEO Commitment to Learning and Development

CEOs said they do the following:

1.	Develop or approve a mission for the learning and development function. Provide input and perspective.	**73%**
2.	Allocate the necessary funds for successful learning and development programs. Initial funding may be based on benchmarking. Later, it is based on value added.	**95%**
3.	Allow employees time to participate in learning and development programs. Encourage, but don't require, a minimum level of participation.	**73%**
4.	Stay actively involved in learning and development programs and require others to do the same. This involves conducting parts of formal programs and getting involved in coaching or mentoring.	**45%**
5.	Support the learning and development effort and ask other managers to do the same. Define and communicate ideal support.	**59%**
6.	Position the CLO in a visible and high-level place on the organizational chart, ideally reporting directly to the CEO or other top executive.	**23%**
7.	Require that each learning and development program be evaluated in some way, recognizing that most evaluations should include reaction and learning data only.	**64%**
8.	Insist that the learning and development programs be cost-effective and require supporting data, including a few ROI studies each year.	**77%**
9.	Set an example for self-development. Show that continuous improvement is necessary in a learning organization.	**59%**
10.	Create an atmosphere of open communication with the CLO. Schedule quarterly reviews with the CLO to discuss progress, opportunities, and issues.	**14%**

The next two were tied. Executives set an example for others in "self-development," but they also support learning and development and ask others to do the same. Forty-five percent indicated that they stay actively involved in learning and development and require others to do the same. Disappointingly, only 23 percent indicated that they position the CLO in a high place. Only 14 percent have open quarterly reviews with the CLO to discuss progress. For this item especially, an opportunity for learning and development improvement is apparent.

Integration of the Data

The insightful and telling inputs and data have made this book in-valuable to the learning and development function. As mentioned in chapter 2, there are eight sources of data for this book. The findings are not just CEO surveys or interviews, but a significant amount of data that has been compiled over a period of time. Figure F-1 shows the eight data sources described in chapter 2, labeled with numbers representing our assessment of the importance of this input. This distinction is risky, because all these inputs are important, and it's difficult to say one is more important than the other.

Perhaps the most unique data is the surveys and interviews. Ninety-six CEOs responded to the surveys and is possibly the largest body of data from this audience. In the interviews, only 22 gave us a chance to probe and find more detail. For most of these interviews, the head of learning and development was not present. These interviews support the tables and charts within this book. However, the comments on the surveys and from interviews represent most of the collection of executive comments throughout the book. Within these comments, we tried to balance the negative and positive. For the most part, negative comments prevailed

Figure F-1. Sources of Data for the Executive View

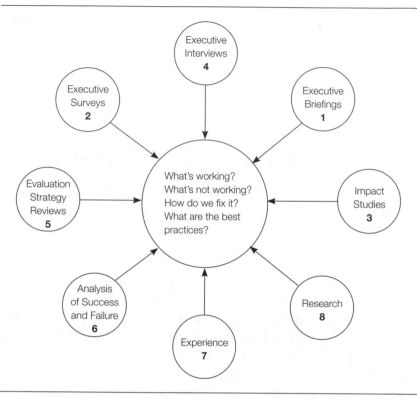

over the positive when an executive expressed concerns about the success of learning and development, although derogatory terms or ultimatums were not offered.

Executive briefings, impact studies, and evaluation strategy reviews are important because they represent face-to-face conversations with executives in the context of presenting results. Typical executive interviews in *T+D* magazine and other publications often feature the executive in the most favorable light. Executives are innately very careful in what they say, as the interviews are often public relations events. The chief learning officers have coached them very well. Any sensitive details or concerns about results will never be revealed. However, within the context of presenting results of a major study, issues are raised and discussed, and even the results are often debated. It is within these discussions where the executives' real concerns and viewpoints begin to surface.

With almost two decades of experience at the ROI Institute, we have witnessed these incidents as a vehicle for collecting our most useful data. During these sessions, we make notes of executives' comments, issues, praises, concerns, and words of encouragement. When any feedback surprised us, we knew that it would be valuable to the learning and development community, and, as a result, we filed these away for later use, such as this book.

Essentially, the last three categories on the list, analysis of success and failure, our own experience, and other research, form the foundation for our examination. The research identifies the issues, concerns, advantages, and disadvantages of different types of data. Our own experience gives us a framework to know and develop issues that are important from both the perspective of the learning and development function and the executive. Both authors have experience as a head of learning and development and as a senior executive. We understand these issues firsthand.

The analysis of success and failures is very important because it forces the examination of both why learning and development is not delivering the value that it should, and when it does, why. Having conducted this type of analyses several times, we've seen that they have yielded insight into the executive role in this process.

Our collection of data from several sources provided an adequate picture of what is needed for improvements. This effort is not meant to support the work of the ROI Institute, Kirkpatrick, Brinkerhoff, or others, but instead complement them and share their same goal of helping the learning and development function show value. We hope this collection of insight, wisdom, and description, based on the input of many others, adds to the literature on this topic and helps move this important field forward.

Resources

Barksdale, Susan, and Teri Lund. 2001. *Rapid Evaluation*. Alexandria, VA: ASTD Press.

Davenport, Thomas. 2006. Competing on Analytics. *Harvard Business Review*, On-Point Article, January.

Dixon, Nancy M. 1990. *Evaluation: A Tool for Improving HRD Quality*. San Francisco: Pfeiffer.

Durfree, Don. 2003. *Human Capital Management: The CFO's Perspective*. Boston: CFO Publishing Corp.

Elkeles, Tamar, and Jack J. Phillips. 2007. *The Chief Learning Officer: Driving Value within a Changing Organization through Learning and Development*. Amsterdam: Elsevier.

Kaplan, Robert S., and David P. Norton. 1996. *The Balanced Scorecard: Translating Strategy into Action*. Boston: Harvard Business School Press.

Paradise, Andrew. 2008. *2008 State of the Industry Report*. Alexandria, VA: ASTD Press.

Phillips, Jack J. 2005. *Investing in Your Company's Human Capital: Strategies to Avoid Spending Too Much or Too Little*. New York: Amacom.

Phillips, Jack J., and Lisa Edwards. 2009. *Managing Talent Retention: An ROI Approach*. San Francisco: Pfeiffer.

Phillips, Jack J., and Patricia Pulliam Phillips. 2002. Eleven Reasons Why Training and Development Fails. *Training*, September.

———. 2007a. *Show Me the Money: How to Determine ROI in People, Projects, and Programs*. San Francisco: Berrett-Koehler.

———. 2007b. *The Value of Learning: How Organizations Capture Value and ROI and Translate Them into Support, Improvement, and Funds*. Hoboken, NJ: John Wiley and Sons.

———. 2008a. *Beyond Learning Objectives: Develop Measurable Objectives That Link to the Bottom Line*. Alexandria, VA: ASTD Press.

———, eds. 2008b. *The Measurement and Evaluation Series: Communication and Implementation: Sustaining the Practice*. Hoboken, NJ: John Wiley and Sons.

Phillips, Patricia Pulliam, Jack J. Phillips, Ron Stone, and Holly Burkett. 2006. *The ROI Fieldbook: Strategies for Implementing ROI in HR and Training (Improving Human Performance)*. Oxford: Butterworth-Heinemann.

Phillips, Patricia Pulliam, and Cathy A. Stawarski. 2008. *Data Collection: Planning for Collecting All Types of Data*. Measurement and Evaluation Series. San Francisco: Pfeiffer.

Rothwell, William J., John E. Lindholm, and William G Wallick. 2003. *What CEOs Expect from Corporate Training*. New York: Amacom.

◆ Index

Note: *f* represents a figure and *t* represents a table.

◆ About the Authors

Jack J. Phillips is a world-renowned expert on accountability, measurement, and evaluation who provides consulting services for *Fortune* 500 companies and major global organizations. He is the author or editor of more than 50 books, and he conducts workshops and makes conference presentations throughout the world.

Jack's expertise in measurement and evaluation is based on more than 27 years of corporate experience in the aerospace, textile, metals, construction materials, and banking industries. He has served as bank president and management professor. This background led him to develop the ROI methodology—a revolutionary process that provides bottom-line figures and accountability for all types of programs on learning, performance improvement, human resources, technology, and public policy.

Jack has written more than 30 books, including *Beyond Learning Objectives: Develop Measurable Objectives That Link to the Bottom Line* (ASTD Press, 2008); *Managing Talent Retention: An ROI Approach* (Pfeiffer, 2009); and *Show Me the Money: How to Determine ROI in People, Projects, and Programs* (Berrett-Koehler, 2007). He holds a PhD and is chairman of the ROI Institute, Inc.

Patti P. Phillips is president and CEO of the ROI Institute, Inc., the leading source of ROI competency building, implementation support, networking, and research. After a 13-year career in the electrical utility industry, she began her work with the ROI Institute's trademarked ROI methodology. Since 1997, she has embraced the ROI process, conducting research on the methodology as well as applying it to a variety of programs in private-sector, public-sector, and nonprofit organizations.

Patti teaches others to implement the ROI methodology through the ROI Institute's ROI Certification Process, as a facilitator for ASTD's ROI and Measuring and Evaluating Learning Workshops, and as an adjunct professor for graduate-level evaluation courses. She works with a variety of organizations as they develop capacity in the ROI methodology.

Patti's academic accomplishments include a PhD in international development and a master's degree in public and private management. She has been awarded the ASTD Certified Professional in Learning and Performance designation as well as the International Society for Performance Improvement's Certified Performance Technologist designation. Currently, she is a board member of the Cambridge-based ABDI Ltd. and the Independent Book Publisher's Association, based in Manhattan Beach, California. She is the author or coauthor of a number of publications on the subject of accountability and ROI, including *Beyond Learning Objectives: Develop Measurable Objectives That Link to the Bottom Line* (ASTD Press, 2008); *The Value of Learning: How Organizations Capture Value and ROI* (Pfeiffer, 2007); *Show Me the Money: How to Determine ROI in People, Projects, and Programs* (Berrett-Koehler, 2007); and the award-winning *The Bottomline on ROI* (CEP Press for International Society for Performance Improvement, 2002).

About the American Society for Training & Development (ASTD)

Through exceptional learning and performance, we create a world that works better.

ASTD is the world's largest association dedicated to workplace learning and performance professionals. ASTD's members come from more than 100 countries and connect locally in more than 130 U.S. chapters and with more than 30 international partners. Members work in thousands of organizations of all sizes, in government, as independent consultants, and suppliers.

Started in 1943, in recent years ASTD has widened the profession's focus to link learning and performance to individual and organizational results, and is a sought-after voice on critical public policy issues. ASTD

- Provides resources for learning and performance professionals, educators, and students—research, analysis, benchmarking, online information, books, and other publications.
- Brings professionals together in conferences, workshops, and online.
- Offers professional development opportunities for learning practitioners, from a Job Bank and Career Center, to certificate programs and the only credential offered in the field: the Certified Professional in Learning and Performance (CPLP).
- Serves as the voice of the profession to the media and to public policy makers in the United States, and collaborates with other associations, organizations, and educational institutions to advance the profession.
- Recognizes excellence and sets the standard for best practices in learning and performance.

Learn more about ASTD at www.astd.org, or call 800.628.2783 (U.S.) or 703.683.8100.

About the ROI Institute

The ROI Institute, Inc., is the leading resource on research, training, and networking for practitioners of the Phillips ROI Methodology. With a combined 50 years of experience in measuring and evaluating training, human resources, technology, and quality programs and initiatives, founders and owners Jack J. Phillips, PhD, and Patti P. Phillips, PhD, are the leading experts in return on investment (ROI).

The ROI Institute, founded in 1992, is a service-driven organization that strives to assist professionals in improving their programs and processes through the use of the ROI Methodology. Developed by Jack J. Phillips, this methodology is a critical tool for measuring and evaluating programs in 18 different applications in more than 40 countries.

The institute offers a variety of consulting services, learning opportunities, and publications. It conducts internal research activities in addition to research for a variety of organizations and institutes. Together with their team, Jack and Patti Phillips serve private and public sector organizations globally.

Learn more about the ROI Institute at www.roiinstitute.net or call 205.678.8101.